INTRODUCTION

In September 1938 Henry Miller announced, among other works in preparation, a book called "Letters to Emil," to be published in the Villa Seurat Series that he was then editing for the Obelisk Press in Paris. The letters, which he had been writing to his friend Emil Schnellock since 1922, had recently been assembled and transcribed; only the task of editing remained. But the next year was a busy one for Henry Miller, and what with the distractions of the Munich Crisis, his struggles with *Tropic of Capricorn,* his visit to Greece, and the outbreak of the war, he never got around to editing the letters.

In the decade that followed, the letters to Schnellock were repeatedly quarried for publication. About one hundred pages appeared in two slim volumes, both concerned primarily with Miller's comments on painting: *Semblance of a Devoted Past,* published by Bern Porter in 1945, with excerpts from letters written between 1930 and 1939; and *The Waters Reglitterized,* published by John Kidis in 1950, a single marathon letter written between February 22 and March 12, 1939. *A Henry Miller Miscellanea* (1945) contained another letter to Schnellock about watercoloring. And *Sunday After the War* (1944) included a "Death Letter to Emil," rambling on about the Spenglerian theories that Miller shared with his friends Michael Fraenkel and Walter Lowenfels. Schnellock himself quoted excerpts from Miller's letters in his reminiscent tribute, "Just a Brooklyn Boy," published in *The Happy Rock* (1945).

Miller and Schnellock had known each other since schooldays at P.S. No. 85 in Brooklyn, class of 1905—a standing joke between them, as the letters show, quoting the principal's admonitions and the school song: "Dear 85, dear 85, we honor thy fair name." They then went to different high schools and lost sight of each other for many years, during which Schnellock traveled and studied in Europe. Thus, when a chance encounter brought them together again in 1921, Miller regarded his old friend with awe, marveling that an ordinary Brooklyn boy should have become an accomplished artist and cosmopolite.

That encounter, as Miller has frequently remarked, had a decisive influence on his life. In *Tropic of Capricorn* he recalls the long evenings spent in Prospect Park, Brooklyn, talking about everything under the sun, but chiefly about foreign lands, about artists and writers. Miller, then in his thirtieth year, was a married man with a good job as personnel manager of Western Union in New York City, but he had by no means settled down. For years he had been thrashing around, trying to find what he wanted from life. Those long talks with Emil Schnellock had much to do with his decision to become a writer.

During the years that followed, the two became close friends, sharing all kinds of experiences that were to become the stuff of Miller's autobiographical romances. They had much in common, they came from the same world and spoke the same language, they had the same earthiness, the same sensibility. Schnellock, a bachelor and a successful commercial artist, was always ready to join Miller in his escapades and to lend him money. But more important than companionship was the intellectual and aesthetic stimulation he provided. Throughout the '20s and into the '30s Schnellock was Miller's chief mentor, the master craftsman who educated him in the visual arts and taught him to paint, the critic to whom Miller constantly turned for guidance—in writing as well as watercoloring.

The most interesting thing about Miller's letters to Schnellock is the record they present of the writer in the making. They begin with his first efforts to write in 1922, trace his ten-year struggle to find his own voice, and culminate with the publication of his first book, *Tropic of Cancer*, in 1934. Actually Miller continued to write to Schnellock until the latter's death in 1960. But in selecting letters for publication in 1938, he limited himself to his apprentice years, 1922–34, a period that closed with his temporary return to New York from Paris. The letters of this decisive period are unquestionably the best and most revealing.

The years that follow are abundantly documented in other published volumes of letters. In fact, the period from 1932 on is in many ways more thoroughly covered in Miller's letters to Anaïs Nin, as she became his patroness and literary confidante in Paris, while Schnellock in New York was a remote and, as Miller often complained, rather infrequent correspondent. Miller's visit to New York in 1935 was amusingly chronicled in an 88-page letter to his friend Alfred Perlès, the longest letter of his career, published as *Aller Retour New York*. And Miller's long correspondence with Lawrence Durrell began in 1935, as did his thousand-page epistolary debate with Michael Fraenkel published as *Hamlet*.

What distinguishes the letters to Schnellock from all these other collections is not so much the period they cover as the evidence they provide of his work in progress. They catch the writer in the act, not only of discovering his medium, not only of experiencing everything that would go into his first books, but turning out rough drafts, some of which were to evolve into finished works. *"Those letters!"* Schnellock exclaimed in "Just a Brooklyn Boy."

LETTERS TO EMIL

HENRY MILLER
LETTERS TO EMIL

EDITED BY GEORGE WICKES

CARCANET

First published in Great Britain in 1990 by
Carcanet Press Limited
208-212 Corn Exchange Buildings
Manchester M4 3BQ

Copyright © 1944, 1945, 1950, 1968 by Henry Miller
Copyright © 1989, 1990 by Barbara Sylvas Miller, Henry Tony Miller and Valentine Lepska Miller
Copyright © 1989, 1990 by George Wickes

British Library Cataloguing in Publication Data
Miller, Henry *(1891-1980)*
  Letters to Emil.
  1. Fiction in English. American writers. Miller, Henry,
  1891-1980
  I. Title   II. Wickes, George
  813.52

  ISBN 0-85635-901-7

The Publisher acknowledges financial assistance from the
Arts Council of Great Britain.

Printed in England by SRP Ltd., Exeter.

CONTENTS

How far does one have to go to find their equal? A cascade, a river, an ocean of words. Stories, prophecies, dreams, ideas, travels, plans, outlines of coming books, adventures, intrigues, expositions of books he is reading, dialogues with new characters he meets up with, reveries, longings, philosophical and metaphysical speculation, descriptions of banquets—everything is in them. Large fragments, too, from books in the making—on Lawrence, Proust, Joyce, Spengler, Balzac—and big slices from the "Tropics" as they took on growth.

Schnellock may not have been a faithful correspondent, but he provided an appreciative audience, for many years the only one Miller respected. Then too, he served a unique function, as Miller observed in a letter written in December 1933: "I am looking upon you as my 'literary trustee' pro tem. I like the idea of knowing that my first drafts are safely somewhere because the temptation is strong to destroy those after I finish the job. But, as you know, there is a flavor about first efforts which is valuable in itself."

By this time Miller had been in Paris almost four years and had sent Schnellock some of the best work he was ever to write, none of it published as yet. He had discovered that Schnellock was the only friend in New York he could count on to look after his manuscripts, the only one to whom he could send his works in progress for safekeeping with the assurance that they would be returned when he needed them. Of all his correspondents over the years, Schnellock was also the one to whom he could express himself most freely in his bawdiest vein.

Not only in 1938 but also in later years Miller wanted to see the letters to Emil published, feeling that some of his best writing had gone into them. In 1968 he asked me to prepare a selection for publication, and I did so the following year, but for a variety of reasons that book never went to press. The present selection is not very different from the one I made twenty years ago, but it does include some personal allusions that would have been omitted then, most obviously the references to Anaïs Nin which Miller was at pains to suppress in the 1960s. Now that she has revealed her passionate involvement with Miller and his wife in explicit detail through the posthumous publication of *Henry and June,* Miller, if he were still alive, would surely no longer feel obligated to protect her privacy.

This book has been edited from the fair copies which Miller gave to the UCLA Library. The Library also has a few of the originals, though most of them seem to have disappeared. In my editing I have tried to follow Miller's original intentions as expressed in several letters to Schnellock in 1938, preserving the spontaneity of letter-writing as much as possible and concluding with the letter Miller wrote on the eve of his return to America at the end of 1934. I have standardized spelling, capitalization, and punctuation somewhat, as Miller would have done, but retained some of his idiosyncrasies in order to convey something of the flavor of his epistolary style. I have used asterisks to indicate major omissions in the text; what appear to be ellipses (. . . .) are actually Miller's punctuations. Chiefly I have attempted to eliminate repetition and obscurity and to bring out the central theme, as it appeared to me, of the writer's self-discovery.

George Wickes

I

JUST A BROOKLYN BOY

1922–25

Fifteen letters survive from the '20s, and of those I have selected six that most clearly reflect Miller's literary beginnings. The oldest surviving letter dates his first day as a writer, when he took a three-week vacation in order to write a book about twelve Western Union messengers, a book that was never published. This and other early letters reveal his tastes at the time, his aversion to Henry James, which is the subject of one letter, and in another his enthusiasm for Arthur Machen's *Hill of Dreams,* from which he quotes for five pages (which I saw no reason to reprint.)

One letter describing the Bowery Savings Bank is the first draft of one of Miller's "Mezzotints," the prose poems which he had printed on colored cardboard and which he peddled from door to door in emulation of Walt Whitman. As the draft shows, Miller's writing at this time was too self-consciously "literary," with exclamations like "pshaw" and "damme" that were not part of his native Brooklynese. In some diary notes he sent to Schnellock in 1923 Miller mused on the words of a friend: "You are doomed to write unacceptable literature," and rather bitterly rejoined: "My literature is no more unpalatable than my living. If they (they being the fruitfully vague image of a vulgar public) push me back into the garbage rucks do they expect me to emerge with lilies in my hand?"

Miller's writing was probably inhibited by his audience as well. His letters were sometimes addressed to several admirers besides Schnellock. And one letter is addressed to posterity—"a sly leaf inserted into my future memoirs"—bemoaning his hard lot as a struggling artist. Some of the less interesting letters (not included) allude to Miller's private life but tell very little, since Schnellock was well aware of the circumstances. In 1923 Miller met June Mansfield, the femme fatale of *Tropic of Capricorn* and other autobiographical romances. In 1924 he divorced his first wife, married June, and quit his job at Western Union in order to become a full-time writer.

March 20, 1922

Ye Gods! The first day of being a writer has nearly broken my back. I have discovered new sets of muscles, new aches, new worries. But I have done my quota for the day, a good eight-hour day such as no union man keeps. I have finished my 5,000 words and made some slight revisions. Tomorrow, if I am like the Lord God, I shall wake and look upon my work and pronounce it good. Tonight I am in grave doubt, in extreme torment. I am wondering languidly whether I have the divine ichor or not. Ah, well, faith's summat, and summat too is the pep! Just now I have the pip and I'm all pap!

Say, many thousands of thanks to you for introducing me to Ezra Loomis Pound. I have him and the whole tribe of modern poetasters on my desk. Eight volumes of modern poetry all at once, and one taken surreptitiously from the public library. Am I nuts? Boy, I can swallow it like Home Brew. And what's more, I can understand it, that's the mystery! Sounds like stuff I say to myself all day long. Maybe, Creeping Jesus, I'm another Lindsay or Masters or Bodenheim, eh? Some day on this golden whale of a vacation I am goin' to shoot you full of my own concoctions—real, red-flannel nightgown stuff, all rheumy and lousy like Dostoievski's prisoners wore. Get me, Steve?

What started me? You can never guess? Commenced writing about a Jew bastard who used to be a messenger and practised the gentle art of Non-Resistance. Wanted a few good lines of poetry to introduce the chapter and lend the mood. Searched my files and hit upon "The East Side" by Irwin Granich—I'll give you two couplets or quatrains or whatever the bunkum is called:

> And there is Sorrow beside the bed of the young
> immigrant boarder on the fourth floor, as he
> tosses on the bed springs, racked and lonely,
> Tortured by the bedbugs and thoughts of his wasting,
> starved life, all the beauty beyond his hands.

Maybe that doesn't convey any imagery to your mind. To me it means worlds. I appreciate that utterly, and my soul is drunk in anticipation of getting more. So out I sneaks to the library towards evenin' and bilks the books aforementioned—*Corn-Huskers, Lustra, Advice, Challenge, The Golden Whales of California, General William Booth Enters Heaven, Smoke and Steel.*

Man, I'll quote you so full of quotations you won't know plop from zowie. I ask myself: Is it for this I have read Haeckel, Darwin, Spencer,

Freud, Huxley, Weininger, Rolland, Dewey, Andreyev, France, D'Annunzio, Havelock Ellis, Forel, Nietzsche, Schopenhauer, Tolstoi, Gorki, Mencken? I ask you as a friend to tell me it is not true!

How does your pale, pink soul react to this, pray?

SOME DAY

Some day, some day
I am going to renounce the gods
And their epical can-cans and lumbering poses,
The houris of mysticism and the planetary
        twaddle of the daily prints,
And the paper-chase for Truth and novels that lie
        about lies.

Some day, some day
I shall forswear the oblique glances of black eyes,
The sedentary paradises in the wine glass,
The frou-frou of the crowds that promenade the streets
Like cranes and penguins in a Cloaca Maxima,
And the "movies" with their phantom kisses and
        phantom murders—
And live with little children in a chink in the sky!
                    Benjamin De Casseres

Some day—I am going to write poetry—just like that! Papa buy me that!

And some day I am goin' to raise corn-fed hogs in Iowa and wear bandanna handkerchiefs; spit huge gobs of spit the while I sing a threnody of Atalanta.

Notice how a vacation will put a guy in tune with the Infinite? And I almost believed I was a business man, one of them there efficient guys, with his welfare didoes and amorous peccadilloes with the gay stenographer. Ho, ho, and a bottle of rum!

Man alive, I am on an intellectual bat. I feel like a gaily caparisoned cacique among cormorants, like a bashaw among bastinadoes—a bat out of hell! Let's sing Goddam and to hell with the Western Union that feeds my brat and all the other slinking mit-glaumers that help the W. U. to do it.

                                    L'Envoi.
                                    HVM

The Hall of the Mountain King
Nov. 5, 1923

Amiel: (Copies to Ross, Stanley and posterity)
*   *   *
Continuing my letter of yesterday, anent the virtue of friendship in old
age. Here are some further thoughts. . . . In point of actual truth I haven't
any further thoughts on the subject, but I am blessed with a new amanuensis and I am determined to give him practice even at the risk of spilling
a little frivolous chatter. Letting my mind, therefore, slide gently down
to the least common denominator, I will impart a few words of seeming
erudition on the subject of *saturation* as practiced by the late Henry James
in his singular style of novel writing.

All great men write to order: Caesar, Balzac, Wells, Shaw, Barrie,
Strindberg and the one-and-only Dostoievski included. The Jamesian
method of approach was to pace up and down the room in a scarlet,
brocaded, velveteen nightgown with a pungent cigarette dangling artisti-
cally between two silken fingers, the while he dictated from an overfed
mind to an undernourished slave. To write a novel of a hundred thousand
words Henry James found the most convenient way was to pour out about
two hundred and fifty thousand. This method has long since been found
meritorious by popular song-writers, as witness the once famous ditty
called "The Longest Way Round Is the Shortest Way Home."

Let us stop for a few moments and contemplate what it means to
squeeze out, weed out, eradicate, eliminate and subjugate a hundred and
fifty thousand superfluous words. What precious offal, what divine excrescences must have been contained in these unique Jamesian "droppings." Take the four walls of your cubby-hole: then imagine, if you will,
what it would look like, if on it we attempted to inscribe the pure didactic
monstrosities of Henry James's artifical distillations, lucubrations and
menstruations. Ask yourself whether you do not prefer the blatant phallic
desecrations on the screaming red walls of the buried city of Pompeii. Or,
if that is not enough of a contrast, choose the urinal in the Houston Street
Burlesque Theatre. Take a characteristic bit of lyric poetry after the
manner of Carl Sandburg, done by an inferior genius—such an inscription for instance as this: "Your Mag has bleeding tits" or "Suck this big,
juicy prick". . . . How pale and anaemic the following from the pen of
Henry James must seem to your sound, substantial intellect:

> Give us that interlude; and then continue like the *curiosity of literature*
> which you have become. For gleams and innuendoes, and felicitous
> verbal insinuations you are unapproachable. But the core of litera-
> ture is solid. Give it to us once again! The bare perfume of things

will not support existence, and the effect of solidity you reach is but perfume and simulacrum.

A brief pause here whilst my secretary rubs his back with Omega Oil and I replenish the gaping maw of the spittoon with a few well-directed gobs of spit. (This is just a reminder that I am still domiciling at Oom Paul's—better known to the initiated as COCKROACH HALL.) Never having read a line of Henry James, and adopting the method of my esteemed mentor, John Cowper Pow Wow, in his late and lamentable lecture (*lame* would have been better) on Joseph Conrad, I will now proceed to wax eloquent on the art of the author of *The Portrait of a Lady.* . . . You recall Hamsun's lines in *Wanderers* about the noise of the forest?—"like the murmurings of a million nothings"?—that is the literature of this effete, expatriated coxcomb, a revised version of *Much Ado about Nothing.*

In the vast desert wastes of that great American novelist's tomes (Theodore Dreiser, I mean), the dull aridity is more than alleviated by the striking verdure of his opalescent oases. In the vast spaces of Henry James' hieratics all is lost save honor. A vast panorama of tintinnabulations, a molten sheen of iridescent acerbities, a mumbo-jumbo of tortured hieroglyphs, a frazzled counterpane of dyspeptic arabesques. Try to pile Pelion on Ossa if you can; subtract the perihelion and add Osiris; multiply by numismatics and divide by hydrated quadratics; then shake well before using. If still unconfined, call Melrose 9693 and Dr. Paul will fetch a straitjacket. In the lefthand coat pocket of the doctor's dirty dressing gown find *Alice in Wonderland;* call for the Prisoner of Zenda; take your place in the solid phalanx of a myriad beasts of the bedstead and hitch your wagon to a star in the best Wordsworthian manner, then tell me if you can hear the clarion call of justice! If not, write Haridas Thakordas Mazumdar and request a copy of the New York *Call.* Read the editorial entitled "Economic Consequences of the Peace Treaty" and try to unravel the involved ethics of the late Separatist Movement in the dismembered German Empire. Failing this, let your eye rove at random until it strikes the advertising section. Read what they say about "mild, pleasing laxatives;" "Are you losing your manhood?" "Do you suffer from lumbago, barber's itch, or internal, bleeding hemorrhoids?". . . .

* * * *

Somewhere in his lectures Cowper Pow Wow hinted at the deep mystery underlying the throes of authorship. Well may you ask on what meat doth Caesar feed that he can spew such vile vomitings. Well then, here you have it: an article of Henry James in the *Yale Review,* long and intimate association of a purely involuntary sort with insectivora, a charcoal acquisition of a Red Indian-like Dante, three pipefuls too many of Prince Albert tobacco, a too eager anticipation over the possession of a Noiseless typewriter, plus an hereditary love of ease displayed in the use and abuse of an unexpected amanuensis, and—a dirty bedspread, a mania for alliteration, a very splendid bowel movement, and the thought that Emil would go Schnellocking thru this jabberwocky chortling chic chuckles.

August 28, 1924

To the last of the Cro-Magnons:
A word or two about this Bowery Savings Bank opposite the Commodore Hotel. The finest commercial building, that is, the interior, in the whole United States. It almost beggars description. Entering it I stood spellbound, the glamour of majestic architecture rooting me to the doorway. One hesitates to enter. The eye cannot take in all the manifold beauties of ornament that surge in and beat against the retina. And yet, it were misleading to leave a statement thus. For this interior, rich though it is in countless ingenious decorations, leaves an abiding impression of simplicity and grandeur.

Imagine a rectangular basilica with noble peristyles flanking the walls. In the center an oval space, encased in delicately wrought bronze and marble, for the corps of clerks and their dollar bills and their adding machines, etc.

Between the columns, which are really pilasters, are noble Romanesque arches and at either end imposing orifices of light. The ceiling is paneled and richly wrought, as are the beams and supports. Curious medieval carvings are embossed on the flat ventilators built into the smooth limestone walls. And underfoot are imported mosaic patterns of pale tints and original design.

The effect of such an edifice is tonic. One easily acquires a feeling of awe and reverence. All except the time-honored lackeys at the door. They grow used to everything, even their horrid false teeth. Damme, if I could forget this fellow's ugly mouth as he prattled on in a sterile way about the marvels of its architecture. His broken hinges, decayed bridge-work, and withering pewter ware disturbed the calm equipoise established by this sanctuary.

He told me that he had verified the various measurements given in the booklet one Sunday when he had nothing to do. Spoke of it rather apologetically as an old man's whim. But he was certain now that the space from the oval to the door was 45 feet, or whatever it was.

I told him in ecstasies that he really ought to pay to work in such a glorious place. He smiled and admitted that one of his customers, a very rich man who had travelled in Italy extensively, had said the same thing. He said he guessed it must be a wonderful place all right. Everybody tells him so. Would I come back another day and he would permit me to sit in the balcony and make sketches if I cared to.

But pshaw, men, this is an idle account and nowise like I intended. I wanted to utter golden pronunciamentos, sing baroque melodies, swell to Scriabin rhapsodies. And all I have succeeded in doing so far has been to recount numbers, facts, items, architectural data which might be found in better style in any *Architectural Forum*.

Again, I wish to allay any suspicion that I am writing this for exercise, trotting out all the newly-acquired terminology of my archtectural and aesthetic divagations. Not so, indeed. What I wish to do merely is to announce to the chosen few—the aesthetic hierarchy of Millerdom—that right in our midst we have a thing so magnificent, so splendid, as to put to shame the endless Palazzi of the Medici, the Doges, the Numa Pompilii. No need now to visit Florence, the Ponte Vecchio, the Duomo, the Campanile, the Arno, the Pitti Palazzo, the Santa Maria Novella, the Sistine Chapel, the Borghese Palace or any of the Numismatica Prophylactica. Right here on 42nd Street and Pershing Square is the genuine, authentic, autochthonous note, the ambivalent equivalent of medieval modernity.

Opposite the Commodore Maximus with its serrated echelon enfilades we have the bronze doors of the Dark Ages leaping at the tremulous moving public that daily throngs the doors. Squat little monsters with a pietic visage poke their ugly gestures at the populace. Misshapen, squat, tortuous, bow-legged, medieval. But beautiful when raised in lacquered bronze on a hammered door. Nothing absent but the ithyphalli from Pompeii. No screaming reds here to insert a lecherous note. Instead, a quiet, even tenor to a monotone floor of intriguing mosaic.

Oh, gentlemen, ere my maudlinity descend to lush Millerics I must close on this solemn organ note. The beautiful, rich organ silence that hangs so portentously over the money-bags in the lacquered bronze oval is broken by a scream, a shrill whistle of some nouveau-moderniter model. The spell is broken. My informant announces that some unwitting fool has stepped on the burglar alarm.

Gone now is Florence and the Arno, dreamy, willowy, Dantesque. Gone now are the Borghese, the Pitti, the Medici. Gone is Lorenzo, Cosimo, Benvenuto, Angelo, Leonardo and the Duomo. Gone, even, is the Third Avenue Elevated which thrust its intestinal tract before the body politic so ungraciously.

Gone is the homunculus. Gone the plebiscite. Gone the duodenum.
        Ave atque vale.
                In the faith.
                    Val Nieting.

P.S. Emil: This fool letter will convince you that I got a thrill nevertheless.
Do see it at once.

                                        HVM

P.P.S. This was a day I missed lunch. With not a farthing in my jeans *I
yet was* able to rise to the occasion.
            ? ? ?
                                        De Senectute!

P.P.P.S. Never mind if some of the words don't belong. There's a lot that
don't belong in this cussed universe. Get me?

[1924 or '25]
Dear Emil:
    Couldn't wait any longer here for you. Took Ned with me (as an artist)
to do up the Houston St. Burlesk. Just received three assignments from
one magazine (*Menorah Journal*) and it included "Houston St." business
and "Night Life on Second Avenue." I am going to interview Minsky,
Margie Pennetti and *Cleo* if I can. Thought I could see your work at same
time, see?
    Tonight I wish you could go with me or rather *I with you* (still flat, you
see) and do up the haunts of the literati—also with sketches. Mind you,
they haven't asked for sketches but if they're interesting I think it will go.
Can you do this? Will be back at 6:00 or earlier. Could go to Joe's with
you or anywhere. Some cheek!
    I have been working my guts out lately—I ought to be dried up but I'm
not. Pounding the typewriter incessantly. Decided to make one grand
stab at newspaper or magazine work. Things look quite bright. *Collier's*
want to see about four of my articles and *Sat. Eve. Post* wants one. Just
finished one on the "Sargasso Sea" for *Sunday Tribune*—*and* have a propo-
sition to write daily feature article of 400 words for a Syndicate—N. Y.
Journal and Hearst Papers. Also, by sending O'Regan round *one* day only
with my MSS he got very favorable receptions and the above contacts with
Tribune and Syndicate. I find that my stuff looks good—only a bit too

high-brow. They don't want literature. They all comment on the versatility of my style. Hot dog! Maybe we'll land on the bandwagon yet. Got lots to tell you.

HVM

P.S. In other words I am free as a lark all day and night till any hour. Let's celebrate and write literature and draw funny pictures. Ask me about Justin Smith and Jac Dun.

March 18th, 1925

Copies to Buzby, Stanley, Ross & Haridas Mazumdar

Papa Emil:

"Stolen this day—3/18/25—from my good friend, Emil Schnellock, never to leave my possession until death and dissolution. No more wonderful epic of the artist's soul have I seen till now."

This I write solemnly in the flyleaf of your book, so generously loaned me and so wantonly filched. But this is a gift from the high places. This is an involuntary gift which can never be requited fully.

Pierre Loti, spinner of the fine fantastic, weaver of such gossamer as *Jerusalem, Disenchanted* and *The Sahara,* must go into the discard with Rolland, France and Flaubert. Not that they are unworthy but that they have been surpassed. For this is indeed—in God's bloody truth—THE LAST LAUGH of literature: a spiritual fiber of teeming eloquence wrung from a great and wracked soul. This is the chaste handiwork of a poet of the imagination, of the most consummate jongleur of Anglo-Saxon hieroglyphics.

Some fool of a critic, hired to beat a blatant hurrah, dubs this honest plainsong of a man a work of "Mysticism." To such piffle I mutter "Bah!" There is no need to drag in harried enigmas such as "Mysticism" in the face of this soul-tragedy. This is, if anything, the grand organ note, the utter diapason of an artist's fretted heart. Who reads this without maudlin ecstasy is a barren, sterile hybrid—no man, not even a werewolf.

Yes, old Poop, perhaps my genius lies in the general direction of emanating "a purposeful, literary buffoonery." Perhaps so. But in my easy chair, in my sumptuous, unearned grandeur, I am eaten by a secret rending desire to write such a book at this. I will not say it is the *greatest* book written in the English language (that for the idle critics) but I can say that it has bereft me of emotion.

"Literature, he re-enunciated in his mind, is the sensuous art of causing exquisite impressions by means of words." Treasure that up, gentlemen. And this: "One touch of art makes the whole world alien." Treasure it up!

And treasure up no less these golden gauds that dangle forever beyond the reach of the literary dogs of today, wallowing in their vomit: "gouts, gallipots, neumes, rath, Pushtu, fortalice, argent, verjuice, whorls, barmy, chrysoberyl, obsolescence, kraal, dingles, spume, ilex, tessellated, fume, glistering, magistral, thuribles, deodar, phantasmal, mullioned, spagyric, cedarn, flagon, jerry-builder."

When you have sickened of polite literature take down these sheaves and reread these purple passages:

"But all the time the flute notes were sounding in his ears, and the ilex threw a purple shadow on the white pavement before his villa. A boy came forward from the garden; he had been walking amongst the vines and plucking the ripe grapes, and the juice had trickled down over his breast. Standing beside the girl, unashamed in the sunlight, he began to sing one of Sappho's love songs."

* * * *

P.S. Don't worry about the book. I'll buy you a new one very shortly!

Midnight—Monday

[Spring '25]

Emil:

As I sat guzzling in the ham-and-egg joint just now I wrote you a letter in my mind, so vividly and swiftly that I can't recall just how it started. However, it concerned your visit tomorrow. And friendship. Oh, yes, I remember now. It started: "Wolf, wolf!" And now I've been crying that so long that nobody believes me any more.

Well, Emil, this time it's but too true. Saturday afternoon (a hot afternoon in Montana, I guess), he dropped in on me casual like, when June was out, and drew a chair up to my bedside while I lay back apathetically, and he told me a quiet little story. He was the best friend I ever had and now he's gone back on me, too. He says the jig is up. Whether I come across with the rent or not, he won't promise whether I can stay or not.

That's about as clear-cut as he made it sound to me. So I leave it to you to figure out what it means.

But, before I go much further, I must make it clear that this is not a demand on sight. This is not even a moth-eaten request for alms. No, friend (how far is it till Christmas?) this is a sentimental outburst in an introspective vein. Perhaps a sly leaf inserted into my future memoirs.

But I got to thinking so hard about your coming that I almost wanted to cry. I got to thinking about the friends I used to have and how there ain't so many as there used to be. Oh, I don't mean to adopt the persecution trend, like a certain friend we have in common. I can kind of figure it all out to myself, if I don't shut my eyes. But I can't stop feeling bad.

So when June told me that "my friend, Emil Snellogg" was comin' over tomorrow night I began to make merry in anticipation. I began to think of how I could straighten the house and make things look bright and artificial. I began to think of how I might dispel this Stygian gloom that hangs like a funeral pall (or shroud) over our fair abode.

When I was a kid and they told me Joey or Tony wuz comin' I used to hop for joy. They couldn't hold me down. I used to go on a mild, boyish sort of rampage. And in my recently acquired habits of being a recluse I suppose I've slid back a ways toward childhood again and become sort of skittish. Anyways, I'm muddled-like about the exact state of my feelings. I know it's a nondescript concoction bordering on tears. Because *now* there's just one friend left me. And that's yourself.

So, in defense of this glorious occasion—the test of true friendship and the passing of the glories of Remsen Street—I say: "Sneak a bottle over if you can." We might slobber over one another more unconsciously if you have it than if you haven't. We might take a drink in memory of the thirty-five Mezzotints written to date. Or another for the Muse that inspired "The Houston Street Burleskers," "Wrestlers," "Diary of a Futurist," "Cynara," "Asphodel," "Chewing Gum" et alia.

You might heave a sigh as I recount the true life of an artist, as practised for six months on nothing but nerve. I could explain more fully what Shaw meant when he wrote, "The true artist will sacrifice everything, let his mother starve, his wife and children go hungry, rather than forsake his vision." Those are not the exact words, but they're near enough. Christ knows, I never expected to eat these words, as I have recently.

We might sing a little song of lament over the friends who so quickly departed: Wright, Dewar, Buzby, Haase, Wardrop, Ramos, Sattenstein, Maurer—why name more? We might hang an imaginary wreath over the shrine of RAPPAPORT and write below the name: "Faithful to the end."

God knows, I'd like to keep my wife home at my side, where she belongs; I'd like to pay the alimony and send my kid to a decent school; I'd like to keep on living in nice clean airy rooms in a respectable neighborhood; I'd like to eat regularly three times a day and not have my food go back on me; I'd even join a Church, everything else being equal.

But when I took the newspaper along with me tonight, to glance at during my repast, I realized what a long way off all that is. I didn't look at the newspaper. I wrapped it up and carried it home again. Newspapers make me sick. What good are they to me? Do I want to know what the rest of the world is doing? There's nothing the matter with my imagination. I know they're buggering one another, bitching up the works, fighting, scrapping, bedeviling themselves and making of this vale of tears a bed of thorns.

Thank you, I'd rather go home, pretend I'm an artist and write some more flapdoodle. I suppose, in the last analysis, it comes down to this: that I really want to escape reality. I suppose I want to dream clean sheets, good meals, happy endings and all the rest of it. And I suppose, further, that I'm one of those lily-livered pups who hasn't guts enough to go out and get a he-man's job and slave eight hours, maybe ten, for some guy who knows a little less than I do.

Well, Emil, I would have liked to fix the house up pretty—have all the pictures I spoke about, sit you down in a cozy armchair and tell you of my successes, past and present. But that can't be. We'll just sit around and look at dirty pictures—done by the great masters in moments like these.

Cabinet Minister

P.S. Another letter that belongs to you.

II

SPRINGTIME IN PARIS

1930

Miller arrived in Paris on March 4, 1930. He had already been there on a visit two years earlier, but this time he had come to stay. His wife June, who had urged him to quit his job at Western Union in the first place and who had supported him most of the time since, was convinced that he must go to Europe if he was ever to become a writer. During the six years he had been struggling with his medium, he had written three novels and countless stories and articles; only a few articles had been accepted for publication.

Paris had the desired effect, liberating Miller psychologically and providing a wealth of material. Though he took to Paris immediately, he did not immediately find himself as a writer. For a long time he continued to struggle with an unfinished novel, still attempting to write conventional fiction. But at the same time he was discovering his natural form of expression in his letters to Emil.

Schnellock, the loyal friend who had seen him off at the pier and loaned him a final ten dollars, proved to be the ideal audience and the informality of letter-writing the ideal medium. Here Miller could shed his self-consciousness and express himself spontaneously in the vernacular. His long, rambling letters to his old friend about everything he experienced led him to the style he had been avoiding in his formal, structured, "literary" endeavors.

Most of the writings he sent to Schnellock during his first three months in Paris were not letters in the ordinary sense but rough drafts of feature articles that Miller intended to revise for eventual publication in a book about Paris. Meanwhile Schnellock was to serve as a clearing house, distributing copies to editors and others who might be interested. Though no editor ever accepted these compositions, they marked the turning point in Miller's career. In fact several of them—notably the one entitled "Bistre and Pigeon Dung"—contain passages that were later to reappear in *Tropic of Cancer*.

The letters written during Miller's first three months in Paris show him responding enthusiastically to everything he encounters: the beauty and squalor of the city, the language, the people, the way of life. "I am overwhelmed," he exclaims, "by the multifarious, quotidien, anonymous, communal, etc. etc. *life!*" He is particularly impressed by the serious interest shown in the cinema and particularly responsive to Surrealism in art and literature. At the same time his letters reflect anxiety about money right from the start. June had promised to send him enough money to live on, but, though she cabled from time to time, the money promised in her cables often failed to follow. A letter written two months after his arrival expresses both his desperation and his determination to stay on: "I love it here, I want to stay forever. . . . god-damn it, I'm going to hang on by the teeth. I don't want to return. Misery there. Here—*pleasant* misery."

I think it's Thursday
I don't know what date!
36 Rue Bonaparte
Hôtel St. Germain-des-Prés
Paris, France
Europe

[March 6, 1930]

Well, Emil—and Ned!—god-damn it, it's wonderful. I feel so good that when I finish this I'm going down and take my first Pernod. Here I am, right up under the roof, five stories up, in a new joint. 500 francs a month, services included, and a bath right outside the room door which I can use at 5 francs the visit. What a room. Dormer windows, sloping eaves, paper peeling off, no carpet—in need of repairs, but excellent for all purposes. Why pay more? Unless you have a weak heart and can't stand the climb three or four times a day. But say—when I look out the staircase window on the surrounding scene I feel glad I am up here in heaven. You can look right into all these French homes and your eyes are rewarded with strange sights. In front of me—on the Rue Bonaparte side—there are various groups of painters. And they have a fashion of putting their canvases out to dry—face front. What's to stop me from doing likewise? Nothing brother, nothing. Downstairs is the most wonderful art shop for supplies. It makes me feel that I want to chuck this crap about being a writer and go in for the painter's life. But no, I must restrain myself. I am only three days in Paris and it is the first day I begin to feel like I ought. I have been pretty punk otherwise. (Christ, my English is deteriorating.)

You see, London gave me a severe cold. The houses are not sufficiently heated. You take a bath and run thru the halls—and br-r—you shiver before you get your clothes on. I don't like London anyhow. I would never advise anyone to go there. It is a wonderful city—but they can have it. They—who? Not the English. Christ, what beggars! The scum of the earth is London's poor—and that means the big majority. Otherwise a fine people.

You said that the gloom was rich. It was. You could cut it with an axe. Ate breakfast at the window under an electric light. However, I saw some *Turners*—and I saw Whitechapel and Limehouse. That was worth the trip. The rest of London didn't excite me at all. Leicester Square, Piccadilly, Charing Cross—just another 42nd Street back in 1895. Of course the alleys and courts off these streets were good—good and ripe. One night, under the arches, I saw a fellow pissing up against a wall. (Of course this could happen in N.Y. too!) But this was a little unusual in that while the fellow pissed his gal kept up a running conversation with him in a voice that all could hear. She said she'd give him a good fuck and suck him off and what not. But he seemed intent only in relieving his bladder, and that brought about a great row in good old Cockney vernacular.

* * * *

Tonight, as I left the restaurant, I passed by Notre Dame and stopped at a pissoir to take a leak. I was torn by conflicting impulses—one, to circle Notre Dame and soak it up; two, to tear off a poster in the pissoir which interested me exceedingly. All over Paris now there are advertisements (London likewise) put out by the municipality, warning the public against contracting venereal infections. And are they realistic? Are they grim? Wait till I get one for you, showing the various stages of syphilis or gonorrhea (from the germ plasm up to the death skull—a leering, grinning figure of death and disease with empty sockets.)

And say—this is a departure from the theme—but! when Marc Chagall calls a picture *From My Paris Window* it means something. This afternoon I went up to Sacré Coeur and looked over the city. It is just such a vision as I have often dreamed. It is all that you wish—and maybe a little more. And I thought (this is literature, because I didn't think any such thing) of how it looked to the Romans when they christened it Lutetia—and how it looked to Napoleon when drunk with the wine of victory he came back from Italy through what is now the Metro Station Place d'Italie.

So, all in all, men, I am content. I will write here. I will live quietly and quite alone. And each day I will see a little more of Paris, study it, learn it as I would a book. It is worth the effort. To know Paris is to know a great deal. How vastly different from New York! What eloquent surprises at every turn of the street. To get lost here is an adventure extraordinary. The streets sing, the stones talk. The houses drip history, glory, romance. Ah well—you think I'm drunk. No, I am dead sober. I paid too much for my dinner (22 francs, including Service.) This must not go on. But after you have eaten one meal "prix fixe" you get hungry. You want food you can eat. I don't know how those students at the Sorbonne, who eat on the Boul' Mich', can nourish their brains. I'm an American, Be Jesus! and I'm not used to eating the intestines of dogs, horses, and guinea pigs. And I'm a son-of-a-bitch if I pay 2.50 any more for a "café crème." There are hundreds of dives where you can get it for 1.25. Why pay more? I've busted so many 100 franc notes that I swear tomorrow and the day after I'll live on 25 fr.—not a cent more!

Emil, I have bad news for you. The Sewers of Paris and the Catacombs are shut down until middle of Spring. But Zadkine says all Paris is practically built over catacombs. So let's do a little private digging before Spring comes.

Ah, Spring! It is here already—almost. Everybody is sitting on the terraces already. It is very mild—rather chilly indoors, but mild outside, if you have an overcoat on. And there lies the principal difference between Paris and London. Londoners secrete themselves in their dingy, drab, sordid pubs. Oh, what vile holes! What craven creatures, male and female. My first visit to a pub shocked me. The women shocked me. Old derelicts, battered, bruised, glum, garbed in greasy black dress with sottish faces and hands gnarled with toil. I'm glad I know what a London pub is like. Nothing I ever read conveyed to me the abject squalor of these places.

How jolly and bright are the French cafés! Last night on the Boulevard Haussmann I sat in one with Zadkine and listened to a Tzigane orchestra. The place was jammed. And all these people had dropped in especially to hear these old folk tunes—they were not squealing for jazz—Plus de Jazz!

Paris does strike me as the most cosmopolitan of all the big cities. Here is the greatest congregation of bizarre types. People do dress as they please, wear beards if they like, and shave if they choose. You don't feel that lifeless pressure of dull regimentation as in N. Y. and London. London really is a bit silly about these perfunctory details. And yet, with all their observance of the amenities, aren't they a dull, witless, shabby, woebegone bunch to look at? Did you ever stop and pike them off at theatre time? Aren't their women frightful? Aren't they the dowds, the prunes, the pain-in-the-ass-es?

Well, fellows, let this hold you for a while. What do you want me to drink—if anything? And *without what flavor?* Give my especial regards to

Muriel, who I know will turn over when she gets these details (not all of them, Poppa!). If there is any special information you all want—anything of a practical or urgent nature—write and ask. A votre service, M'sieu, Madame!

Say—that French! The first night it just broke down on me. I couldn't remember how to say beans. Principally because the fellow (the patron of the hotel) looked so blandly stupid when I rolled it off. We commenced jabbering at each other—making signs like two god-damned apes. O, it was comical. But I felt like 30 cents. Since I changed my quarters I am doing better. I even get a civil response from the gendarmerie.

I guess the only way to learn to talk French is to talk it, eh? I must go to hear a French talkie.

Man, I know a letter like this doesn't make you feel good. Forgive me if I seem to rub it in. I don't mean it that way. I just wanted you to know that when you decide to come it won't disappoint you. Even if you forgot your umbrella, or your rubbers! So that's all. Best wishes. Let me hear from either or both of you occasionally.

HVM.

[March 9, 1930]

First Sunday in Paris

Perhaps the most wonderful Sunday of my life! Awakened early by the cries of the street vendors, each of them singing a different tune, a beautiful tune to my alien ears. Plunging into the street and wondering suddenly if it is Sunday, so many shops open, housewives prowling through the narrow streets in their carpet slippers, arms laden with provisions. The air is light and the sun out strong: a typical Paris sky, not brilliant as in the South, yet blinding, perhaps owing to the reflection from light gray walls. I walk toward St. Severin, determined to have a look at it before breakfast. The street cleaners are busy with their long brooms made of thin bunches of coarse hemp. Tiny streams of water flow along the kerbs, carrying the refuse of the streets down into the famous sewers, which alas, one cannot visit now until Summer.

St. Severin is there in all its crumbling beauty—very worn, very aged, very beautiful on this lovely Sunday morning. I am almost tempted to go in. But why should I? Outdoors it is even more wonderful than amidst the smoke and prayers of the faithful. I step into a café at the Pont St. Michel—"Au Départ" it is called—for my croissants and café crème.

There is a great bustle at the bar, doubtless because it is Sunday and everyone is up early to take advantage of the holiday. I study the healthy, homely faces about me—these peasant faces, so sturdy, so animated, so expressively sensible and normal. They are happy as we Americans will never be. They seem to be enjoying each day as it comes along, finding their pleasures simply and naturally, asking nothing more than being in each other's company, to converse, to drink their excellent wines, to taste the flavor of their rich tongue, to go to the bird market perhaps and bring home a canary or a cooing pigeon. The bird market is not far off—just across the bridge a little way, on the Ile St. Louis, almost in the shadow of Notre Dame. How much it tells us about the French, a little thing like this bird market, or the flower stalls abounding everywhere. Violets for one franc a bunch—not for special occasions (when you take your girl to the theatre, or you suddenly remember your wife's birthday) but for every day, for everybody.

It is tranquil and beautiful along the Seine. So many bridges, each of them christened with an imposing name. They look this morning as they have often looked to me on a canvas. The water is slightly ruffled and the shadows under the arches waver and tremble. Men are fishing with long poles on both sides of the river, all along its course as far as one can see. Beyond the walls of the river, following its gentle curves, the houses lean lazily on one another, and glow with a soft, mellow light. One wonders how old they are, how long they have stood thus in their serenity and vividness. In each age there have been writers who have deplored the passing of the old Paris, the Paris that was familiar to them in their youth, or that was pictured to them by their parents. And yet it is difficult to conceive of a new Paris. I believe that Paris will always look aged, like her old painters with their hoary beards and twinkling eyes; I believe that she will always have a wonderful savor like her beautifully colored liqueurs.

I am on the Right Bank now, have passed the Hôtel de Ville, and suddenly find myself in a squalid, moldy district off the St. Antoine Quartier. Children are plentiful here and one is bound to observe them because one may walk for miles sometimes without ever stumbling on one. Here the streets are frightfully crooked, dismal and narrow. The houses seem to converge above one's head and as one looks up the walls show dreadful scars, are grimy and discolored. Here the scum thrives, in the very heart of old Paris. Here on a day in July the citizens rushed to arms, thirsting for vengeance; through these very streets they poured like rats deserting a sinking ship. It is only a short distance to the Bastille from here. Up the Rue Antoine, crowded now with pushcarts. A typical ghetto scene, yet distinctly Parisian. One observes the gendarmes, just as in every big city, harrying the poor vendors, squabbling with them disgustingly about the miserable articles of the law. And since they are frequently

Jewish, these poor creatures of the kerb, one is delighted to observe the repartee that goes on—the grimaces they make behind his back, the way they stick their tongues out and thumb their noses. Indescribable the merchandise amassed along this crowded lane. Oranges with the peels already removed, skinned rabbits, shellfish of all denominations, wooden shoes, mushrooms, silk stockings at seven francs the pair (!), and so on. Best of all are the wines and liqueurs: Old Port, very aged, genuine, original, etc. at less than fifty cents the quart, Malaga, Burgundy, wines of Anjou, cognac, brandy, whiskey, Benedictine, Chartreuse, Curaçoa, Crème de Menthe. I bought a little flask of Benedictine for two and one-half francs (10 cents) and drank it down at lunch time. Finest stuff in the world, warms the gizzards, makes the entrails glow. Had enough left to give the waitress a snifter, because it doesn't do to walk into a restaurant and bring your own cordials.

At the Bastille I feel that I have strength enough (seeing that monument to courage and defiance) to continue a little further. The bus carries me for three cents to the Porte St. Denis, a grand, battered relic of crazy Louis' day. I know now that I am standing on what is regarded as the oldest street in Paris: the Rue du Faubourg St. Denis. And what a street it is! One of the great streets of the world, no doubt, verily more interesting than anything I have ever seen in London or New York. It is positively rancorous with age, or is it rancid? More pushcarts, more shops, teeming multitudes in the gutter, trampling through garbage heaps. And at frequent intervals, passageways leading to neighboring streets, some covered, others open to the sky, the sunlight beaming strongly on the stone flagging. I duck into these passageways and peer into halls and stables, touch the dripping walls and study the signs that hang in the entrances. Foul places these, where midwives advertize their calling, and professors of the dance guarantee to teach all they know in a dozen lessons. Lazy dogs lie on the sidewalk and refuse to budge. You have never seen the dogs of Paris? Ah, they are a breed all by themselves. Slovenly, cowardly creatures, full of lethargy, constipated too, and yapping because they have nothing better to do.

It is getting on toward eleven o'clock so I return to my room and work for a few hours. After lunch I take my manuscript with me and search for a quiet café where I can sit in peace and correct what I have written. I notice now, as I walk along, and since most of the shops have their shutters down, how many little galleries there are scattered everywhere. It is probably so, as someone has said, that there are fifty thousand artists living and working in Paris. Around the Gare Montparnasse, just below the Rotonde and the Select, there are exhibitions on the street. An amazing quantity of canvases, some excellent beyond cavil, others atrocious, abominable, eyesores even to the bourgeoisie who are out in mass to view the work of their citizens artistiques. The painters themselves are even more interesting than their canvases. Many of them are typically Mont-parnasse, garbed picturesquely in corduroys and black hats, wearing long beards and smoking huge pipes. Others, the obscure, sensitive ones, elicit one's deepest sympathy. What must it be like for an artist to stand all day Sunday peddling his wares like a common huckster. Some of them look at the crowds timidly as if apologizing for being there, and scan the stupid faces wistfully, hoping that there is something not too unintelligible among their works to appeal to those pocketbooks bulging beneath the black frock coats. For the most part the street show is conservative. The water colors are especially good and draw enthusiastic comments from the onlookers who are quick to recognize their beloved streets. The still lifes are very still, très mort, despite all that Cézanne preached about pitching planes, etc. But there is this to remark in connection with the open air galleries—the public displays a critical acumen far above the level of our bourgeois herd. There is no scoffing and wisecracking going on. One has only to think what the comments would be like if outside the Carnegie Library on Fifth Avenue, for instance, a similar show was staged.

Well, we must be getting on, to a nice, quiet café, and so we go along the Boulevard Montparnasse, past the insufferable idiots at the Dôme and the Coupole, until we reach the Closerie des Lilas. I take a seat near the window facing the Bal Bullier, and as I sit studying my manuscript, I can see on the greensward outside a weight-lifter, clad in full tights, amusing the crowd with his stunts. After a while I go downstairs to the lavatory and by mistake walk straight into the ladies' room. The ladies smile and take the faux pas good-naturedly. When I get through with my business I bunk into the madame of the toilet de cabinet, seated at her little change table, writing a note to her sweetheart. She looks spic and span, her hair is coiffed and she seems as happy in her little quarters, happier I should say than a dizzy stenographer on the top floor of the Woolworth Building. The little plate has only a fifty-centime bit on it, so I add my pourboire and get a pleasant thank you from madame. Possibly madame has chil-dren waiting at home for her; possibly she has business to transact after hours. It is well to think charitably of these toilet keepers. Their life is scarcely what one would call wholesome.

Possibly you think I had a few liqueurs to drink upstairs. No, I drink two cups of coffee nature, finish my work and saunter down the street again. I go back past the Dôme and the Coupole and turn up the Rue de la Gaîté, which is very gay now and jammed with theatre-goers. The shops are wide open and have special bargain sales on—they always do on this street. Blood-curdling posters are displayed outside the cinemas, and I see Bebe Daniels' name in big letters and William Haines playing in *Jimmy le Mystérieux,* which is French for *Alias Jimmy Valentine.* On the French posters our cinema stars don't look the same any more. They have become very roguish looking, very froggy, and one can pay all sorts of prices to have a look at them. Sometimes one takes a "promenoir" for a franc, or one can sit in the rear of the orchestra and pay top prices. I like the Rue de la Gaîté because it is alive and colorful. It is also one of the queer streets of the world again. One can dive off it quickly into country stables, or into a little park like Bowling Green, where they still play at bowls. There is a police station on this street, planked between the busy shops, and looking very spanking, very red, white and blue. You can see a handsome gendarme outside, twirling his mustache, his cape slung nonchalantly over his shoulder and a cigarette in one hand. It is a wise government that permits its policemen to smoke on beat. They look contented, these Parisian cops, and for the most part, they mind their own business. At night I see them prowling about with big pipes in their mouths, sometimes ducking into a bar to have a drink, or swinging on their heels holding animated conversation with a citizen.

The sun is going down now, and before diving into the populous quarter beyond the Avenue du Maine, I peek through the cemetery gate, the Cimetière du Montparnasse. There is a convenient little pissoir, one of the very open sort, right at the gate of the cemetery—very thoughtfully located. I go in and soil the cemetery walls with another bucketful of urine. Then I lose myself in an absolutely strange district which burgeons out in all directions starting from the Avenue de l'Ouest. I find that I have struck another rich vein, a quarter whose existence I had never even suspected on my last visit to Paris. The sky has turned slate-gray—a lazy, listless sky that seems all one with the houses and lanes into which I am steering. Here all the stores are open. The horse butchers are doing a tremendous business; the huge carcasses hang in the street in ghastly abundance. It is only when the horse is seen split open, and hung from a peg, that one realizes what a big animal it is. Beside the other creatures, the rabbits and sheep, the fowls and pigs, he seems positively antediluvian in size. And now again the eye is filled with curious sights. Always in these squalid districts the streets reveal the grotesque aspects of humanity. The imbecilic dwarfs of Velásquez, the wretches and cripples of Fantin-Latour, the idiots of Chagall, the monsters created by Goya—all these pass now in review, brush up against one in filthy tatters, mumbling to themselves, singing or cursing, staggering under heavy burdens or stopping to pick a crust from the gutter. It is cruel, no doubt, to call all this glorious, but I must confess that in contrast to these sights the glitter of the grands boulevards seems pale and lifeless. This is humanity in the raw, the endless procession of that prolific spawn at the bottom on whose backs the boulevardiers climb in greed and lust. I stand outside a common bal in the neighborhood and watch the antics on the floor. The place burns with a red glow. The smoke is cloudlike and settles over the place like a heavy vapor. From the far end of the hall comes a queer burst of music, and straining my eyes I can dimly make out a tiny group of musicians isolated in a little loge. I hear an accordion, a violin, a drum, perhaps a piano also. On the floor the couples are spinning giddily to the tune of an old-fashioned waltz. The men keep their hats on and they hug their women unashamedly. Grouped around the floor are rude tables and benches, such as one used to see in German beer gardens or picnic grounds. Everyone seems to be drinking beer, everyone is flushed and happy. This is not a den of vice. I see mothers leading their daughters to the tables, and old gray-beards getting up to dance with round-bellied matrons. This is one of the ways the common people of Paris spend their Sundays. "Very conservative," the waiter tells me in the café next door, "very orthodox." Very, very. . . .

At the Restaurant des Gourmets I have an excellent meal for twelve francs, including wine, butter, bread, serviette and pourboire. Unbelievable—becoming a gourmet on a 48-cent meal! This is a dirty little place, with sawdust on the floor and flies even in the winter, but the onion soup is delicious and only sixty centimes the bowl. While I sup a conversation takes place beside me between an American and a Frenchman. I hear the word "theosophy" over and over again and then the American asking the Frenchman (in English) if he can't sum it all up in a few words. I don't get what the Frenchman says, except through very significant gestures— and a blank stare on the American's face—that nothing worthwhile can be put in a few words. The American is evidently an artist: very gentle, mild face, wrapped in a rufous beard that makes him look like one of Holbein's men. Astounding what the barbe does for our native sons! Especially when, to begin with, they are endowed with a sensitive organism. One sees them everywhere, here on the Left Bank, cultivating their beards, wearing their berets very rakishly and gargling their throats while they practice the French rrr. It is great not to be a simple "où est, avez vous" guy here. You can get so damned much out of a Frenchman when you expatiate delightfully. Every day I ask for butter and every day I have to make gestures with the bread or with a knife to convey what I mean by my "du beurre." Wines are easy and Benedictine—also "les haricots verts," or "Place de l'Opéra."

After dinner I take the Metro to Rue Blanche and search for Studio #28. Montmartre is simply lousy with whores. Little bars, hardly bigger than a coffin, are jammed with them. They seem to be the only customers in some places, and there is always something doing here, as there is around the Columbia Burlesque in New York. Just as I dive off the Avenue de Clichy to mount the Rue Lepic, a very steep pass that only goats can manage speedily, I see one of these unfortunate women of the streets leaning against a wall, weeping, her coat all muddy, and her face bleeding. Nobody pays any attention to her. But wait! Suddenly as I walk on, wondering what has happened, I see a garçon dragging a young ruffian by the scarf, and clamoring for a gendarme. They don't walk up and sock the guy, as a New York cop might. They don't even swear, or swing a club maliciously. I gather that the roughneck has had an altercation with the woman because she gave him a disease. I hear the other women, who have crowded around now, jeering and muttering coarse jibes. "Too bad," they seem to say to each other. "Did the poor little fellow expect to get diamonds for his money?" Wow! they make you shiver, these dolled-up specters. They sit in the cafés and beckon to you from the window, or bunk smack up against you on the street, and invite you to come along. However, Studio #28. . . .

This is *the* intellectual movie of Paris. It is deserted, as intellectual places should be, or generally are. And what a program! I have only space for a few words on *Un Chien Andalou.* I shall say beforehand that never in America do I expect to see such a picture—not even when the millennium comes. What is *Un Chien Andalou?* I don't know. I don't know what it was all about, except subconsciously, if I may use that word glibly.

* * * *

In the lobby of the theatre is a machine from the year 1905. A machine for "making noises." Used, it appears, in those days in moving picture houses during the vogue of the slapstick pictures. People push knobs and pull cords to test it out. What kind of a noise would you like to hear? Broken plates, raspberries, snotting glissades, sandy floors, shattered glass . . . ? There are over 57 varieties.

I trudge down the hill and walk all the way home. The Seine is dancing with colored lights as though the city were celebrating a perennial carnival. I have a letter in my pocket which I want to post. Drop into the spacious Gare d'Orsay, on the Quai d'Orsay, looking for a letter box. The station is deserted. No, not entirely. On a bench near my letter box two lovers sit, fastened in each other's arms. A gendarme stands nearby, watching them quietly. The woman has her head way back, her lips parted, waiting for him to commence all over again.

I leave them to their joy, terrifically stirred by the sight. I walk along the quai, stop for a few moments at the Pont du Carrousel and look over the water toward Notre Dame, barely visible, ghostly, and vastly quiet. I am on the verge of tears. The beauty of it all is suffocating me, and there is no one to whom I can communicate even a fraction of my feelings. Even now, as I recall it all, my eyes swim. I can't go to bed yet. Now I am fairly intoxicated with the glamour of the city. I remember suddenly a place that of all my previous impressions of Paris lingers as the most beautiful, the most vivid. I go searching for this place. Further along the quai, past the Pont Neuf, back again somewhere in the vicinity of St. Severin or St. Julien-le-Pauvre. I don't care any more to know precisely where I am walking. The sky is dark, charged with heavy storm clouds; the air has grown chill and the dampness penetrates. But if it had been hailing rabbits my enthusiasm would still persist. Every once in a while, the narrow passages open up, and there is a charming square, a place or a circle, and things seem to spin.

At last I am there, at l'Odéon, and I find my little Café Voltaire, all shuttered up. The moon breaks through the clouds as I stand there, recalling wonderful memories. The statue in the center of the Place grows with a wan light. It is still just as beautiful as it was on that summer's night when three of us sat drinking beer on the terrace talking of Spengler and Aristotle. I walk over to the theatre, and in the dim light, try to read the billboards for the coming performances. I can make out names like Racine, "après Balzac," Victor Hugo, etc. I try to think what it must be like to witness in this theatre one of the old French classics. Who played there? Will I ever get to really understand the true spirit of this people?

Everything is closing down. I must go back to the room. Along the Boulevard St. Germain I can hear the bells tolling. Strange sounds they make, almost Oriental at times. Some roll long and lingeringly, some chime melodiously or break out with a clangorous peal; and some barely puncture the stillness of the night—just as a faint, high gong, and the sound is snuffed.

I have made the grand tour. I am back again in my attic room at #36 Rue Bonaparte. There is the chill of the grave in the room, but the portières have been put up in my absence. They are stiff and starched-looking and have a quaint colorful design, like rustic tablecloths. I hang up two of my watercolors. They still look good to me. The rest I can throw into the Seine some night. (Catch me!)

And this is Paris after the third or fourth day, a somber cough racking my chest, my blood in a fever, and all my days of labor lying before me.

Au revoir!

P.S. Emil: Is it!
P.P.S. Sending it in two separate envelopes to save postage.

[March 1930]

Apocryphe Hebdomaire, Parisien avec Sang et Feu!

* * * *

Well, let's try another literary indulgence. . . .

Boulevard Malesherbes. C'est minuit. The asphalt gleams like the black helmets of the mounted police. Indigo sky swept clear now of those fleecy clouds which hang all day over the city. One sees so much more of the clouds now, walking between low buildings, debouching onto huge carrefours. It is winter and the trees do not obscure the sky. One can look between the naked boughs and observe the colors changing from rust and purple to lilac, to Payne's gray and then to deep blue and indigo. Along the Boulevard Malesherbes, long after the crepuscular glow of evening, the gaunt trees with their black boughs gesticulating, stretch out in infinite series, somber, spectral, their trunks vivid as cigar ash. Where is the Seine? I inquire at intervals. Tout droit, monsieur, tout droit. On, on, under the arch of twisted boughs, a silence supreme and altogether European. The shutters drawn, the shops barred, a red glow in some window where some mistress enchants her lover. Brusque the façades, forbidding, and pure as the immaculate conception. Night seems to refresh the buildings. They slumber granitically in the moist air. And now which way shall I go? I have come again upon a round-point. An enormous wheel with spokes running out along all the meridians of the compass. If I take the wrong spoke and walk away from the hub, I may end up in Père Lachaise, or Clignancourt in time to see the Flea Market open. But when in doubt it is always safe to *bear* (as the Londoner says) tout droit. "Là-bas c'est la Seine." Nobody understands my "Seine" at midnight. It sounds to les oreilles françaises like "Sévigné," or "Vincennes." I make a noise like running water and draw bridges with my cane. It is difficult for me to imitate the colored lights. "Compris, monsieur?" AH. I have come upon the Jardin des Tuileries. There are two Greek temples perched upon the top of the ramp. One is the Musée de l'Orangerie where for another few days the centenary of Camille Pissarro's birth will be celebrated. Camille Pissarro! Now another Paris comes into my memory—one that I have seen almost as vividly as this living one. It is a Paris of literature, a Paris etched upon the page of *Human Bondage*. Going back a few decades, when George Moore was engrossed with his *Confessions,* when "Les Fauves" were the intransigeants veritables, Somerset Maugham was then a student of painting. He had etwas zu sagen von Camille Pissarro, and about another terrible Spaniard who was startling the world with his acrobatic leaps from style to style—these "styles" which Spengler has so well said are no style at all since each one decides for himself each day of his life what the style shall be. In the grand manner the style is gone. With the death of classicism the culture went under. Do I think all this as I walk along the embankment? Frankly, no. What do I occupy my mind with? With the magic of the night, with the inexorable, wounding beauty of this little stream whose glancing waters reflect a neo-Grecian world. Here the trees bend slightly as if in homage to the miracle of the Seine. In summer they will bend still more under the weight of leaves and blossoms, and when the wind rises in the evening, circulating through the brilliant foliage, they will perhaps shed a few rustling tears and shiver as the water swirls by.

Pont du Carrousel—Pont Solférino—Pont des Arts. Cabs moored to the sidewalk, dozing under the arc lights. In the little box behind the windshield sits monsieur le conducteur de voiture—avec handlebars, un type très curieux, comme les caricatures de Peter Arno.

Notre Dame rising tomblike from the waters. The gargoyles leaning far out from the white façades, grimacing fiercely, hanging there like an idée fixe in the mind of a monomaniac. On the port side, stretched out on the cold, shallow steps, the old women of Paris are sleeping, newspapers under their rags for mattress.

Twenty centuries of Christianity with its relics of bloodshed, its architecture and acres of linen madonnas hanging in all the mausoleums of art the world over. And still it is permitted that women with white hairs should sleep in the cold, beneath the gargoyles and cluttered friezes, beneath the graven disciples who stand with hypocritical saintliness, or advance from the crowd with severed head in hand. What is the meaning of all this? Has it any meaning? What does architecture signify to a frozen body, or the mummery of the Mass where under the splintered beams of light streaming from rose-colored windows a satyr in hood and cassock swings the odorous censer?

*   *   *   *

A bookstore with some of Raoul Dufy's drawings in the window. Drawings of charwomen with rosebushes between their legs. An album of Cocteau's *Dessins*. Exhibition inside of Kandinsky's latest. A treatise on the philosophy of Jean Miró. Then my eye falls on something of rare interest: a book by a Frenchman, illustrated by himself. It is called *A Man Cut in Slices*. Each chapter begins "the same in the eyes of his family," "the same in the eyes of his mistress," etc. I read a few lines and my heart leaps with joy. It is another piece of Surrealism. I believe in it with all my heart. It is an emancipation from classicism, realism, naturalism, and all the other outmoded isms of the past and present. Why must literature lag behind painting and sculpture and music? Why must we consider always the intelligence of the reader? Is it not for the reader to endeavor to understand us? This is the day for the senses to have their innings. After one understands the soul one must grapple with the emotions, with art, with the eternally changing formless forms.

A Prayer: That I may yet live to write such an oeuvre about New York or Paris. That I may describe incomprehensibly the drama going on in a soul standing at 42nd Street and Broadway. That I will not have to explain why he suddenly took it into his head to go home and chop his baby into seven parts.

* * * *

And heavens what a wonderful jolt I got when in Morand's *New York* I stumbled on Walt Whitman's "Crossing Brooklyn Ferry," translated into French—and recognized it, rolled with its rhythm, tumbled into its grand sonorities. Following this excerpt, which I could see moved Morand deeply (since he himself admitted his thralldom over the sight of this marvellous scene) he adds with that keen perception of a true Frenchman: "Dreiser, Dos Passos et bien d'autres ont, depuis lors, chanté le port de New York, *mais ils n'ont fait que paraphraser ce poème de Whitman.*"

A little more: of Bowling Green he remarks in passing—"the oldest of New York parks, the matrix out of which Broadway is born." And later chanting the praises of the gratte-ciel—he describes them variously and singles out the square phallus of the Equitable Building.

* * * *

And if sometimes these accounts of foreign visitors read like enchanting fairy tales, if they seem a trifle grotesque, bizarre, fantastic—I forgive them because I know that to my vision Paris is also a chimera (not shimmera!). And it is all the more truly veritable Macedonian, or was it Thessalonian chimera, because it is all Greek to me—the language, the customs, the pissoirs, the labels on the bottles, the sliding scale of tips, the courtesies that are not courtesies, the radiators that give milk instead of heat, the procession des noctambules, the chanteurs ambulants, the calliope that wakes me up every morning, wheezing the same tune yesterday as today.

Au revoir
HVM

[March 1930]

Spring on the Trottoirs

Je commence: Spring is here! It came in like a swallow during Mi-Carême. It threw spangles of gold on the Place du Tertre where all Paris seemed to flop on the benches and lap up beer. I am talking of the afternoon of Mi-Carême before the debauchees desecrated the Roman bath corner of Boulevard St. Michel and St. Germain. Children float through the underground dressed like fairies and fairies float through the cafés gloved in tights. In the foaming shadow of Sacré Coeur artists stab at their easels to entertain the butchers and drovers who flood the pissoirs and choke the gutters. An Aztec with a flowing mane, his feet shod in carpet slippers, stands outside his dive and barks at the passers-by. He is a composite of Guido Bruno, Oscar Wilde and George Sand. There is just a drop of Buffalo Bill in him also. Inside a German is singing the ancient songs of France, accompanied by a wheezy accordion, a zither, and a flute. It is a ballad in Ut Minor. A heavenly ballad in Springtime, in Paris, the cold walls flecked with dazzling rays, the basilica of Sacré Coeur floating among the clouds just above one's head. The taxis are pouring into the Square. There is no room for them in the narrow passageways so they climb up on the sidewalks, mount the walls, overrun the benches, scratch your back—all in good spirit.

I order a bite in a little den where the menu is chalked up on a blackboard. The walls are crowded with fresco work, the ceiling is a smoke brown, and the little zinc bar where the bottles are submerged in cold water is no bigger than a coffin. I have everything I want, coffee and Benedictine besides, for ten francs. In a corner a group of French artists are collected—their wives and mistresses are with them. They are all a little zigzag and very dramatic in their gestures. They have frank, intelligent faces, extremely mobile and plaster of Paris. They are discussing America. Everywhere one hears this word "America" on people's lips. Usually the remarks are uncomplimentary, accompanied by shrugs of the shoulder, emphatic grunts, leers, devastating grins. I should like to throw in a few myself. I feel deeply this day how pernicious is the influence of our country. I see its paralyzing, stultifying effects. We are dead and Europe is moribund. Somewhere a new people must arise, with vitality, with original ideas. For two thousand years we have been looking for Resurrections, Renaissances, etc. We should junk all this rot in our museums, forget that there ever was a Jesus Christ, a Gautama, a Mahomet—to hell with Michelangelo, Da Vinci, Rembrandt. Take all these madonnas that litter the walls and chuck them into the ashcan. Give us a fresh start, somewhere, somehow. We need it. We need a reforestation of ideas. We need to come down to earth again.

Something of all this went through my mind as I stood in bewilderment, trying to embrace the fertility, the grandeur, the scope of the Oceanic and African Exposition at the Théatre Pigalle. Here was assembled the genuine, the archetype of what we so glibly refer to as Primitive Art. The very term has an invidious ring. Primitive! Elemental would be better. Direct, autochthonous—the unified expression of peoples in various strata of civilization who have not been touched yet by the white heart rot of a bogus white culture. Not yet. Alas, I am thinking back a few hundred centuries. Some have disappeared entirely, like the islands in the Pacific. Others are going the syphilitic way of all white flesh. Africa, which seems to us so dark, so aboriginal, so pristine in its backwardness, its lethargy—Africa has contributed to this enormous collection a variety and wealth of art which is truly staggering. And yet Africa, glorious in its eloquence, pales somewhat beside the vigorous, the more stark and terrifying products of Oceania. This Africa has already shown signs of deterioration. Its message is diluted. The Oceanic Archipelagos, remote, isolated, deriving from God knows where, were more fortunate. There is scarcely an interruption in the brutal, frenzied rhythm of their spirit. One looks at these images, these idols, fetiches, totems—whatever they be—and one's heart quakes. They are not beautiful as we understand the term. They are powerful, effective; they evoke that universal awe which slumbers in the breasts of all of us, refined or barbarous, pagan or devout. Without knowing a single thing about their history, their traditions, their involved and inexplicable customs, one can become saturated, standing before these works, with the fulness of their life. One can grasp intuitively the relationship that existed between man and nature, between the soul and the divinity. One must say above everything that here stands an integrated world, a world enigmatic and cruel, a world divided into extraordinary patterns, but an intelligible, meaningful, rich and vital world. Such a world exists no longer anywhere on this earth. The Primitives are collecting Easter eggs. The super-Nordics have grown two heads, one looking forward, the other looking backward, and when they advance they move crab-wise.

*　*　*　*

But at the Club de L'Ecran, Salle Adyar, Square Rapp, near the Tour Eiffel, the real treat awaited me. Here, in a beautiful Theosophical Centre, is a little meeting hall with a screen where the intellectuals meet to discuss the affairs of the cinema. To hold a post-mortem, as it were. (Usually one or two short films are projected also.)　*　*　*　*

This was a lively, amusing, and intelligently conducted affair. The audience participated. Some of them were actors, some literary men, and some painters. As far as I could make it out they were clamoring for the survival of the authentic French film, an expression of French genius, French traditions, French life through and through. They wanted to put a curb on the importation of American and German films. They wanted the pictures to be made for the French exclusively, and to disregard all thought of foreign markets. There was much talk of direct appeal to the emotions, hitting the reflexes, mécanique, industrielle, comique, Nordic, Anglo-Saxon, artificial, Surrealism, etc. Charlie Chaplin—admittedly funny, a universal mime, etc. They dragged in classicism and realism, discussed Rabelais and Boccaccio, spoke of the advance wing and Studio

28. Of Germaine Dulac, who writes scenarios on the order of the Count de Beaumont. (I saw one of hers at "The Eye of Paris"—called *Theme with Variations.* Quite a beautiful thing, with a woman dancing throughout and for variations on the dance shots sandwiched in of machinery in motion, often very direct, obscene, scarcely symbolic at all. For instance, she is bending backward on her toes—a crazy shot, up-ended—her arms flutter ecstatically as if she held something unmentionable in her grasp. Presto! a huge piston rod, thoroughly greased, shoots insistently backward and forward, plunges into a groove, comes out again black and greasy, to plunge forward once more.)

But—the meeting. Alongside of me sat a painter with his mistress. He wore a sardonic smile throughout, and listened impatiently to an actor in the front row who seemed to monopolize the meeting. Finally he demanded to have a definition—a definition of the comique. Everyone laughed. The chairman tried to pass it off lightly. He repeated the question a few minutes later. The chairman seemed nonplussed. He worked his arms excitedly and finally asked the interrupter to come to the platform. No, the painter didn't want to do that. People began to clap, remarks were hurled. He got angry and bounded from his seat. Someone said something as he passed down the aisle. Like a tiger he turned instantly, went directly up to his man, and gave him a short, brusque, vigorous retort. It must have been excellent because the house burst into a tremendous spontaneous applause. He got on the platform, took a drink of water, mopped his brow, and cleared his throat. He was uneasy. His voice sounded a little dry, it threatened to break. He began falteringly. People bent forward in their seats. He seemed to be getting up steam. He made some magnificent gestures, gave his face a vigorous massage as if to loosen up the muscles of his jaws, and then began in earnest. And my God, never have I listened to such oratory. It was superb, overwhelming. A torrent broke loose inside him and simply deluged the audience. He hurled questions, answered them himself, singled out this one and that one of the previous speakers, challenged their statements, went into long criticisms of their remarks, went back as far back as he could go into the history of the theatre, discussed the classic period of French literature, poured all his vitriol on Anglo-Saxon trash, jeered at the Russians, spit on the Germans, talked of the decadence of art, of painting particularly, mentioned Elie Faure and André Salmon, referred to the Oceanic Exposition, tore the Chien of Andalou to pieces, mocked at Maurice Chevalier, called Chaplin a clown, praised Max Linder, dragged in Cyrano de Bergerac and Sacha Guitry. . . . God, must I give all he spilled out in these ten minutes? Never a pause, never a false move, never a loss for the right word. . . . The audience rose and cheered, stamped and shouted—a tremendous uproar. Tears were streaming down his face as he marched to his seat. His beard was dewy, he was blushing like a schoolboy. And his mistress? She sat there proud as a peacock, or a peahen, wrapped his muffler around his neck, patted his hands, and beamed at everyone benignly.

This is how the French are taking the cinema today.

* * * *

It is Saturday night, after the cinema. Avenue Wagram, near the Arc de Triomphe. The streets are sprinkled with lights. One theatre after another here. Great crowds, well dressed, animated, jovial. People in masks going to a fancy dress ball. Everything wide open. The picture has got me by the throat. I take three beers in succession and start to do the circle of the "Etoile." Impossible. There are too damned many spokes to this axle. I shoot off onto the Champs Elysées and talk out loud, to myself. The Champs Elysées too gets me by the throat. I had never believed it to be so beautiful. It is like people imagine Fifth Avenue to be. It is one of those highly civilized, extraordinarily immaculate highways in which, as Morand well says, "everything breeds but nothing grows." It is like Miami, and it is like Michigan Boulevard. It has been sterilized, cauterized, and polished like a piece of old silver. There is no noise except a scarcely audible fizz from under the glittering awnings where the rich spawn. Is there any boulevard anywhere more refined, more sophisticated, more glittering than this? Through and through it remains the same—like Tiffany's show windows. Here at midnight the streetwalkers are thick as flies. You dodge one only to bunk into another. They tackle you in twos, jab you below the belt, wiggle their tongues promisingly, and ask you if you are a student. A student of what??? Several times now I have been asked that question—by waiters, by gendarmes, by streetwalkers. I have learned how to answer it. I take off my hat, and pointing to my few hairs, say: "Terminées, les études!" That goes over big. . . .

* * * *

You all know where the old Porte St. Denis is? Well, just a stone's throw from the boulevard, between the Rue St. Denis and the Boulevard Sébastopol, you will find the Rue Blondel, and also the Rue Sainte Apolline. This is a typical red-light district. Reminds me a little bit of certain vague areas off Chatham Square.   * * * *   I walk away from the Market along Boulevard Sébastopol. This is an ugly street, very ugly. Off it are innumerable smaller streets, gloomy, drab, and smelly. Around Réaumur-Sébastopol station on the Metro things begin to look up. That is, it gets thick. It gets rotten. Whores dive out from the hallways and cafés. Not the sort that hail you on the Champs Elysées. Broken down voitures, in raincoats, and without hats. One of them came up to me nonchalantly scratching her ass. She looked like a certain character I am writing about. Her face was swollen, as if she had just done crying, her eyes swam about like big onions in a plate of soup. . . . A little further along, I begin to see flaps instead of doors, red lights swinging over tiled walls, numbers in red lights, and a depressing silence on the streets. It is all very theatrical, this setting—like an Ufa design. I see doorways that tilt up and backward, precisely like those cubistic settings in the Krause-Veidt classic long ago. (My memory is growing terrible, especially on names.) Oh, I have it—*Dr. Caligari*! Yes, these are Caligari doorways. Caligari walls and windows. And the people one encounters are somnambulistic. I haven't the nerve to venture in alone. I parade up and down and watch the taxis roll up with Americans and Englishmen. These are the places one can find in Nagasaki, Singapore, Marseilles, San Francisco. . . . Here they speak the universal tongue. Here Sodom clasps hands with Gomorrah. I wander back to Les Halles and study the vegetables piling up now in huge mounds under the electric lights. The horses whinny to one another, the big tumbrils tilt backward, empty. Green canvases are spread out, and the streets resound with the clatter of wooden shoes, with the sharp cries of the market women, and the screams and pompoms from the little toy engine that drags the freight cars up to the sheds. I go take a look at the meat division. Again I see those enormous carcasses of the horse, very red, still dripping blood, so huge that they trail the ground though they are swung from hooks far above one's head. They swing in a dazzling, eerie light, all stiff and cold. Men walk between the rows of cadavers in white aprons with pads in their hands—counting the ribs, most likely.(?) A gruesome, impressive sight. They should call it the "Morgue for Horses." Off the Market are crooked streets, ill-lit, very dilapidated in character, and full of refuse. There is a powerful stench in the air—so powerful, in fact, that it steeps through to the Metro station. At first it seems like stale urine, then it changes to fish, and then to cheese and leeks. It brings back tender memories of Delancey Street Bridge, under the span on the New York side.

Well, Spring has come and flown again. It is now the 11th of November, 1929, Avenue Président Wilson, quatre-vingt-douze. I am thinking of Masaccio and the men of the Quattrocento. My kidneys are thumping because this is all in one stretch. On the corner, in the vestibule of St. Germain-in-the-field, the blind man is sitting; on the steps below him sits a little old woman with a black shawl over her head. They sit there eternally, I never see them stir. On the trottoirs feet are passing, some in fancy slippers, some in sabots, some with run-down heels. They never look any higher than the waist. The blind man doesn't look at all. I always want to draw this picture, but I haven't the courage. Somehow it seems blasphemous to be studying the pose of two miserable ones, just to decorate a piece of paper.

Finis.

April 1st, 1930
Restaurant Louis Varnier
12 Rue du Pont
Suresnes, France

[To Ned Schnellock]

Ned, today is really the first of April. It is more like the first of June.
Hot as blazes. I close the window to keep the room cool. (At night you
open it to get warm!) Today is a day for loafing. I must get out on the
highway and feel the sod under my feet. I decide to take a boat up the
Seine. (Up? There is no up or down; the Seine winds like a great intestine
thru Paris, thru the suburbs, and thru France.) Down at the Gare d'Orléans there is a gaily decorated boat which looks as if it took public
passengers. I step aboard and inquire. The man says he speaks English.
Good! "Where does this boat go to?" "Maurice Dekobra," he replies.
That's hardly a place—but I get the drift. Dekobra is being feted today
on this little river boat. Women are busy hanging up garlands of flowers—the tables are spread up forward. The glasses glitter. There is even
a piano on the main deck. Jesus! if I only had my nerve—I'd invite myself
to go along.

Anyhow, down where the Salvation Army keeps a floating hotel (Armée
du Salut—Asile Flottant) are more boats. (The floating hotel, however,
reminds me vividly of that belle ship *Floridan* in Jacksonville!) But I can't
find out when the next boat goes. It looks as if the service were "interrom-
pée" for several hours (probably to give the captain a chance to catch a
bite). I am right down on the wharf—under the Louvre. Men are fishing,
sketching, painting. These bridges of the Seine—how many thousands of
times they have been done! I think of the marvellous Turners I saw in the
London galleries. Pictures of the quais here in Paris. A Paris of a hundred
years ago. A totally different Paris.

Well, I take the trolley for St. Cloud. I am in the trolley. It is sweltering.
I wish I had a bicycle. If I could cut out smoking Camels perhaps I could
afford a second-hand "bicyclette." It takes about ¾ hour to reach St.
Cloud. One ought to do it in ten minutes in the subway. You approach
the hills that girdle Paris. I don't know why it is but these low hills
fascinate me. They remind me of old engravings which show an ancient
town nestling in a hollow—columns and altars all about, women in Greek
costume, etc. Do you know what I mean?—a classic scene! And I think
too of back in 1917 when the Germans hid behind these hills and shelled
Paris with the Big Bertha. Right near where I *dwell* (St. Germain-des-Prés)
the shells fell and killed 200 people outright!

Well, St. Cloud—I am there! Everything is jake. How can I describe it?
Unless you have seen a small French town along a river it is almost

impossible to visualize it for you. It is a little bit like Sheepshead Bay here, only not quite as colorful. The Seine is less active, less crowded. On the banks workmen have flopped to eat their lunch. Bottles and salami and great hunks of bread spread out. They rest. We don't know what that word means. How they rest! It makes you envious. Canal boats, houseboats, tugs are moored to the shore. One of them is called *Surprise*—but I doubt that it means surprise. You never know what these familiar words are going to turn out to be.

Now I am walking. Walking toward the next town—Suresnes. Only a short distance. I have my manuscripts with me. I think I shall do some work in a nice shady spot. I begin to think of America—home—of all the highways and byways I have trudged along, looking for hitches. I think of you and Joe, of our trip to Florida—and then of Nice and Monte Carlo—of days flat broke, wondering what the morrow has in store. Now I am safe for another ten or twelve days. It is a glorious feeling—being that far ahead. I wonder if I ought to buy a bicycle. I already have maps, fountain pen, watch, etc. All I need is a bike. Fellows are mooching along this riverbank in sweaters and khaki trousers. It reminds me of the Rhine and my envy as I watched these cyclists keeping up with the boat on which we were travelling. Yes, there is nothing in the world like travelling— going hither and thither, taking a knapsack and a pad—perhaps a hunk of boloney and a bottle of red wine. You remember the pages I read to you one night from Hilaire Belloc (*The Path to Rome*)? Can one say that there is anything more wonderful than this experience? Ned, you should read that book. You should follow him as he crosses the Alps, sleeps in the forests, drinks the wines of Anjou, of Burgundy, of this place and that. This world is not just a dirty hole like New York—or that morgue, Brooklyn. God, this is a glorious world, especially when the sun shines and you can speak the universal tongue.

I am nearing Suresnes. I have already written six pages to you. And three other letters besides! One to Cocteau, one to Paul Morand, and one to the author of *Madonna of the Sleepings*. If Anatole France were alive I should write him too. After all, we all have something in common. What it is, I don't know precisely. But I think they would understand me if I had five uninterrupted minutes alone with them. I must be an awfully reticent cuss. Here I am, three weeks in Paris, and still friendless. Not unhappy, mind you—but isolated. Nobody decorated any boats in honor of my coming. Besides being sensitive I guess I am a typical Dutchman, too. I notice that I am not the regular, the orthodox American type. The waiters invariably mistake me for a Heinie or a Swede. I lack that carefree, audacious air of the average American. Even the Americans ignore me. They talk English at my elbow with that freedom which one employs only when he is certain his neighbor does not understand.

Well, this is not the day nor the place for self-commiseration. I am on my second bottle of wine and the waitress (who would be good-looking if she had all her teeth) is looking at me with sparkling eyes. She knows I am an American. She knows she will get a generous tip. I try talking to her about the "Grand Guignol" which I visited last night. I ask her what this means and that. She only laughs and scratches her ass. It must be too funny for words—my "parlez-vousing." When I want to say dessert I usually say warehouse, which in French is quite similar. And when I want to say "drunk" I say "fuck" (Zigzee for zigzag!) Imagine telling a waitress that you were well fucked last night. As a matter of fact I haven't been well fucked at all. I'm beginning to doubt that I have any manhood left.

* * * *

Well, this just a scratch while I am eating my déjeuner at the above. I wish I were wealthy, famous, etc. and could say—"Ned, here—here's a couple of thousand. Take the next boat! I need you!" If I ever strike it right I shall certainly buy a home over here and keep open house—I can't understand my failure. Somewhere there must be an audience waiting for my words. Where? I read what Morand says about New York and honestly (forgive this egotism!), but I have said it all a long time ago, and better. Why does nobody want what I write? Jesus, when I think of being 38, and poor, and unknown, I get furious. I refuse to live this way forever. There must be a way out. Well, now for some Benedictine and "café nature." Greetings, Ned, and write if you have the desire.

HVM

P.S. And that brother of yours?—Emil? Is he still taking his afternoon naps? Tell him to work night and day, to kill himself, but to get here. Get here before old age comes on. It is still glorious. It will still bowl him over. Don't stick in New York leading the advertising life. Get out! Thumb your nose at them! There are men exhibiting here in the galleries who can't hold a candle to Emil. This is a free-for-all world. Stick $5,000 away and take a vacation. Do it, and regret it afterwards, if you must. Don't debate. Don't figure. Don't get tied up. Strike out!

Allons nous! Tout droit! Vous avez raison! Goddamn it, even the French fails to express what I mean!

[April 1930]

The Romans and the Wops

Lunch at 3:30 P.M. in the Patisserie Alsacienne. Lunch too well, so decide to clean up a number of miscellaneous items in the notebook. "See the wine merchants at Bercy, visit dog cemetery of St. Ouen, l'Arène de Lutèce, etc. etc." Passing the planimeter at St. Germain and Rue Bonaparte I look up a few streets whose location I am unfamiliar with. Meant to see if there were any streets named after Balzac or Rabelais—these names do not bob up constantly like the others. What is wrong with these two giants?

Starting out to hunt for Rue Jacques Callot, right in my own neighborhood I change my mind and go hunting for that art gallery where the Surrealists are exhibiting. Can't find it. Don't see the Rue Jacques Callot either, though it must be right under my nose. The notebook says, "Visit the private gallery of Yves Tanguy, 16 Rue Jacques Callot. He and Marcel Duhamel are two very important young men in Paris today." Don't know where I picked up this piece of change. Who is Yves Tanguy and why don't I see his name more frequently?

Well, I'll have a look at the Roman amphitheatre in daylight. Last time I went there it was midnight and the gates were closed. I get a little shock when I discover that there is no charge for admission, and a further shock when I look down into the little bowl and see children playing ball there. I had expected something entirely different. Nevertheless I get a thrill out of it. It is a piece of history, it is quaint and charming, well kept, and above the topmost layer of seats are mounds of grass covered with shrubs and trees and dotted with benches. Along one arc of the arena houses are built close, their open windows giving out on the little bowl, permitting a view of the lovers whom one finds anywhere in Paris where there are benches. Beneath the tiers, on a level with the bowl, are the cages where the wild animals were kept—and perhaps a few wild Christians too. They have thrown open a subway station (Monge) right at the amphitheatre, corner of Rue Navarre and Rue Monge, a rather woeful, run-down district not so far from the Place Maubert where the clochards congregate, not far either from the Cluny Museum and the Jardin des Plantes. Ask the artists up at the Dôme where the Arena of Lutèce is and they shrug their shoulders. No one has anything more than a vague idea. A great pity. The arena is an idyllic spot around midnight; the ghosts of the slain seem to rise up out of the mist that hangs between the trees, there is an awesome silence broken only by the rustle of the leaves.

The Jardin des Plantes is so near that I give up the idea of going to Bercy and dining with the wine merchants. This makes the seventh time I have started for Bercy and done something else. Too many in-between places. Too many exhibitions, too many famous spots and deserted alleys.

It is near closing time at the Jardin des Plantes. And it is raining just a little, not enough to scare people away. At once I am enthralled. This is a civilized zoo, it invites you to witness the birth of the swans, to see the insects in their original habitat. Beautiful pelicans here and geese from the Museum of Chapultepec, Mexico. Peacocks screaming with lust—or hunger—spreading wide their enormous studded fans, mythologic statues vomiting green water, brown polar bears rubbing their shaggy sides against the stone walls of their sunken cages, children everywhere playing in that civilized manner that only French children seem to possess. It is too late for me to see all the insects or even to see the monkeys but I can hear them chattering, screaming with lecherous joy and it is not difficult for me to imagine what their obscene antics are like. Park guards, garbed in semimilitary fashion, stroll about nonchalantly, puffing away at their short butts. These are not the perverted faces of the cops in Prospect or Central Park—the guys who crawl on hands and knees between the bushes in order to pike you off before pulling you in. These are honest, intelligent, serene faces—pensioned for life in one of the prettiest parks in the world. Old age has no terrors for them. They are as safe as the animals.

* * * *

Now I am at the Gare d'Orléans, studying the map at the Metro station. Would like to see the famous prison here—La Santé, not far away, on the Boulevard Arago—near Tihanyi's workshop. A Boulevard de l'Hôpital—all around are hospitals, old women's homes, insane asylums, broken-down manors, farmyards, restaurants for the provincials and by the provincials. I ought to cut off down the Boulevard St. Marcel, but one look down this street and I lose heart. It is too much like some of the streets in Harlem or Yorkville. Yes, there are here and there in Paris dreary streets, wide, colorless, insipid streets that might have been transplanted from Brooklyn or Hoboken. Not many, thank God. I think immediately of the Rue Soufflot and Boulevard Raspail. How I detest these streets! And St. Marcel is another—only worse, emptier, drearier. So instead of heading for Boulevard Arago and the prison, I keep going along Boulevard de l'Hôpital toward Place d'Italie. After a while, very quickly, the odor of hospitals wears off, the atmosphere becomes more vibrant, energetic, living. The Italiens make themselves felt, especially after you reach Campo Formio district. Girls appear with smoldering eyes set in enamelled faces: their eyes are warmer here than in Greenwich Village—they stare at you hard and insolently. They know what they want. Good, my spirits begin to revive. Wherever the Italiens are out in numbers there is always something doing. They breed excitement.

*   *   *   *

And now here we are at the rond-point, the carrefour, the étoile. Little
Italy! Under a glowering sky, torn to shreds, whipped to a milky foam and
sprinkled with arsenate of lead. Life is whirling here—madly, in the usual
Italianated way. Every bench is occupied in the little place where the cars
draw up, right at the Boulevard de la Gare. They are standing on one
another's feet, they are sweating and pushing, cursing and loving each
other, and they are either exhausted from toil or happy because the day
is finished. Most of them are jubilant and excited. There is another place
a little further off, still in the circle, where a few ugly black trees, perfectly
nude, claw the air. Here there is plenty of room but no one seems to care
about sitting there. It has a sombre aspect indeed—almost a demented
appearance, if we can ever refer to Nature as being crazy. This wheel is
enormous, like the Bastille and the Etoile. Ever so many spokes radiating
out in every direction. You look down one street and it seems like the end
of the world is at hand; down another and you feel that you are standing
at Eastern Parkway near Atlantic Avenue, Brooklyn; down another and it
is Bensonhurst or Ulmer Park. You want to go down all of them at
once—but each of them requires a day in itself. This is one of the reasons
why I seldom get back to the same place twice. I am always going off on
a tangent. Each street promises the end of the rainbow. And while I stand
here, wondering whether to find a seat or dive into the subway, Jimmy
Pasta's person comes to mind. I must write him a letter and tell him how
I feel about his lively compatriots—especially about those dark-eyed girls
down on the Boulevard de l'Hôpital who glare at you with smoldering
embers set "en cabochon" in their white enamelled faces. Jimmy will be
promising me another job with the Democratic Party out at Queens. And
soon it will be time for the Park Department to get out another Annual
Report—with lots of photographs. How far away this all seems to me now.
What have I to do with Annual Reports and the Borough of Queens? I
am thinking of tomorrow: finding that gallery with the Surrealist show,
eating with the wine merchants at Bercy, meeting that very important
young man, Yves Tanguy (who I bet will turn out to be a woman!). Yes,
and there is La Santé to visit—if they will permit it. I hope they don't turn
me down, as they did at the "Abattoir Hippophagique." And I must find
out if there are any streets, avenues, boulevards, rond-points, squares,
places, carrefours, parks, statues, or monuments dedicated to François
Rabelais and Honoré de Balzac!

Note to the municipality: "It is a disgrace to have a mustard-colored
building on such a good street as that bearing the name of an honored
painter like Edouard Manet. Please demolish it at once!"

P.S. Emil: Here is another to keep the ball rolling. Sent Elkus one a few
days ago to show you. You please show him this—and keep George Buzby

posted. Schöner Wetter heute! (Have a fine article, with good etchings, for you on your beloved "Marais Quarter." Hope to mail it soon.

P.P.S. Listen, Emil—those art objects at the Flea Market in Clignancourt—they are O.K. and very reasonable. Do you want me to plunge? And for how much?—only on African and Oceanic things—fetiches, masks, statuettes, etc.

Hôtel Central
1 bis, Rue du Maine
[April 1930]   Paris (XIV), France

Bistre and Pigeon Dung

* * * *

Sunday Morning. Have just had breakfast and loaded up with oranges and bananas. God knows when that cablegram is going to arrive. I'm down now to fifty francs, which is two bucks in American spondulix. For four days hand-running I've been trotting over to the American Express. Tuesday I get a cable saying the money is being telegraphed that day. Saturday six o'clock still no signs of it. How long must I hold out? Begin to think about selling my winter clothes, my heavy Montagnac, my old valises . . . the trunk, if necessary. Can't understand the delay. . . . However—it's Sunday morning. I won't starve today, nor tomorrow either.

The Rue de Buci is alive, crawling. Bars wide open and curbs lined with bicycles. All the meat and vegetable markets in full swing, arms loaded with truck bandaged in newspapers. Oh these Catholic Sundays! How I relish them! How dreary, how pale and sanctimonious are our goddamned Protestant Sundays! Here one jumps from the church to the grocery store and then a little rest in the café, or a quiet snooze in the park.

I want to go back to the room and work, but here I am standing at the confluence of all these crazy streets off the Boulevard St. Germain. On one corner is le Hôtel Confortable, opposite it the Hôtel de Louisiane, grim old hostelries known once to the bad boys of the Rue de Buci— Carco, Max Jacob, MacOrlan, Picasso, etc. . . . At the Boucherie crockery is being given away with the meat. Yes, given away! Put that down in the notebook. Something for nothing! In France! I tell you, on Sunday mornings there is a fever in the streets. Nothing like it anywhere, except perhaps on the East Side. The quiet little Rue de l'Echaudé St. Germain, where every evening after ten o'clock the streetwalkers congregate and follow you until you shake them off, is now seething with activity. The streets twist and turn, at every angle a fresh hive of activity. Here Heine could have exclaimed anew: O, the grand swarm of Israelites. I come upon the Square du Furstemberg. Have I ever spoken of it before? Here is where I should like to take rooms. A deserted spot, bleak, spectral at night, containing in the center four black trees which have not yet begun to blossom. These four bare trees have the poetry of T. S. Eliot. They are intellectual trees, nourished by the stones, swaying with a rhythm cerebral, the lines punctuated by dots and dashes, by asterisks and exclamation points. Here, if Marie Laurencin ever brought her Lesbians out into the open, would be the place for them to commune. It is very, very Lesbienne here, very sterile, hybrid, full of forbidden longings.

*   *   *   *

Let's go back to yesterday. Sitting in a cheap restaurant near the Metro du Combat, saving three francs in order to squander five on a taxi. Yes, that is what happens. I get so damned chock-full of ideas that I am afraid they will dribble away before I get back to the machine. You would think I was a correspondent rushing back to the office, that what I had to report must reach the N. Y. office before the finals. The tablecloth is paper, and I begin jotting down my notes at the far, upper, left-hand corner. I order any god-damned thing, and consequently get codfish again. But the ideas are streaming out of me, exhaustless as a supply of radium. The waitress looks at me benignly and smiles. She has wild Circassian hair, red elbows, lead pipes for legs. I put this down too on the tablecloth. She doesn't understand anyway. And while I write the lights are suddenly switched on and the glare of the unshaded bulbs strikes the water carafe and spreads over the back of my hand, over the stained paper, gorgeous geometric designs. The refraction made by the curvature of the bottle splinters the prism of light and throws dancing jewels of color into the penumbra made by the carafe. I have one of those mad Strindberg variations.

*   *   *   *

I climb up instead of down to take the Metro, at Jean Juarès. Twilight hour, Indian blue, water of glass, trees glistening and liquescent. Juarès station itself gives me a kick. The rails fall away into the canal, the long caterpillar with sides lacquered in Chinese red dips like a roller coaster. It is not Paris, it is not Coney Island—it is crepuscular mélange of all the cities of Europe and Central America. Railroad yards spread out below me, the tracks looking black, webby, not ordered by engineers but cataclysmic in design, like those gaunt fissures in the Polar ice which the camera registers in degrees of black. I have gotten into the first-class compartment by mistake. No, not altogether by mistake. My aesthetic instincts had prompted me unconsciously to follow in the wake of a beautiful woman. She is the first beautiful woman I have seen since I am here. She is with a French officer, and he in a masculine way is almost as beautiful as she. The colors of his uniform are so harmonious and yet variegated: stiff, vizored cap of taupe embroidered with heavy braid, boots lacquered and adorned with spurs. She has the eye of an aviator, her breast is full and quiet as a thrush. Is this a French woman or one of those Amazons from below the equator who fly to the Rue de la Paix with jewels under their wings? And while I make mental notes I also try to figure out how I will say without stammering: "Can I not pay you the difference?" Meaning, of course, when the conductor approaches me for the fare. I also think that the military hat is very much like that "cheese-box on a raft, the *Monitor.*"

Before reaching the hotel I have thought of a lot of other things which pass through my head in bed, or at the restaurant—"Go to the Bal Java, Faubourg St. Martin," see *Les Criminels,* who is Loulou Hegoburu, meet Mr. Zero, titles for books: *Mon Venus, The Ur Country, World Without Women, Amen!* Can I *"utilize"* a little of all this later? How can I acquire a secretary and a battery of stenographers? I feel that I could turn out a book a month here. If I could get a stenographer to go to bed with me I could carry on twenty-four hours of the day. But when I see one of Dufresne's wet nudes I think that I have made a grand mistake in choosing literature. Knowing principally his pastels what a shock I received when I saw the oils! Especially one noble canvas, a sort of déjeuner intime, repast in the 13th century sans vin (as the Ligue contre Alcoolisme would like to have us believe). In the foreground, reclining on a bench, he puts a nude, solid, vibrant, pink as a fingernail. Her flesh rolls in glistening billows, she has all the secondary characteristics and a few of the primary. Her body sings, it is moist like a Vlaminck landscape, the flesh is quartered and palatable as a good still life, only nothing is still, nothing dead here. The table creaks with food, it is uptilted and slides out of the frame, and though we are in a room, a very humble room, there is in this canvas again all those luscious jungle notes which we saw at the Modern Museum—the one particularly in which the zebras and the gazelles nipped the fronds of the palm trees.

Well, I must positively call a halt, even though I have one more note about "swarthy Lascars and the odor of sanctity." Morand crossing the Delancey Street Bridge gets a whiff of the fish market below. He speaks of the odor of the melting pot, a celebrated commonplace. He looks down upon the tumble of buildings and sees in them the colors of dry blood, bistre, and *garnet.* Garnet? He saw garnet? Jesus, where was he standing? Not even in a Jewish beard can one find such a hue as garnet. No, sometimes Paul Morand is a little careless. I don't mind him talking about the square phallus of the Equitable Building, nor calling some of the

skyscrapers feminine and others masculine, but garnet for the ghetto—
impossible!

* * * *

Listen everybody—until further notice my address is American Express, for both letters and money transfers—the latter preferably. I need a stout pair of secondhand shoes and some shaving soap. Don't let me get lost "in a bohemian world."

HVM

[April 1930]

Dégringolade, Tintamarre, Salmongondid, Chinoiserie

For five days and nights there was a great darkness over all the land and I did not eat, nor sleep, nor do anything but lie in bed concocting telegrams that would bring results. It is very hard when you are three thousand miles away and there is nothing but a vast ocean and a vast silence separating you from home—it is very hard, I repeat, to think of any other words but "desperate," "hungry," "prisoner," etc. But now the silence has been broken. I can breathe again, and my bowels are becoming more regulated. It was fortunate too that during that interim I had a mild attack of dysentery and could stomach nothing but oranges. What would have become of me if I had wanted "cervelles" or "entrecôte grillée" or "bifsteak rôti pré vert, pommes nouvelles," etc.?

Easter came in like a frozen hare—but it was fairly warm in bed. Today it is lovely again, and along the Champs Elysées at twilight hour it is like a plein air seraglio choked with dark-eyed houris. The trees are in full foliage and of a verdure so pure, so rich that it seems as though they were still wet and glistening with dew. From the Palais du Louvre to the Etoile it is like a piece of Debussy's music—for the pianoforte. For five days I have not touched the typewriter, I have not looked at a book, I have not had an idea in my head—except that one of going in the morning to the American Express and asking for a cablegram. At nine o'clock this morning I was there, just as the doors opened, and again at one o'clock. No news. (And no news is what killed the dog!) At four thirty I dash out of the hotel, resolved to make a last-minute stab at it. Just as I hit the street I brush against Alfred Pach but he does not recognize me and as I have nothing important to say to him I make no attempt to refresh his memory. Later, when I have the solidarity of five hundred francs in my wallet and I am stretching my legs on a bench in the Jardin de Paris the figure of Alfred Pach reverts to mind. He was a little stooped, pensive, a sort of serene yet reserved smile on his face. I wonder, as I look about me, look up at this softly enamelled sky which has so much pale green and mauve in it, which does not bulge today with heavy rain clouds but smiles like a piece of old china or a bit of beaten brass—I wonder what goes on in the mind of that translator of the four thick volumes of the *History of Art* when he takes in this blissful cosmos with his drooping eye?

At the Palais de Glace there is an announcement of a coming exhibition of "Humoristes." Must see it! Fall into conversation with an old letter-carrier, a sort of Crainquebille, an old "combattant" and a very good ami of les Américains. What a cordial chap! He clutches me by the arm and points out this and that as we go along—things I am well familiar with, but which I marvel at just the same, out of courtesy. (I feel like saying, "Jesus, brother, you don't know the half of it! Come with me some day and let me show you Paris.") But this old grandfather is so benevolent, so courteous, so affable and effusive, that I can scarcely believe I am talking with a Frenchman. Every few moments he releases his clutch and takes a stand in front of me, like old man Carey of the Western Union used to do: "Attention! Many thieves in Paris . . . Attention! Champs Elysées very charming, very beautiful . . . Attention les prostitutes, les chanteurs!" The latter are the pervert-solicitors who hang around the urinals. He urges me to be very careful with my money, always to ask directions of a gendarme—*jamais* un civilian! "Every day at six o'clock I pass here . . . every day! Avec plaisir, monsieur!"

I take a seat outside the Palais de Glace under a horse-chestnut tree. Attention! Beside me comes to sit a young lady with monkey-fur trimmings, very svelte, distinguée, not too much rouge, a little stiff in the legs, air triste. She waits for me to look at her twice so that she can begin to speak to me. Attention! I think of Old Bill and I open my Paul Morand and commence to read about the grand hotels where one can buy everything from soup to nuts in the lobby, where there are wonderful telegraph counters, open all the time, and where the Americans send dispatches of all sorts at all hours of the day—because the Americans *never write, they always telegraph*. If this is the case I am a super-American, because I not only telegraph but I write too.

If I dare to look up from the book I am sure this one will start talking to me. She waits maybe fifteen minutes and then she gets up with a little frou-frou and a delicious pout and saunters off on her high wooden heels. (Only the old women of Paris wear rubber heels, and then usually it is a felt slipper which is entirely lined with rubber, a sort of pantouffle for street and house wear, bien chaussée.) No respectable prostitute would think of easing her aching arches by wearing O'Sullivan's rubber heels. This is why at night, when the streets are dead, it sounds so queer to hear someone walking. You can follow the sound for blocks before it finally

dies out. Paris is so very dead after eleven o'clock. All bosh, this talk about
a gay, wide-open city! New York is the wide-awake place, the all-night city,
the city of noise. Here, when I start coming home, no matter from what
direction, it is like walking between the walls of a mausoleum, no sounds
except the honk of an occasional taxi, no music but the music of the
drains, the gurgling of the sewers.

"The town was a shambles; corpses, mangled by butchers and stripped
by plunderers, lay thick in the streets; wolves sneaked from the suburbs
to eat them; the black death and other plagues crept in to keep them
company, and the English came marching on; the while la danse macabre
whirled about the tombs in all the cemeteries. . . ."

Paris in the vicinity of Saint Paul during the time of Charles the Silly
who, poor fellow, was practically a prisoner in his Hôtel St. Paul, deserted
by his wife, his shameless wife, Isabeau de Bavière, his only companion
being the lowborn Odette de Champsdivers, with whom he played at
cards. . . . In the last ten days or so I have done some prowling about the
vicinity of St. Paul, back of the Place des Vosges, in the heart of the Marais
Quarter. I have sat in the Square du Temple which was once the garden
of the Grand Prior in the days of the Knights Templar. I have mused over
the doings of the horse-knackers led by Jean Caboche and thought long
and ruefully over the sad fate of Charles the Silly who prowled about the
halls of his Hôtel in filthy rags, eaten by ulcers and vermin, gnawing his
food with canine greed. At the Rue des Lions I felt the stones of the old
menagerie where he fed his pets—his only diversion outside of those card
games with Odette de Champsdivers.

*   *   *   *   I had hardly started down the street—just a stone's throw
from Boulevard de Sébastopol—when someone whistled after me. I
looked around and there stood a brazen wench, leaning against her door
like a lazy slut, cigarette between her lips, sadly rouged and frizzled, old,
seamed, scarred, cracked, evil greedy eyes. She jerked her head a few
times inviting me to come back and inspect her place, but my eyes were
set on a strange figure tugging away at some bales. An old man with
enormous goitres completely circling his neck, standing out below the
hairline like huge polyps, from under his chin hanging loosely, joggling,
purplish, veined, like gourds of wine—transparent gourds. Here the
breed is degenerate and diseased. Old women with white hair, mangy, red
lips, demented, prowl about in carpet slippers, their clothes in tatters,
soiled with garbage and filth of the gutters.   *   *   *   *   They have
bedbugs, cockroaches and fleas running all over them, they are syphilitic,
cancerous, dropsical, they are halt and blind, paralyzed, and their brains
are soft. They are the same now as when Quasimodo looked down on
them from the towers of Notre Dame. They are not a whit above the level
of those poor devils in the Middle Ages who lived in the forests of this

vast morass and preyed on dogs and cats, or chewed grass. They are not even as intelligent as these savage tribes of Parisii who inhabited the banks of the Seine and resisted the onslaughts of Julius's legions, forcing him back on the Ile de la Cité where he was obliged to erect ramparts and fortifications.

Oh yes, I haven't done much reading in the last five days, but the little I have absorbed has been profitable. This time I look upon an entirely different Paris. When I walk down the most wonderful street in the world (St. Denis!)—and also the oldest in Paris—I know that I am taking the road of the Roman legions, the road of the Knights Templar, the road that the fearsome Saint Denis himself trod, head in hand. And when I come out under the arches of the Louvre on to the open square at the Théatre de la Comédie Française I know now that it was here Joan of Arc fell, struck down by an English bolt, in her valiant attempt to save the city of Paris. And along the Quai des Celestins I know that François Rabelais once walked, that somewhere along here he died—no one knows exactly the spot any more. And I make a vow that some day I will journey out to Chinon, his birthplace, and drink some of the good wine of that country, and pay a pilgrimage to this healthy, sane, normal intellect of France. About the patrons and *prodromes* of the Renaissance I know little. (I haven't come to that point yet!) For the present I am all fed up with Saint Denis and Saint Martin, with Madame Pimpernel, la belle boulangère and Maître Jehan Crapotte, l'Orfèvre. Not forgetting Charles the Silly and his lowborn companion, Odette de Champsdivers, or Gus Bofa and Moholy-Nagy, or Rodin, the evil genius of *The Wandering Jew* who practiced his nefarious ways until "the day when he was enflamed and outwitted by the octoroon Cecily!"

* * * *

This is all somewhat of a hodgepodge because I can't remember any more what I said in my previous letters and what I put down in the manuscript of the book. I am still waiting to know how to solve the problem of distribution. I can knock out a long letter at least once a week and use it for material later. Would rather do that than keep it on cold storage in my notebook. Everything dies after a time—even the most vivid impressions. Each day I go out nets me at least ten or fifteen pages. What am I to do about it? Putting it in book form is vastly slower, though rapid, considering everything. In a letter I can breeze along and not bother to be too careful about grammar, etc. I can say Jesus when I like and string the adjectives out by the yard.

Here are a few of the things I am in doubt about: have I touched upon them yet?

The Lion of the Louvre

Dog of Andalouvre

Lovers in the subway, Parc Monceau, under the Eiffel Tower
Six Day Bike Race—Mlle. Lou-lou . . . Allo, Allo!
The Legend of the Pissoirs
Ham and Iron Fair, Boulevard Richard Lenoir
Flea Market, Clignancourt—veritable objects of art for a song, including Oceanic, African, Melanesian, Siamese, etc!!
Kandinsky, Lurçat, Miró, Czobel, Dufresne
Surrealism—2nd Manifesto (Aragon, Breton, Soupault et alia)
Abattoir Hippophagique, Ville Malakoff, Place Violet
Place Vauban—Last Man of Europe sleeping under the Capitol
Willy—"Le Troisième Sexe"
Charlemagne's Chess Pieces—the macaroni guy at Bibliothèque
Rue Blomet and other rues
Grand Guignol—Cent Lignes Emues and "Le Griffe"— Stupendous!
The Mummies at the Trocadéro—where Zadkine, Maillol, all of them, big and little, got their first inspiration—and their last. . . .
Germaine Dulac—premier creator of artistic films—personal interview
The Mussulman's Cemetery at Père Lachaise
Toilets on the Right Bank and toilets on the Left
Conversation with Hickok about Spain, the Basque country, etc.
The Idiot in French—with a French Madame for Nastasya Fillipovna
The Madone des Sandwichs—Rue Mademoiselle
The Lesbians at the Jockey Club and the fairies at Rue de Lappe
The Cosmos on the flat at Galerie Zac—Mexican show
Dufresne's marvellous pink-meat nudes—big canvas, déjeuner

Saturday [May] the tenth, 1930

Personal—to you, old poof:

Jump right on the boat. There are no extra charges that I know of. And you don't even have to lay out $125 for the passage. Get a freighter and eat with the crew—good stuff, I am told, and under $100. Above all, do not take an American liner. I will show you how to live on less than $25.00 a week here. And comfortably. Don't worry about the cost of living—it is still dirty and cheap. Meal this noon: 8 fr. 25 centimes—including vin blanc, café, banana, tournedos bouquetière, bread, napkin, tip. . . . $.33! You can have a good room in this hotel (better than mine) for the same price I pay (495 francs per month). I have a large room with two windows. The main thing is not to suffer from chilblains. Theatres? Had a front row seat in the Grand Guignol for a dollar, or a dollar ten. Cinemas—anywhere from two francs a seat to 80 francs. Whores? Anywhere from 30 francs up. . . . Taxis? From here to the Opéra, about five francs in the daytime. Laundry, about a dollar a week. This is high. What else? Metro? 70 centimes a ride. Beer anywhere from 50 centimes to 1.75, or 3.75 (Löwenbrau München). Does that convince you? On forty dollars a week you could have a swell time. You could be cockeyed every night in the week, you could buy the best French literature, you could pick up objets d'art, Oceanic, Egyptienne, Afrique, anything your little heart desires. For Christ's sake, don't spend any more money on chess sets. I haven't seen anything here yet (principally because I haven't thought a great deal about it), but why buy extra chess sets when you can buy the world over here?

I am living a dog's life (because the money has been coming very irregularly), but even I manage to have a swell time. Guy Hickok of the *Eagle* says nobody deserves to have such a good time as I am having. He ought to know. We had a great day together recently. He showing me spots and I showing him. Get out the map. Somewhere below Buttes Chaumont look for a winding street, small, Rue Asselin. Steps leading up, down, and around it. It is coming down soon. A street packed with the lowest dives where the Algerians and Arabs get their hump. Look for Rue de Meaux nearby, and then to the right of it a sort of court, "Cité Nortier." Had to show this to Hickok—and even he was amazed. This is the Ufa setting I mentioned in a recent letter. Hickok is a great guy— knows everybody (including Allan Quatermain and Bob McAlmon). I think he's cunt-struck too. Anyway he's a good guy to know.

Yes, I got your letter this morning, and I was astounded. I didn't think you could pull yourself together and write three whole typewritten pages. I don't believe you wrote it. It was great. Cheered me up no end. (I am in the dumps, you know.) I think of so many things I want to spill. For instance, I have been wanting, ever since I arrived, to send you a copy of the Surrealist Manifestoes, of *Un Homme Coupé en Tranches,* of the brochure by Aragon: *La Peinture au Défi,* of *Photogénie,* of *Frou-Frou,* of the article on St. Merri district, of *La Semaine,* of the magazines devoted to the cinema, menus, announcements, back pages of *Sourire,* etc. etc. etc.

Am frustrated by lack of funds. Paralysis of the periphery. And no joking. Anyhow, I am having some fun reading the French. Would you believe it, I picked up André Gide's *L'Immoraliste* and read it—I might say—almost with ease. Simply told, beautifully told. A blank here and there matters little. I am carried along, can read thirty-five or fifty pages at a crack. That spells progress, nicht wahr? And oh—when I stand in front of the window and look at copies, handsomely illustrated, of Pierre Loti, and of Pierre Louÿs—read for the first time the opening pages of *Aphrodite* in French. Ready to tear my hair out. Marvellous. I say to myself—another year and I will write in this wonderful language. I love it. I love the way the adjectives pile up, and the modifying clauses, the swing, the sonority, the elegance, the subtlety of it . . . Yes, Emil, the French machines have the accent marks (must have them!) and they are used everywhere. Where it derives from I don't know. But you can readily see the necessity of it.

The language! Just left the restaurant. Had to smile. The waitress, who rattles it off like telephone numbers, tried to tell me that she had something I was asking for the other day. I didn't get it all—trop vite. She walked away, and then suddenly it dawned on me. Everything fell into its proper place. And a broad grin came over my face. I thought of you and I began to smile still harder. And I was staring all the while at a beautiful blonde who ogles me every time I walk in. She got rather confused. Perhaps she thought I was a bit derisive. Anyway, I plucked up courage later and went over to her. I said, in pidgin French, that she must not think I was laughing at her. I was very happy, I said. She laughed and squeezed my hand impulsively. Told me she was very glad too that I was glad. We were all glad. "Have a Benedictine!" Sure, we sat down together and had a couple of Benedictines. She wants me to take her for a walk some day in the Jardin du Luxembourg. Why not? I'll take her to Asnières, St. Cloud, the Batignolles . . . anywhere. Have you ever noticed this type—the fair-skinned, milky, creamy complexioned ones, with peroxide hair and dark brown eyes, perhaps heavy eyebrows? This is a type I adore. I think it is truly French. The delicate skin, almost blue as skimmed milk, makes me feel brutal—want to crush them tenderly.

I said at the opening "Personal." Remember that. Don't make a mistake and pull it out sometime in June's presence. I am going to tell you a few interesting episodes.

Women! I haven't said much about women in the carbon copy letters. Naturally! But what wonderful times I have sitting with the whores . . . everywhere: back of the Gare de Lyon, around the Bastille, Closerie des Lilas, Champs Elysées. . . . I made a little compact with one, Germaine (Mme. Daugeard, she calls herself). Factory girl type. Met her one day on Boulevard Beaumarchais. A Sunday afternoon—heavenly Sunday, just after an excursion to Clignancourt. I liked her at once. Stopped and waited for her to pick me up. We sat in a café and talked things over. Told her the situation very frankly. Couldn't afford it. Would take her to the cinema, if she liked—or a spin at the Rue de Lappe.

She said she was a model—gave me some fake name, I suppose, of the Danish artist she was posing for. Anyhow, not to prolong the suspense, she invited me up to her hotel and said twenty francs would be O.K. (Seeing that I was a writer!) We had an awfully good time (the room was only five francs, Rue Amelot, and the preservative 2 francs). We went to dinner together, talked a hell of a lot of French (learnt a barrelful that afternoon), and promised to meet again. I get little pneumatiques from her, in quaint, illiterate French. She is my "grande amie." Well, I go broke, as you already know. I have fifteen francs in my pocket. Go to the Café l'Elephant again and wait for her. (She asked me to wear my knicker-bocker outfit, so American, she was proud of it, I guess.) "Germaine," I said, "I am broke, but I love you a whole lot. Do you want to take a walk?" Germaine takes me up to the hotel again. No money. She says: "I have the greatest respect for you, I trust you implicitly. When you have money we will go to another hotel, stay all night, lie in each other's arms. . . ." Nothing could be fairer than that, eh? I like this little factory kid. She's sincere. She seems like one whore who has a heart.

Last night up at the Dôme, discussing with a Mr. Fred Kann the prospect of opening an academy for American students here. He has broached the idea to me, wants my assistance, says we could make a humble living from it without devoting too much energy to it. O. K. with me, I am waiting to see what will happen. Am to go with him Monday and make a tour of the big French academies, Grande Chaumière, Beaux Arts, etc. Meanwhile, at the Dôme, a Swiss girl comes in and sits between us. He knows her because she comes every day to his studio to take a bath. Betty is a little lit up. She gets up every few minutes and says: "I must peepee, another fifty centimes." Then she sits on my lap for a little while and I give her a grand feel. Kann says to me: "If you want her go ahead and take her . . . I have no sexual feeling toward her." (Jesus, why not?) But Betty is one of those hungry son-of-a-bitches. I get too worried watching her eat. At the end, she pays her own bill, and then I feel sorry I hadn't spoken about the other matter. However. . . .

Another night . . . Champs Elysées . . . a little lit up . . . the world spinning, thinking of Ned and what a grand letter I would write him about this street. Topnotch form. I am grabbed, after dodging six in a row. Walk a long way to a hotel. Twenty francs, the room. Preservative five francs, tip to the maid, two francs. Price for the dame: 150 francs. Wow! But she was a lulu. The wildest thing you ever saw, jabbing at me continually, rolling her tongue, grunting, groaning . . . Start off by letting her get down on me. She has it down to a science. But when the thing goes off and I hear her hawking it up, looking a little bilious, I lose all my passion and get up and get dressed. She looks at me mournfully. "Don't I please you?" she asks. "Are you too tired?" No, I answer, I'm just sad. . . . Ride home in a taxi, thinking about the posters in the pissoirs. Will I get the syph, etc.??? (When you see the manuscript on Paris, the chapter dealing with the American Hospital, you will understand everything.) Fortunately, I was O.K. I just imagined everything. The doctor finally looked at me as if I was a mental case. Fuck him. I had a good scare—for 177 francs, not including the taxi.

You write me about Joseph Stella. Strange, I was searching on the Rue du Faubourg St. Honoré only yesterday for the gallery where he is at present exhibiting. Yes, I remember his work well. I have a fine regard for him. Did not know that he could write so well, either. That was a splendid passage . . . made me feel quite ashamed of myself. Here I am supposed to be a literary guy, but I have never said anything about the Brooklyn Bridge to equal those lines. And as for the book of mine, which you read, I can guess (from what you have omitted) that it was pretty crummy. Perhaps a few fine passages, descriptive, moonlight and flowers, but for the rest, perhaps a flop. Just now that manuscript is in Berlin, with the biggest firm in Germany. What will come of it, I don't know. Nothing, doubtless. The second novel is much better, firmer knit, racier, more integrated. I am almost done with it. So near the end that I tremble. It is hard for me to sign off . . . Finis. But when I am through, I think I will be through also with realistic literature. I don't think it is the highest plane. I think it is perhaps all too egoistic, too vain, too presumptuous. Who am I, after all, that I should think to make literature of my life? "Have I a right, a place, a value, a mission among men . . . ?"

As for Tihanyi—know nothing of his whereabouts. Don't believe he is here in Paris, or I would have bunked into him. Have not seen Zadkine but two or three times. The enclosed note will show you. So this afternoon, in response to his message, I will visit his studio. Truth to tell, I was a little let down. I may have been over-sensitive, as I do get sometimes. Anyhow, I thought he was just tolerating me. Perhaps I was cockeyed. You see, I have a feeling, where these guys are concerned, that I am just as good as they are. And I want them to realize it. So I just stay by myself and wait for them to make the first move. Is this rather petty? Am I developing an ingrown soul? Alors! Friday next week I see Germaine Dulac. There is a woman, one grand Lesbienne, who really wants to see me. I know we are going to have a good time together. What I don't know about the American Cinema I will invent. If that woman would pay me $15 a week I would go to work for her. I would be proud to assist in the production of such films as she turns out. Emil, you have yet to see another realm of film magic. Thoroughly French, absolutely artistic, unsentimental, and beyond realism. When I get some of her brochures I will send you a copy or two. Judge then for yourself. (Meanwhile I have learned that that film *Un Chien Andalou* made a great impression on Cocteau, and that he has written on it at some length. Would be interesting to see, eh?)

Neither Cocteau, Dekobra, Buñuel (author of *Andalou*), St. Cyr, have answered my effusive letters. Think they must have me down for a nut. People here don't write two- and three-page letters to people they don't know. Perhaps too I was a bit boyish. But they were good letters, Emil— especially the one to Buñuel. I will show you it some day. It was as crazy as his film, and crazier.

* * * *

I am looking at the notes I made at lunchtime, ever since reading your letter. These notes! They pile up like dirty linen. I hope the stuff on Paris *is* good. I should like to make a rollicking book of it . . . something popular, saleable, palatable . . . Is it that, do you think—from what you have read? I know you have caught the gusto? But do you think it is too personal, too limited in appeal?

* * * *

Then there were some letters which I sent to Elkus for him to show you, or have copies made for you. Did he do so? And have you taken care of Buzby? I suppose not. I suppose, in a way, I am a god-damned pest too. What I need are secretaries. Well, when we get that academy started (with the help of John D. Jr.) perhaps we can get a few nudes, if not secretaries. One good nude is always worth three secretaries.

* * * *

Well, the last note is about "desperation." I dare not look further ahead than the end of the day. If I were to look into next week I should go crazy, or jump in the Seine. I do want to remain here . . . I believe I will. I think I can say confidently, "Come along, Emil, you will find me here." If I should prove to be a liar, it will not be through wilfulness. I will take anything to keep afloat here. Believe me, when I think of what can happen to me (for instance, when the Patron puts me out!) I can assure you that you will have a much better time of it than I am having. You will at least have a bankroll (and maybe you had better not look me up, after all). You see, old top, I don't know at all where I stand, now less than ever. Have not had a line from June, as I may have said, except for some cables. You say you telephoned her. Good. I didn't know that you could find her. Is that joint still operating? June means so well. She is probably having a tough time of it. If she would only say to me: "Live on twelve dollars a week, that is all I can send you," I would be satisfied . . . I would know what to do. But all the messages are full of hope,

rainbows, courage—hell, you know. And then the money doesn't come
. . . big gaps, debts roll up, I go three times a day to the American Express,
looking for that cable which should have been due last week. All this is
enervating. I can hardly write some days. I am thinking only of that
cable—where is it? (Jesus, this begins to sound like Van Gogh.) And don't
think I am laying it on when I tell you this: The other day my shoes busted
through frightfully . . . the socks were sticking out. I went to the shoe-
maker and asked him to put patches over the holes. When I got them back
they were neatly sewed up . . . you could hardly see any sign of reparation.
Would you believe it, I almost cried. I was so damned happy about this
little thing. I kept saying to him and to his wife: "Très bien! Très bien!"
So they asked me six francs for the job, which ordinarily, I suppose, would
only have cost three francs. When I go Sundays to Clignancourt I look
longingly at the secondhand shoes there. They are so sturdy and comfort-
able-looking. I will wear anything so long as my ass doesn't stick out. And
I guess if it comes to the worst, and I have to leave the hotel without
baggage, I guess then I can find some studio where I can sleep on the
floor. I am quite ready to do that. I tell you, very, very frankly that sticking
up billboards for a few francs a day would not intimidate me in the least.
I don't want to starve, that's all. The rest is nothing.

So you see how Paris has made me. You see that you would not be
disappointed. I may write some day and say that it is terrible here, that
I cannot tolerate it, that it looks lousy to me . . . Don't pay any attention
to that. That is just the belly talking. Fear, discouragement, desolation.
. . . Nobody has a right to feel miserable here if he only has a few dollars
in his pocket.

* * * *

Final: Have a few funny letters from Frank Harris in Nice. I am dunning
him for the old man. He writes that he is 75 years old, and his memory
is not as good as it should be. Says if I would stop in on him in Nice his
wife would cook me a fine meal . . . that she is proud of her cooking, etc.
Then he adds that he is doing a biography of Shaw and hopes to get a
little money, and settle all his debts before he dies. . . . Christ!!! What
a life!

Amen!

P.S. Am walking around without a card of identity—if I get nabbed
around the Rue de Lappe, the Bastille, or any of those "camelot" streets
some midnight, it is *jail* for me. Isn't that a hot one? Jesus, Jesus, where
are we going to lay our heads? * * * *

[Spring 1930]

With the Wine Merchants

At noon the sky is as dark as the back of a mirror, the Seine livid, snot-green, reflecting nothing of the ghastly color radiating from the walls back of the embankments. The river is turbulent and filled with traffic. It is a river of commerce now, below the Gare de Lyon, below the Pont Austerlitz, on the way to Bercy. But it is a mild frenzy when I recall that other river lined with mile after mile of docks and steel girders, with enormous gray tugs and barges drifting under bloodred sails. Is there any river to compare with the Thames as a symbol of power—as a symbol peculiarly significant of our modern industrial era? The Thames, on the morning we pushed up to the Albert Docks, was a symphony of fog and mist pierced by the music of giant cranes wheeling in tons of axle grease; only Monet could have done justice to it, not Turner, Whistler, Pennell, all of whom lacked the full measure of vitality and lust, all of whom were architects first and artists later. The Seine is not even a feeble echo of the mighty Thames. The Seine is a dirty creek in a picturesque setting. The Seine always reminds me of an old hag squatting in the gutter to void a little urine. But where the old hag squats may be in the shadow of a crumbling cathedral, the porch stuccoed with kings and saints, with monsters gripped by hate or lust, the ceiling ripe as a nut, bitter as must.

Never have I seen the Seine as it looked today. The ground was all prepared for a revolution. If only the machine guns were to start their put-put the sky would drop and we would have a deluge of lead and dishwater. The quai is deserted, cars are racing along under the stalwart trees whose trunks are exposed and gleam with a sick, ashed hue. Behind the high rail that encloses the warehouses of Bercy are touches of savage color—raw blues and siennas, murderous pinks, Spanish yellows, nauseating mustards, steel blues. The buildings are scrambled together, ornamented with huge, flamboyant signs bearing the marks of all the liquors of the world. The yards are stacked with huge barrels which, if they were ever set in motion, would roll as far as Constantinople and around the Horn. One gets excited looking at the miscellany of objects cloistered in this vast district. Every drink known to civilized man is stored here and waiting to be consumed.

I find a few of the wine merchants gathered around the dinner table in a little double pavilion exactly like one would expect such a rendezvous to look. On the one side is a bistro and an eating room for the workers, on the other side a sort of old English tavern with heavy rafters, fine silverware, heavy brocaded tablecloths, napkins with a heft to them, and kerosene lamps fitted with parchment shades, all lit now and glowing with a steady, warm yellow light. It is only two o'clock and the rain is still holding off. Men and women are gathered here in this quaint little tavern, all of them waiting to see what will happen when the sky breaks. A little while ago the Graf Zeppelin had circled over the city. I was walking toward the Obelisk then, and the Zeppelin was directly over my head, following the same course. Everyone stood and watched, the balconies were crowded, the traffic cops forgot their business—it is still an event, the coming of the Zeppelin. But there was not that keen joyous animation, that ringing cheer which seizes the New York crowd. The feeling awakened in me was rather this—that it was with apprehension and misgiving that the Parisians looked on this spectacle of the air. Perhaps they were thinking of the next war and the quantity of explosives capable of being stored in such a vessel. And they are damned right in thinking this way. Because, as sure as we live, Germany will convert this air fleet into an armada of vengeance and destruction. The war is not over—it has only begun. Not many years hence the yellow-bellies will be swooping over Europe, and Germany may be the leader of a new and more vital hegemony. England is finished. France will have to become a neutral zone like Switzerland, a grand museum of romantic art and a hostelry for the rich tourists of Asia and America.

This is a pleasant interlude while dining at Bercy. Perhaps it is the women here who make me feel this way. They are magnificent peasant types, gowned at the Rue de la Paix. With their bobbed hair and razored necks, their strong arms bursting through the sleeves of their skin-tight frocks, they seem like the advance guard of that coming third sex. They are all male except in first and secondary sexual characteristics. Nothing is on their minds except frocks, fucks and food. They know no future and own to no past. Their eyes are hard and glittering, faces pleasant, friendly, very frank, very outspoken. "For a new coat, monsieur, I am yours—tonight!"

On every table is a bucket of champagne, and on the center tables where the fruit and cheese is laid out are bottles of staggering size, taller than demijohns and as thick, labelled with years like 1880, 1894, etc. Rums, cognacs, liqueurs—God only knows what all. I am the only one drinking wine, and it is "piccolo" they have brought me instead of the white wine which I ordered. However the color of it satisfies me—an old rose turning to garnet; it has a rare, mellow flavor and the savor of an excellent bouquet. Just the ordinary table wine, nothing special. It will cost me a franc and a quarter. The whole meal, in fact, only comes to thirteen fr. 25 centimes. And for this I get a wonderful lettuce salad especially prepared for me by the proprietor's wife. And she is a Mademoiselle LOU-LOU! A woman of the Quattrocento, heavy with sap, feet moving in blood, busts stiff as a fist. From somewhere she has gotten herself a hideous Nile-green gown which is wrapped around her strong flesh like a bandage. Her teeth are perfect and she knows how to use them. When she talks to me she puts her hand on my shoulder and her weight almost crushes me. And yet, strange thing, these people are not breeding. What a race they would be, these authentic French people, if they began to think about increasing the population. I cannot help making frequent comparisons. I think always of the great shame it is that the English, worn-out, emasculated, parasitic, blood-sucking, should be dominating the world. Oh, I admire the English in many ways, chiefly for their civilized virtues, their grand air of calm superiority and all that stuff—but, when India slips out of her hand, when she is reduced to an island power and will be obliged to use her fleet for excursion boats, what then? Man for man the French are superior, as a stock, a race, a nation. More intelligence, more hardihood, more vitality, more aggressiveness. As time goes on I am changing all my preconceived opinions of the French. I admire them. It is only that they lack sound political instincts—in other words, the technique of the vandal—that holds them down. Neither England nor France is touched by the St. Vitus dance of America. In England however the indifference is more closely allied to lethargy. I think what they refer to proudly as "insularity" is only a mask for feebleness. About the French I feel differently. In them I sense a spirit of resolve—a deliberate hostility, based on sound judgment, against American hysteria. And what does all our *push* amount to? Deep down I have a suspicion that it is a feminine taint. I don't believe at all any more in the legend of vigorous youth which America is supposed to represent. More and more she seems to me like the madame of a whorehouse elbowing her way to the bargain counter. And when I ride into the bay again and see the old blowser standing in her nightshirt holding aloft the torch of liberty I will simply give her the raspberries.

*   *   *   *

June 18th

Dear Emil:

*   *   *   *

June has been cabling me that she might come any day—"without funds." Tell her not to do that. I have already warned her. I can't seem to find a job here—much as I've tried. But I am firmly expecting to receive money through the books in a few months—I feel pretty sure I can demand a little "advance royalties." It is on that I base all hopes of remaining here longer.

If June burns the bridges behind her now, we are both out of luck. I can't write, or do anything, when I'm broke.

Only a little while longer it is necessary for me to hold out. The stuff is pouring out of me like diarrhea. Tell that to June—she will understand. I don't know where she is living now—she told me to mail my letters c/o The Pepper Pot—which I did, but still no answer.

If you are able to sit down with her somewhere (preferably in a public place!) please put a pen in her hand and make her write a few words right under your nose. Then walk her to the P.O. box and see that it falls in. Don't leave anything to chance. Attention! Attention!

You don't know how tough it is to have to write this. I get letters from all over the world—but the one letter I look forward to never arrives.

*   *   *   *

Finis!

P.S. Am paid up at hotel (Alba, 60 Rue de Vanves) until July 14th. But I will commence getting hungry about time you get this letter. Come on over!

III

CANCER AND DELIRIUM

1930–31

Soon after his arrival in Paris, Miller began leading the life recorded in *Tropic of Cancer*, often going without food and worrying about where he was going to spend the night. During most of his first two years in Paris he led a precarious existence, resorting to all sorts of shifts and dodges, sometimes finding odd jobs—as the servant of the Hindu he calls Mr. Nonentity in *Tropic of Cancer* or as a proofreader (of stock figures!) for the Paris edition of the Chicago *Tribune*—but most of the time relying on friends to take him in and feed him. The friends also turn up as characters in *Tropic of Cancer*.

During his first winter in Paris he was rescued by his friend Richard Galen Osborn, who invited him to share a comfortable apartment and provided food, drink, and entertainment. Osborn, who worked in a bank by day, led a bohemian life by night. The entertainment included a Russian princess whose dialogue, reported in one of the letters, reappears in *Tropic of Cancer* almost verbatim.

Other friends were painters and writers, some of them vividly described in the letters. Miller hung around the Montparnasse cafés and made many friends who looked after him, enjoying his good company and conversation. With these friends he worked out a rotating dinner schedule, dining with a different one every day of the week.

Of all these friends Alfred Perlès was the one who remained closest to Miller throughout his Paris years. Perlès, who had been living by his wits for years, proved to be a kindred spirit who understood Miller's predicament and outlook. He shared his room in the Hôtel Central, helped Miller earn a little money by writing feature articles for the *Tribune*, which as a staff member he submitted under his own name, and eventually helped Miller to a proofreading job like his own. Miller also did some ghostwriting for a journalist with the unlikely name of Wambly Bald who produced a weekly column called "La Vie de Bohème." In fact Miller himself appeared as the subject of one of these columns, portrayed as one of the picaresque characters of Montparnasse. In time Miller repaid the compliment by portraying Wambly Bald as the most unsavory character in *Tropic of Cancer.*

But while he was leading the life depicted in that decisive work, Miller was still laboring over the novel he had brought with him from New York. As he finished it, however, he had serious doubts about it, finding it too carefully controlled, and decided to "explode" in his next book. His letter of August 24, 1931, makes a momentous announcement: "I start tomorrow on the Paris book: first person, uncensored, formless—fuck everything!"

In addition to his contributions to the Chicago *Tribune,* Miller published two other pieces during this period, both of them in a little magazine published in Paris, *The New Review,* both of them indicative of the direction he was taking. The first was a relatively brief commentary on Luis Buñuel, whose Surrealistic cinematography Miller had admired from the time of his arrival and would later recognize as a profound influence on his own writing. The second was a story about a Paris whore, "Mademoiselle Claude," which had all the earmarks of the later *Tropics* and could well be hailed as the real beginning of his literary career.

The editor of *The New Review,* Samuel Putnam, made the mistake of entrusting an issue of this magazine to Miller and Perlès while he was away on a trip to America. Gleefully the two friends threw out some of the contents which they found boring and substituted some of their own, adding as a supplement a bawdy parody of all literary manifestoes called "The New Instinctivism." Unfortunately, Putnam returned in time to suppress the supplement, and Miller could only turn to Schnellock in hopes that he might find a publisher. "The New Instinctivism" is lost to posterity, but like everything else dating from this period it can be said to have found its way into *Tropic of Cancer.*

8/9/30
Chez N.P.Nanavati
54, Rue Lafayette
Paris, France

Dear Pop—or What Have You!

I have been writing everybody under the Sun (June, Elkus, etc.) to find out if and when you are really coming to Paris, because if you don't come soon I will be here in the skeleton, at Père Lachaise or Cimetière Montparnasse—wherever it is they bury starving, or starved authors, of no consequence.

Alors! it is Monday high noon, and I am chez Mr. Frank Mechau, an American painter of much promise and a big heart who, together with his wife Paula, look after me in physical ways—food, drink, et cetera. I have just eaten and *drank*. Good red wine of Burgundy—marque "Macon." Tout ça va bien!

I have been thinking a great deal about your coming—about a clean bed to sleep in, about a good meal for 12 francs now and then—about trips to Chartres and Beauvais, the dungeon of Vincennes, etc. I know all the places but I "manque" the carfare. Right now I "habite" chez Monsieur Nanavati, a dark Hindu of no intellect or anything else. Life is very hard for me—very. I live with bedbugs and cockroaches. I sweep the dirty carpets, wash the dishes, eat stale bread without butter. Terrible life. Honest! Worse than Florida. Only a pair of flannel trousers and a tweed coat to cover my nakedness. I can't go any more bohemian than this.

Frank here is a great painter. You should see the walls. Paris is full of great painters, past and present. That is the trouble with Paris. Otherwise everything is fine. I hope you are fine too. I know you are. In this life one must have hope and courage. One must believe in tomorrow, even though tomorrow never comes.

Yes, I ask you—when are you coming? I am ready to act as guide, interpreter, or what you will. I know where to get ass cheap, and where it is plentiful. Everything is beautiful, except the hardships. How is Ned and Muriel? Don't they ever think of writing a fellow? It is tough to go every day to the American Express and not to get the news. I am very sad sometimes. Today I am very happy. Today I don't give a damn. Let them do what they will. In a little while I am going to take Frank to Mr. Zadkine's studio—there to see the sculpture. Maybe he will have some Cinzano or Pernod to drink. That will be very good. Because it is necessary once in a while that man should drink a little alcohol. Man is not a beast. He is just a little lower than the angels. Play that on the cymbalon. At Moshowitz's.

Yes, Emil, I am thinking of you today very strongly. I hope you are not going to get cold feet. I will show you how to live *very well* on $25.00 a week—including a little snack for me now and then—for friendship's sake. I will take you to the Bal Nègre and turn you into a corkscrew. Or I will take you to the Rue de Lappe and let you lap it up with the Apaches. Or, if it is a Sunday, we will go to Charenton and eat pommes frites with the holiday throngs and dance with a grisette in a Bal Musette. I know Paris now like I know the dictionary. I know everything but how to earn a living—tant pis! In other words I am the same miserable failure as always. No money—no hope. I will sing you a Russian song in French which Eugene has taught me: "Je me souviens toujours, toujours!" It is wonderful. But it does not put money in your pocket. So, then, when you get this you will cable me perhaps—care Amexco (American Express). I am no longer at the Hôtel Alba—because I was kicked out recently. I now live with Nanavati, 4th floor—rear—at 54 Rue Lafayette, near Metro Cadet. Look me up when you come to Paris. Always yours sincerely for a glass of beer, or a ham sandwich.

Maybe some day I will become a respectable member of society. I hope so for your sake. I think there is nothing finer in this life than to be a good citizen, a self-respecting member of society.

Read this out loud—it has a noble ring!

Maybe when you come we will really see Paris. I know all the places—from the outside. I know a couple of places where we can dance with a naked woman (white or black) who will hold your "little frère" while you dance—for 2 fr. the glass of beer. It is chalked up on the wall—no cheating! Or how would you like a nice refined whorehouse for 20 fr.—to the Madame and 10 fr. to the girl. Take your choice! That's $1.20 in American money. Vouvray or Anjou here is about 35 or 40 cents the bottle. Enchanting—dry with a fine aftertaste. The Boulevard Malesherbes very black at midnight. Sacré Coeur always white. The Dôme always open.

What a feller needs in this life is a friend. That's why I appreciate all the big letters I don't receive. Tell Ned the last letter was great. No, I am not homesick, only I would like to see a smiling face—a friendly face.

If you don't find me at Nanavati's look me up, by letter, at the American Express. I go there daily for the letters—or money orders. Or try the Dôme any time after 8:00 P.M. on the terrace, drinking a beer or a "café nature." Or try the American Students' Club at 107 Boulevard Raspail.

Only come!!!

Yours anxiously,
HVM.

P.S. Il me semble que les oiseaux sont ivres.

10/23/30
Hôtel Central
1 bis, rue du Maine
14ème Arrondissement

Dear Emil:

Started a letter to you on the back of a menu somewhere the other night but can't locate it. So here's another—with an enclosure from Elkus that ought to make you die laughin'.

The thing is—are you really coming in November? Christ, I'm eager to know. I feel more than ever lonely now that June has returned. She was here for three weeks and had to leave Saturday morning. *Reason:* lack of funds!! Tough, tough, and then that isn't half enough to say. One calamity on top of another. As for me, I'm virtually a prisoner here, you see. I can neither go forwards nor backwards. Believe me, it was hard to put her on the train. Seemed like the end of the world.

Anyway, I'm staying on, and the hope is that June will return sometime toward the end of the winter. She is going to try to make the theatre in N.Y. I succeeded in getting a promise for her of a job in the first English talkie to be directed by Mme. Germaine Dulac. But that won't be until January at least.

Saw a great picture this morning at 10:00 A.M. at Cinéma Panthéon—special invitations from the Viscount and *Vicomtesse de Noailles* (the great Lesbienne)—on the part of Monsieur Luis Buñuel who created *Un Chien Andalou.* This one was called *L'Age d'Or.* I am going to write you more about it by machine soon. Something extraordinary.

Jesus, Emil, it's raining like hell, and I feel like I want to go out and buy a pair of rubbers. (Don't forget to bring yours when you come. You'll need them.) At noon it was so balmy and wonderful. I was on the *Rue des Carmes* looking at some ancient "impasses." The old Latin Quarter is still glorious, but they're pulling down some of the very rare old sights.

* * * *

I have been looking for a good cheap hotel the last three days. Have visited over *100* so far! Believe me, I will be able to tell you a thing or two about rooms when you arrive. This dump I am in now is only "en passant." Have been living in about five different hotels during the last three weeks. Don't let that worry you. Maybe we'll still go skating together in the Bois—or the Vélodrome. The *Dog of Andalou* is still on at Studio 28. And the Surindépendents have just opened their show!

I gave June a book by a humorist, Rudolf Bringer, for you. Be sure you get it! But don't ask for June at the *Pot.* She doesn't want them to know yet that she has returned. Sorry I couldn't send you anything more than that, but I just couldn't. June arrived without a cent and left the same way.

I had 50 fr. when we parted. Why should I read any more romantic literature? Why? Write soon, will you? Regards to Ned and Muriel. Where are you living?

HVM.

Monday 10/26/or 27/30
c/o American Express
11 rue Scribe
Paris, France

Emil:

At the Rotonde, a new stamping ground, better whores, rotten paintings by La Horde. Sick of the Dôme, the Coupole, the Select. Just a little giddy from the five vins ordinaires I had at des Gourmets. Also from the compliment which Madame la Propriétaire hurled at me. "Monsieur," she smiled, "il me semble que vous êtes tout-à-fait Parisien maintenant."

* * * *

Attention ce soir! Only 60 francs above the rent money. Attention! Today, for the first time in ages, I feel like my old swashbuckling self. Maybe it's because I've begun to work again. Very enthusiastic tonight. Maybe two days from now down in the dumps again—have to look for another hotel, etc. etc. It's like having a black eye, this life. You turn all the colors of the rainbow. But shit! *Merde!!!* Right now I feel I'm good. A very knowing young man has been reviewing the MS of my epic work— this novel that I've been dragging about from one hotel to another, across the ocean twice, thru bordellos and carnivals, a pillow at night in the movies, and under the bridge at the Seine. Stop! Cut the sentimentality! That's one of the weaknesses of my literature . . . my crap.

Well, he said it was something extraordinary! Something new in American literature—altogether original—epic sweep—vital—throbbing.

Well, if it's only *fair*, I'll be satisfied. But just to show him what a cockeyed liar he is I commenced quietly, on my own, to prune it down, to mutilate it, to reduce it to skeletal strength. Jesus, I'm getting a masochistic pleasure out of it. I wipe out whole pages—without even shedding a tear. Out with the balderdash, out with the slush and drivel, out with the apostrophes, the mythologic mythies, the sly innuendoes, the vast and pompous learning (which I haven't got!). Out—out—damned fly-spots. Here I am, and I am only beginning to recognize it—a very plain, unvarnished soul, not learned, not wise, no great shakes any way you look at me—particularly *"comme artist."* What I must do, before blowing out my brains, is to write a few simple confessions in plain Milleresque language. No flapdoodle about the sun going down over the Adriatic! No entomological inquests, no moonlight and flowers. After all, I know only a few things. I've had a few *major* experiences. I'm no Shakespeare, no Hugo, no Balzac. Something a little higher than a louse. That's not overestimating myself, is it?

Alors! Il faut boire quelque chose!

Un Cointreau!!! Triple Sec!

* * * *

I lie in a wet bed nights and dream of taking the train to Monaco. I'd like to see Monaco once again—the little café near the gare, at the foot of the bleak hills, the harbor underneath the Prince's gardens, the two French boys who took us to the bullfight. I'd like to go to Spain, to smell the flowers pouring out of the windows in a ceaseless cascade of perfume. I'd like to smell Naples and Capri, and Anacapri. I'd like to hang for a melancholy hour over the yellow waters of the Arno—go to the secluded Republic of Andorra. Christ, I'd like to do a million things.

But every morning, rain or shine, I get up and go for croissants and coffee. And every morning Paris exerts its same fascination. The day slides by. The rent comes round. The dirty laundry has to be taken away—one has to splash a little water under his armpits to get that garlic smell removed. And once in a while one has to go to the theatre, or the cinema, or a Bal Musette, or just go on a bust. Just drink. Guzzle it, swill it, get boiled.

You know, when I look at your lovely script, I realize the fine balance you have. Jesus, what a hand! Impeccable! The perfect letterer! Honestly, I like it. It's clean, frank, straightforward. It knows its direction. Mine is like some old whore's. Waiting for someone to wink at her. That's me— waiting!!!

* * * *

This, ladies and gentlemen, concludes the performance for the evening. I think Paris is a lovely place. I think the French are so nice. So polite. I think I'll drink a Pernod. Attention! Deduct 4 francs. Oh hell, I'll skip lunch tomorrow. I'll go for a walk on the street of the Mauvais Garçons, or Le Roi du Sicile, or Les Quatres Vents. Hell, I might even stroll along the Blvd. Jules Ferry, or look for the ferryboat on the Rue du Bac. No, I changed my mind. I'll shake hands with the discoverers of Quinine on the Blvd. St. Michel, en face Posilippo's. Maybe I'll do a Zadkine or a Lipschitz. The Superindependents are having their autumn fling. Café l'Avenue has just opened. The heat is turned on in my hotel. A Frenchman just smiled.

HVM.

P. S. A painter named John Nichols has arrived. Perhaps you know him? From Woodstock or Provincetown. Dark glasses, ruddy beard, funny shirts, loud ties, very droll—we are good friends.

P.P.S. Did I give my regards to Ned and Muriel? Why don't I ever hear from them? Why don't you send Muriel over in advance? Or just send a shirt or a pair of trousers.

P.P.P.S. If you want to see how rotten Paul Morand can be read his *Champions du Monde.* I prefer Chirico. By the way, was flirting with Chirico's wife at the Dôme the other night!!

Nov. 18th. 1930
c/o American Express
Paris, France

Dear Emil:

You said once that rather than "kick off" I should try you by cable. Here's an appeal for whatever aid you can summon. I have decided to try to return—despite everything. Can't stick it any more—a life more miserable than a dog's. I won't go into that, however. Right now I have enough in my jeans to last me ten days—by pinching and scraping. There is a cheap boat—America-French Line—leaving every Saturday for New York. I want to make the boat leaving Dec. 7th. Need a hundred dollars. Today I wrote Elkus and my folks to see if the money could be raised. I think my folks would come across with half of the sum. Suggested to Elkus that he get in touch with O'Regan, Conason, Lyons, June and yourself for the balance. Between you all it might be done. *   *   *   *

Believe me, I didn't want to return but I simply must. I'm worn out with the daily struggle for meals, with the uncertainty of a room, etc. I think the book will be finished when I sail. And when you read some day about how certain famous authors wrote their books you will know that I am in the same line—that my struggle with this has been as picaresque as any of them.

And Emil, the book is good. Not only I say so but everyone to whom I have shown it. It is just likely it will create a sensation. It is just possible I will be made. And then maybe it will be I who can do a little helping—for a change.

The book on Paris I can write in N.Y. just as well—the material is all there—a few months of comparative security and I can finish it.

Alors, do what you can. Am bringing you two swell volumes on Paris of the year 1909—in French: the Right and the Left Bank.

HVM.

P.S. Tonight at Cinema Vanves I am seeing one of Emil Zola's pictures—*Au Bonheur des Dames*.

[Dec. 14, 1930]   Sunday, 14th
                                           #2 Rue Auguste Bartholdi
                                           en face Square Dupleix
                                           Quinzième Arrondissement

Feeling very French today and why not? Le bon et joyeux Noel viendra bientôt, dans une dizaine ou comme ça. Ça y est! Et merde, alors! Prière de laisser cet endroit aussi propre, etc. etc. Drinking champagne this morning with my bacon and eggs chez nous. Très bien, papa, believe me. Très bien! Formidable! Ooo la la, la la. . . . So, in the true spirit of Christmas, thinks I, what could be better than to finish off, polish off as the literary eggs say, that article I commenced a few nights ago apropos of *L'Age d'Or.* So here is the copy of the rough draft, old top, and know ye, that when I rewrite it the thing will go to print in one of the best magazines Paris has seen in many moons—Samuel Putnam's own little hobby, with the alienation and conspiracy of Ezra Pound, he with the Provençal complex and the Phillidulla poems. Yes, Cocteau is writing for it too, and Bodenheim, the little shit-heel. I am feverishly scratching out all the pricks, balls, cunts, Fallopian tubes and whatnot that cluttered up the original. Sam wouldn't like that, nor Ezra neither. Observe the amenities, observe the amenities. By Simon Stylites, but I am running good these days—oh, it is not this lousy little article, think not that. No, I have gotten back into my old form. The sap is running again, I wake up with semen in my hand, I get ideas in the toilet, on the Metro, in the telephone booths, etc. Good sign. Great tidings. I will write again. Yes, a new world is opening for me. (Champagne talk!) No kidding, Emil, I am writing you like a friend of old standing, like a brother before whom I was not ashamed to weep on occasion, etc. etc. etc. Spiddividdibeebumbum. . . . Merde, but I've done a lot of work in the last few weeks. Wish I could have sent you copies of the various articles I have written—you would have enjoyed them. But I am sending them all to George Buzby in the hope that he will get them published. And some direct to literary brokers whose names have been furnished me. Stop boasting. . . . All right, I will. How is Ned? Good old Ned. Why doesn't he ever write me? And Muriel? Did she ever get the letter I wrote one hot afternoon outside Père La-chaise? I suppose I'm the sort of guy who shouldn't expect return letters, since I never ask how is Aunt Mary or what is the weather like in New York? Just the same, I want to know. I'm burning up with curiosity. Jesus, write, everybody, write. . . . Don't treat me like some poor god-damned son-of-a-bitch who will get along anyhow somehow or other. Maybe some day . . . stop boasting. Full stop!

Merde alors! Always a good paragraph opening. Merde! Osborn (he's my room-mate) still refuses to believe that it means shit, et pourquoi?— because it doesn't sound like shit. Isn't that good? Today I bought eggs— des oeufs coque. Had a long conversation about coque. Sounds like cock to me, but I discovered it wasn't. Now Osborn is just showing me a page out of *Bravo*—I will send you a copy shortly. Good pictures of great artists in their dens. Zadkine with a leather cap on. Foujita with his bang. Kiki with her aurora borealis. And then a fine nude—a wow—all ass, and I don't mean maybe, papa. "Is it Mlle. Claude?" he asks. "Mlle. Claude?" Jesus, maybe it is. And who is Mlle. Claude? Ah, the prettiest, juiciest, cleverest little cocotte in Montparnasse. Osborn and I share her once in a while. Such taste, such discretion, such politesse. And intelligent? My eye. Knows how to talk like a master of politics. Reads everything. Even Huysmans. Anyhow Mlle. Claude is sort of low-swung, red apple but-tocks, taut teats, pearly teeth, fine tongue (with needles in it) and plenty of sparkle and animation. But so goddamned refined that you don't want to take advantage of her. "You go home now and get dressed, Claude." Claude looks up at you drowsily. "Tu ne m'aimes pas?" Sure, sure we do. But a fellow gets tired sometimes. And then there are the other customers waiting for her at the Coupole and the Rotonde. Give her another ten francs for a taxi. Throw in a pair of silk stockings. Jesus, but those little things tickle Claude immensely. Even more than the big things. What? Excuse me. Anyhow, Claude likes me to write her letters care of the Coupole. There they are, stuck on the bulletin board—I sometimes see them before she has a chance to catch her mail. She gets up late, you see. And then, sometimes, I'd like to snatch them back. My French isn't so hot yet. But Claude doesn't mind a grammatical error now and then. So long as you pay in francs, and remember the pourboire for the taxi. And then with Mlle. Claude you don't need to employ any extra precautions. "You see Mr. Osborn, he is not ill." All right, the hell with the condom. Save it, I might be hungry tomorrow. It's fine once in a while to work your way in without any mucous membranes interfering. Jesus, what am I saying?

You might get the idea that I'm screwing Mlle. Claude. No, Jesus, don't go thinking anything like that. Mlle. Claude is a fine gal . . . the finest little piece of ass in Montparnasse. A letter chez la Coupole will always reach her. Drop her a line. Tell her you're a good friend of mine.

* * * * Osborn has good taste. Parallel with mine. A Connecticut Yankee, with a slip in the ancestry somewhere. Bon vivant. Likes his wine, and likes his ass. Great spieler. Strong on Anatole France, on the culture of the French. Every night he comes home from the bank and says, in his rotten French, "Tonight, Henry, we must *fait un rigolo*"—which is simply untranslatable, even by Mlle. Claude, but it means that we must go out and have a good time.

Saw Zadkine at the Dôme the other night. Called me back just as I was sortieing. "Henry, why do you stay away from me?" he says. "You know where I live. Why don't we go out some night and have a little fun?" Yes, Herr Zadkine hat dies gesagt. You know me, soft guy . . . almost melted. The truth is I'm abashed in the presence of great men. I avoid them. Nobody takes me for a great man—I'm not saying I am, be Jesus. Whoa. . . . Stop. . . . So Zadkine adds, "Henry, how do you make so many friends here? Do you know I am very lonely? I never think of speaking to someone unless I know him. I am very lonely, really. Why don't you take me out with you when you go on your *folklore* expeditions?" Folklore expeditions! Cripes! That was a good fifty-cent word for Zadkine. Meant to impress me, I guess. Anyway, I don't need an introduction to go up and talk to people. Some of my best conversations are with the women who sit in the toilets and empty the little coins out of the saucer. Very human, believe me. Marcel Proust knew what he was doing when he added that little scene in the privy house. Where was it again? I should like to go there. Methinks it must have been near the Rond-point des Champs Elysées. Am I right? Or was it near the Trocadéro?

* * * *

Well, remember me this Christmas, and get your skin full. I know you will without any urging. Are you a poor man by now? What has happened to you—with all the banks closing and sales stopping? No more ketchup bottles to paint? How about Arrow collars? France is still in good condition. Of course if America blows up there'll be trouble here. But—there is no danger yet of Communism, is there? Tell me what you think of Buñuel. Do you believe in the Age of Gold? Or should I have put a little more hair on it? (Note the artists' names who contributed the sketches.) Anyway, Merry Christmas—and to Mr. Scrooge too, merry Christmas. Old 85 and the Santa Claus on the blackboard in colored chalk.

HVM.

P.S. Got a couple of Hindu outcast whores from the Vale of Cashmere coming to dinner next week. They wrestle with guys like Augustus John, etc. He's a big horse's ass.

P.P.S. A gang is pouring in—Merry Christmas from all Montparnasse— and from Mlle. *Loulou!!!*

2 Rue Auguste Bartholdi
Quinzième Arrondissement
Feb. 16th, 1931.

Well, well, well. Blow the grampus! Three boatloads of mail arrived today and in all the bloody swill there was nothing but your letter. But! You don't know what your letter has done for me. Voici! I almost ran back to the house. Ran all the way along Boulevard Haussmann to the Metro Station Havre-Caumartin, and at Trocadéro, where I change, almost forgot to get off. Dreaming about the lovely words you put down in that careful, calligraphic script. Did I say calligraphic? I meant Caligari. Pardon. . . . Saturday I had a letter from George and answered it immediately, saying toward the end, "What's the matter with Emil, is he dead, down and out, or sore?" Didn't you get a big clump of mail from me around Christmas, and some magazines and a poster or two from Cinéma Vanves which I expected you would put up on your wall along with my water colors? And did you get the stuff on Buñuel? Or have I been dreaming that I sent all this to you? Couldn't understand your silence at all. Ned and Muriel—I can understand their attitude. Procrastination . . . deep, inrooted. But you! Jesus, man, you have no idea what a letter means. It makes me hysterical.

 * * * * You talk about form, style, etc. Why yes, these things have been occupying me frightfully. It is the entire meat of our discussions around here. Discussions with the artist John Nichols, with Frank Mechau, with Tex Carnahan, and my room-mate, Richard Galen Osborn, friend and benefactor, patron of the arts, etc. etc. And, to show you that you have not been out of my thoughts, I will say that only last night I fell asleep pondering over the question of how I would mail to you the two beautiful volumes on Paris which I have been talking so much about from time to time. The books are crowded with pen and ink sketches and the city is covered exhaustively—the city in the year 1910 or thereabouts. I have another curious book for George—given me by the author, in which, among other things, there appears the songs of the shit-pumpers—songs as they are still sung in the cafés around Belleville and Place du Combat.

Irene is sleeping in the next room so I must try to tap quietly. You don't know Irene? George has a few pages about her in my diary notes. Be sure you get these from him soon—about 40 pages. More about John Nichols there, too. At any rate, the life as we live it in this studio is far from dull. Irene has the clap, Osborn has bronchitis, and I have the piles. Just exchanged six empty champagne bottles at the Russian épicerie across the street. Not a drop went down my gullet. Strict diet lately—no meat, no wine, no eggs, no rich game, no women. Fruit and paraffin oil, arnica drops and adrenalin ointment—seulement! Right now, writing this, I am propped up like a pasha. Can't find a too comfortable seat. But I feel that I'm going to break out soon. Last night I dipped into a bottle of white wine and took a slice of veal with pommes frites. Feel none the worse for it today. Live and let live, be Jesus!

Nichols ought to be here soon to add the finishing touches to my portrait. I think it is a Renoir, with a slight element of the caricature, à la Grosz—if that conveys anything to you. The underlip is very prominent and the dome bulges out eloquently, very like the Invalides. And then there are the whiskers. Yes, I have a full-grown beard now, mostly dark red, but peppered with gray and white. The concierge doesn't like it at all, and my laundry woman says every time we meet: "C'est pas beau, monsieur. Vous êtes vieilli"—or something like that. But it's my beard and I'm very proud of it. It's untrimmed, you know, and in a few more weeks I'll be another Dostoievski. I can't stand these Montparnasse beards—they look so damned artificial.

Am I going to stay, you ask? Emil, I don't know a thing. I face each day as it comes along. I have no plans. Certainly I have no wish to return. It's only a question of being able to hold on. I owe my friend Osborn here over a hundred dollars. Owe other people too. As long as I have a roof over my head I will stick. By the fourth of March we are to get out of here—the painter who owns the joint is returning then from the Midi. Haven't the slightest idea what I will do then. Go to the American Express daily looking for money. June wires every now and then—"Hold on, money soon." A few weeks elapse and then another wire: "Hold on, sending you money in a few days." And that's the way it goes, week after week, month after month. I'm always living on the edge of disaster. If I were ever picked up by the police, for instance, I could be shipped to the frontier at once. I haven't had an identity card since landing.

Of course my principal obsession, as always, is meals. Osborn has been feeding me for weeks and weeks. Nichols too once in a while, and Fred, the journalist, with whom I have written some pieces. Everyone counsels me to stick it out. I'm supposed to be a guy with promise. Besides that,

I'm supposed to be a *romantic*. People wonder and shake their heads. How
is it that things happen to that guy the way they do? Always in the midst
of exciting things, adventures, confessions, etc. But the question in my
mind is: what am I doing for literature? Here I am, still muddling along
with the book. At the very tail end and can't put the word Finis to it. And
sick and sore about it . . . disgusted . . . hate it . . . think it the vilest crap
that ever was. You mention my enthusiasm. Somehow only a meager
portion of what I feel and think gets expressed, and that nearly drives me
crazy. Sometimes I believe it's because of the form I have chosen. This
book, for example, has been so carefully and painstakingly plotted out,
the notes are so copious and exhaustive, that I feel cramped, walled in,
suffocated. When I get thru I want to explode. I will explode in the Paris
book. The hell with form, style, expression and all those pseudo-para-
mount things which beguile the critics. I want to get myself across this
time—and direct as a knife thrust.

    *   *   *   *   Have been up to the ears in Lawrence lately. Understand
him better than ever. Yes, I know his limitations. Limitations! What's
that? We all are prone to limitations, eh, old pfoof? The worst thing about
Lawrence, as I see it, is his use of the orthodox form. That was especially
a great pity in the case of *Lady Chatterley's Lover*. There he had hold of such
a wonderful idea. And he marred it by using the old schema. All the stuff
about the colliers, about the intellectual life of the parlor, about democracy and Communism, etc. Fiddlesticks! If he had just confined himself
to warmhearted fucking all the way through, what a book it would have
been. But when he describes the forest there, and the forester, when he
opens up the whole heart of nature like a vein filled with blood . . . God,
then you have the real Lawrence, the mystic, the son of Nature, the phallic
worshipper, the dark flower and the Holy Ghost.   *   *   *   *

Marlene Dietrich! I have her here on the wall, over my bunk. Did I see
The Blue Angel? Man, I saw it three times—twice in German and once in
French, with English songs, But I prefer the German. That voice! "Ich
bin von Kopf zu Fusz auf Liebe eingestellt. . . . und sonst garnichts!" I
have been driving the guys crazy around here with talk of *The Blue Angel*.
Not Jannings—though he had superb moments—Lear-like in the Cori-
curcuroo business . . . but Marlene. Ach himmel! What blissful sin. What
carnality. What a voice! Emil, the thighs almost killed me. I studied them
from every angle of the theatre. I dream about them at night. It's hard
for me to say much now about the picture. . . . I've exhausted myself on
it. About Heinrich Mann I know nothing. I see the cheapness of the plot,
the Hollywood trappings, the meticulous Jannings dramaturgy, and all
that. But, as you say, what a performance! A vaginal catharsis, old man.
As story, very unconvincing. As drama, superb. As sex, ovum and testes.
Wish I could splurge here and let you know the occasions on which I saw

the film. How we drank at a little bistro on the Rue Guy-Lussac before and after the second visit. How, after the third visit, the Negro and I went to a peep show on the Rue St. Lazare, watching the man and beast act. How, after the first time, I ran into Mlle. Claude at the Coupole, and after taking her to the Hôtel Vavin, sat up all night talking about life (in French), so that when Mlle. Claude left she was almost in tears, and gave me a great big hug and kiss and said that I was very human and very wise, etc. etc.

To come back to Lawrence—and the great painters. Was reading in the restaurant last night a few passages from his collected papers. Read how he stumbled on painting at the age of forty. Water colors. Thomas Girtin, copying the old masters, trying to "make pictures." Gave me a tremendous kick. Saw myself all over again. Clinton Street. Joe O'Regan . . . water colors . . . still lifes . . . turning out pictures. . . . I understand Lawrence perfectly, perfectly. He did exactly what I feel I want to do. If I haven't touched the brush since I've been here it's only because I felt I had too big a job on my hands with the book—and the problem of living. I dream of buying new tubes, new brushes, and starting all over again. But I resolve steadfastly not to commence until I have finished the job in hand. Job I call it. That expresses my inner feelings. Sometimes when I think of doing a water color I get such a furious hunger and rage that I could destroy the book. I want to paint—if only water colors. I know I will paint again. And I don't give a damn whether people will recognize it as painting or not. It gives me great joy, and that's all I ask of it. Wish that writing could do the same thing for me. I'm almost losing faith in myself, in my ability. You said a hell of a lot of fine things. But are they true? Do I know anything about writing? I feel I am becoming a critic instead of a creator. I see all the faults in the other guys but can't profit by them myself. In the mornings I feel like a reservoir of energy, and at night when I look at my pages I see that I am nothing but a constipated windbag. Here in Paris I have done more deep, serious thinking about writing than ever before in my life. Certain things are beginning to clarify in my mind. I think I know the direction I want to take. Unfortunately, it is a direction that will further alienate the reader. It's almost as though I had made up my mind to prevent people from liking me. For example— you know how I revered Thomas Mann. The other day I got *Death in Venice* from the library in order to bedazzle Osborn. And I read a few pages at random before handing it to him. And lo and behold! to my own absolute astonishment, I saw that Thomas Mann was dead . . . finished . . . *for me.* I saw all his faults and damned little of his virtues. I saw that glorious story, which I once swore was the finest novelette ever written, as a tedious, pompous, pedantic, piece of German sentimentalism, outmoded, outdated, outworn . . . ausgespielt. It's difficult for me to understand my former enthusiasm. *The Magic Mountain*—I still believe in that. But I am almost afraid to approach it again. Nor can I tell you whom I would put in his place. Joyce too has lost his charm for me. I see him as a broken vomit, a precious sewer, a medieval stew. There remains Proust and Spengler. Spengler emerges biggest and best of all still. Have reread him here—the first volume. Swiped it, in fact, from the American Library. There is great music, great literature, great ideas. Will I be obliged to retract this two years hence? Well, anyway . . . for the time being . . . big man!

Of course I really don't think I'm going to degenerate into a critic. As a critic I'm lousy. And so, I'll stop about ideas—with just this parenthesis that John Nichols (wish you could know him!) has been giving me more ideas about art—all art—than anybody I have met in ages. Imagine the guts of a man to go every day to the Louvre, rain or shine, for four months. Studying the old masters. And in the Metro, when he wants to close his ears against his wife, opens a book on the Louvre. I feel convinced, when talking to him that I am standing in the presence of a genius. I can see in him another Van Gogh, or better. Because, except for the beard, he is very little like Van Gogh. Yes, traces of Van Gogh in the early paintings, but the spirit of Van Gogh is missing. Nichols is a deeply cultured guy, a rich, ripe guy of the autumnal cities, a man of feeling, of intuition, of instinct, but also of great intellect, and of great ego . . . charming ego . . . charming effrontery. The child-man, the wonder-man, soft-voiced, musical, sure, suave, convincing, and never-ending. And most of his conversation, when it is not about me, is about himself. He hobnobbed at Woodstock with John Carroll, Speicher, Zorach, Kuniyoshi, and that gang. Believes himself leagues ahead of all of them. I too. And though sometimes his paintings are so putrid, so vile and amateurish, so weak and wobbly as to make me burst out in laughter, I know that other things of his are on the very finest level and they fill me with reverence and awe. He says, of course, that I know next to nothing about painting, that I see it only as literature—and he applauds that, because in his own deft fashion he construes that to be witness of my fine creative instincts. He tells me about Cézanne (and he has the most original dope on Cézanne that I have ever encountered), about Renoir, about Picasso, as if I had never heard of them before. He's a great Renoir man, I must tell you. He has a self-portrait which is magnificent in sensuousness. He doesn't give a damn about being impressionistic. He doesn't draw very well. He loves color. He hasn't much use for Picasso. He will stand for days in front of Titian, Piero della Francesca and Rubens. Why Rubens? You ought to hear him extol Rubens. In fact, the amazing thing about him is that he can find something to marvel at in nearly every one of the great fellows. And he's strong on going to the originals. . . . You know, he says up in Woodstock they were telling him the Louvre was a waste of time, and he was thinking all the while, "Well, if Cézanne spent so much time there he must have found great things in it." He mystifies me at times . . . much too often, in fact. He adores Faure and Spengler. He misquotes them. He will say, "As Spengler says," and then introduce his own private thoughts, and if you trip him up, he will right himself easy as a feather. Great guy. Warm, human personality, thinker, artist, scholar, sensualist— *and has a private income!* Therein lies his great blessing. He has time to do what he wants. Painting can wait on him. He holds the future in his hands. * * * *

Well, Emil, you said it was the longest letter you ever wrote. So is this. I hope you're reading it over a bottle of wine—preferably Anjou. Just before the piles began enjoying Mousseux. Want to try Asti soon and Château Yquem, which I had a sip of New Year's Eve. Nearly killed New Year's Eve in a taxi smashup. Ran full on to another car, tipped it over. The glass smashed to bits right beside me, but I got off without a scratch—only to come down with the piles. And never felt the least nervous afterwards. As though it happened on another planet. Can you beat it?

Just had a great fright. Washed my face, after lunching on fruits, and when I put the towel back saw that it was Irene's. Can't educate Irene to use the right towels. She says: "My dear, if you could become blind from that I would have been blind years ago." I speak to her fatherly about the toilet seat. "You know, Irene, it's dangerous for us, having you around." "All right," she says, "I won't use the toilet. I'll go outside to a café." "No, don't do that," I say, "just clean the seat each time you use it." "Oh, my dear," she says, "I'll not sit down on it . . . I'll stand up." The house is all cockeyed with Irene around. Osborn picked her up one night on the Champs Elysées. First she wouldn't fuck becase she had the monthlies. She had them for eight days and we were beginning to think she was faking. Then we found cotton batting under the bed, all full of dark blood, and we knew it was no fake. Everything is thrown on the floor, or under the bed: orange peels, wadding corks, empty bottles, scissors, old condoms, pillows. The bed is only made up when it's time to retire. "My dear, I wouldn't get up at all if it wasn't for me Russian newspapers." That's it—no toilet paper. . . . Nothing but Russian newspapers with which to wipe your ass. Anyway, after the menstrual period, Irene still wouldn't fuck. Said she only liked women, or if she took a man, she had to get excited first. Wanted Osborn to take her to a whorehouse and watch two women doing it so that she could get excited. Osborn couldn't see it. Then just when he was mounting her one night, she tells him she's still sick—with the clap. Six months old. He fell off her like a log. Narrow escape. Next night he decides to risk it, with a condom. But Irene is too

tight. So one thing after another failing, he just gave it up. And now they
lie there like brother and sister, with incestuous dreams. "I'm telling
you," says Irene, "in Russia it often happens that a man sleeps with a
woman without touching her. He can sleep that way for weeks and
months. Until—well, once he touches her, then paff! after that it's paff,
paff, paff." "Paff" is her favorite exclamatory expression and very expres-
sive. The other night Osborn kicked her out. Bawled hell out of her on
the street in front of the Select. "I don't want any of your high-ass Russian
variety," he yelled. "Why should I feel sorry for you? What have you ever
done for me? You're no better than a French prostitute . . . you're not
so good. Get away from me." And Irene walked off, crestfallen, humbled,
dejected. Two nights later Osborn meets her again on the Champs Elysées. "Hello, darling!" Go off together to Le Boeuf sur le Toit—a Cocteau rendezvous infested with perverts. I come home and find Irene in
bed again. "My dear," she says, "I just couldn't stay away from you. I'm
sick of all this fucking around." We read her a few passages from Lawrence one night. She thought it great. And now, ever since, it's nothing
but fucking, fucking, fucking. "My dear, I don't want to see my movie
director today. He wants to fuck me, and I don't feel like fucking today."
We urge her to go. We want her to get work and clear out. "Go ahead,"
says Osborn, "see your movie director and give him a little warmhearted
fucking." "Darling," says Irene, "you are so brutal with me. You want that
I should go out the whole afternoon fucking and bring home to you the
money." Last night Irene was perplexed. She had a suppository of some
kind, with a string attached to it, which she was supposed to put inside
her and pull out full of pus in the morning. "My dear, where is the string?
I can't find the string." "Oh, let the movie director find it," we yell. "But,
my dear, I am bleeding again. I just had my menstrual period a few days
ago and now there are gouttes again. I must stop drinking. I can't bleed
to death." The story is that Irene committed suicide for her movie director. Jumped in the Seine. Was fished out. She remembered that there
were a lot of people watching her, cheering her, etc. "My dear, my life
is always like that. I am a neurasthenic. The whole day I am running
around and at night I am drunk. Just imagine, I was an innocent girl when
I came to Paris. I knew nothing. And as I had 300,000 francs, Swiss francs,
I enjoyed myself. And what happened? I fucked around with this one and
that and then I met my movie director and he gave me the clap. And now
I want to give it to him, because it's all his fault that I committed suicide
in the Seine. But darling, I must first have a new dress. I owe my dress-
maker still 30,000 francs. . . ." Irene's lawyer, who is trying to collect the
money which is hidden away in the Midland Bank of England, and in the
Swiss bank, and in the National City Bank, N.Y., is a timid, young Frenchman who idolizes her. "He kept begging me always to fuck **him. I got sick**

and tired of hearing him with his fucking all the time, so one night I said, 'Yes, come upstairs and I will fuck you.' And so I fucked him and a few days later he calls me up and says, 'I must see you.' And then he shows me a paper from the doctor and it's gonorrhea and I had to laugh. 'My dear, I didn't know that I had the clap. You wanted to fuck me and so I fucked you and that's all. Paff!' So now he's cured of the fucking business and he gives me only a hundred francs when I see him because he wants me to behave myself and not run around Montparnasse drinking and fucking the whole night." And from this Irene will calmly switch to an affair with a Lesbian. "Yes, my dear, I picked her up in Le Fétiche one night. She was drunk and she made love to me all night from the tables, so that at last I couldn't stand it any more, so I said, 'Come with me.' And then I gave her 200 francs and I let her suck me off. Paff! But I don't care so much for Lesbians. I tell you, I would rather have a man, but when I get terribly excited—three, four, five times, paff, paff, paff, I bleed and that's very bad for me because I don't want to bleed to death. So you see why once in a while I let myself to be sucked by a Lesbian. . . ." We don't see at all, but we nod our heads. Now the arrangement is that Irene must find another victim and sleep elsewhere, because Osborn has just been promoted to a bigger and better job and has to get sleep. So Irene has picked up a sculptor who is castrated and she will sleep with him—only he keeps her awake all night, kissing her. "But darling," she says, "you will let me come here once in a while to take my douches? The sculptor he has no hot water and I can't take my potassium permanganate regularly." Furthermore, she is so tired from being kissed all night that she wants to come back here to rest up. "Besides, darling, I luff you. You have such a nice body. You are just like a woman. Only don't put that candlestick next to me, it makes me nervous. Always that candlestick. Why don't you become a fairy so then I could love you? Wouldn't you like me to suck you off?" Etc. Etc. Etc. . . .

Do you begin to get Irene's character? Sorry I can't expand at length. My back is sore. Going to close now. Sure, I'll write again and I won't wait exactly for your responses. But try to write once in a while. If only on the back of a menu—a little scrawl over the wine bottle. Anything to keep me on the jump.

*   *   *   *

Love and more blue angels. Thighs. Big business and fornication.

HVM

March 10th [1931]

Emil:

* * * *

As I sit and pose for my friend Nichols—working out the food and laundry problem—I am regaled with divagations from the lips of all the celebrities who ever held brush to paint. Nichols and his wife are working on new portraits of me (wife is Frances Wood, née Ginsberg). * * * *

Great days—full of missing meals—but rich in paint, verbiage and local scenery. Getting into such a bummy condition that people everywhere nudge one another and point me out. Cold days—real winter's frost—and everybody rushing to the warm cafés to breathe the sour breath of stale, smoked bodies bombinating in the void. People coming back from Cagnes, Nice, Menton, London, etc. "Hello Henry—you still here?" Etc. The glad hand and a free drink. Maybe a croissant now and then. Everybody digging in and getting sociable. Frank painting his grand abstracts, à la Chirico—with concrete walls, swimming pools, stereopticon views and Neanderthal dolls. Nichols working with his left hand and lots of fine little brushes which he loads with a pale impasto. Francie slapping the canvas, à la Titian, until it sings with her bludgeon strokes.

Kann—panjandrum of Pantheism—with whom I am now living, wants a good skeleton to put in his latest Lurçat picture. "Find me a dealer, Henry, and I will turn them out like hot cakes." Osborn opposite me, cockeyed with Cointreau, writing to his gal back in Connecticut about the phallic writer—the great American novelist—Henry Valentine Miller. Mlle. Claude sitting on the terrace near a brazier at the Coupole, pulling her fur wrap around her tender loins. Archie Giddes standing at the Dôme bar, talking about the Tate Gallery in London. Sandy Calder walking in here with a wire creation from the Bal Nègre. Zadkine in his cold studio looking at his Trocadéro Museum. Irene wandering in the snow looking for a little coldhearted fucking. Derain going to the Guimet Musée to get new ideas for his coffin portraits. Fred, the journalist, just coming out of a tunnel where he has been raping Pavlova in her last swan dance. Sam Putnam getting drunk at the Rotonde with a newsboy fifty years old.

Just sold about 350 francs' worth of writing to the Chicago *Tribune.* Printed a Lulu by me yesterday, called "Paris in *Ut Mineur.*" Nobody knows who the author is. The great anonymous art of the 13th century.

* * * *

Anyway the problem is to live. What we artists need is food—and lots more of it. No art without food!! I have doped out that I could live now on practically six dollars a week. But even if I said three dollars a week, it would bring me no nearer to a solution of my problem.

We must get Madeleine Boyd definitely and vitally interested in the great American novelist. If Madeleine would only stake me to that *sine qua non* I would write anything, including Dante's *Inferno*.

Just answered an ad by a Count Vladimir de Cykowski who wants to teach painting in exchange for English. It is getting to the point where I will actually have to earn a living, mal gré, bon gré.

* * * * You know I have had a pretty rich life thus far. Well, this last year has been the epitome of all the years preceding. I feel now exactly as all the great vagabond artists must have felt—absolutely reckless, childish, irresponsible, unscrupulous, and overflowing with carnal vitality, vigor, ginger, etc. Always on the border of insanity, due to worry, hunger, etc. But shoving along, day after day. I think when you see my face you will recognize the toll. I have crammed so damned much in that I am on the point of snapping. If I were told tomorrow that I must hang I would say O.K. I've seen the show. And fuck you, Jack!

* * * * I tell you, if I ever get a break, and a chance to tell the story of my tribulations in the pages of *Vanity Fair,* I will be the romantic guy of America—*sans doute.*

I went recently with Nichols to the Cirque Medrano. We sat in the stalls for five francs and had a fine Seurat night of it. I will probably write something about it for the Sunday *Tribune.* Especially about the trained seals—a sheer plastic delight. I believe I could make everything live again as it lived in the days of Renoir, Manet, Degas, et cetera. I have still a fine, fresh vision, and when I am not ridden by phagomania, enjoy every minute of the day to the fullest.

Cafés, cemeteries, bistros in an orange light shedding a medieval aura of sanctity over the rubber black pavements. Prostitutes like wilted flowers and society dames glowing like gardenias. Pissoirs filled with piss-soaked bread and feuilletons of futile journalists sweating in cold garrets. Beyond the portes the "cold mournful perspective of the suburbs—by Utrillo, bastard son of Suzanne Valadon. The Seine running like a twisted knife between the Right and the Left Banks. Sacré Coeur white in the night of Montmartre. Belgian steeds prancing with all their testicles thru the empty streets of midnight. Lesbians at the Dôme working off their excess lust in charcoal and ambergris. The Boulevard Jules Ferry still as a murderer's heart, emptying into the Abattoir de la Villette. Cold Greenland women at the Viking blazing under polar ice, their blonde wigs refulgent with exotic heat. A whore opposite me smiling lasciviously and scratching herself under the table. At the Rotonde, after three A.M., they lift up their dresses at the bar and run their fingers thru dark rose-bushes.

Count Stablowski, Polish artist sawing his easel in pieces before evacuating his too expensive apartment-studio. Kann and I making off with the pillows and bed linen.

Just saying to Osborn—"Tonight I'd like to live. Where the hell's Mlle. Claude." Would she trust me for once? Why not? Didn't I give her a pair of cotton stockings as a little *cadeau* the last time?

Fred says: "Write a letter to Buzby. Make it twenty pages long. Maybe he'll send you another five bucks." Good idea! A letter to Buzby. *Sub rosa, Emil! Sub rosa!* Must live. Must live. All Paris before me—Right & Left Banks. And the Bank of Indo-China. Let's go! The checks are piling up. Twelve beers between us, and more to come. Make a night of it! Don't forget the starving artists of Montparnasse. Address care American Express. Cable *Amexco.* Unscrupulous, adorable, loving and amiable. Great nights. Remember me to everybody. I wish you all were here.

Love and kisses,
Henry

24 Août, 1931
Hôtel Central
1 bis, Rue du Maine
Paris, xiv. Arr.

Dear Emil:

Getting this letter off is somewhat of a task. I just finished the book and must wait now until payday for funds wherewith to mail it. Meantime I have been making notes—for a grand letter covering the interim since the previous one. I am going to give you a few brief notes immediately, as I know that it will be days before this is finished. (I start tomorrow on the Paris book: first person, uncensored, formless—fuck everything!) So. You understand that my life has not become any easier because I have a job. Au contraire, I am worse off than ever. Everyone expects me to pay back what I borrow, whereas heretofore—well, you know what I mean. However, there is the life at Gillotte's nightly (that is, the little bistro around the corner from the office). That compensates for everything. There is the walk home with Wambly Bald and Fred. There are the sick whores at the Dôme just as dawn comes up. Oh, there are numbers of things which seem to make everything all right—particularly Porto Sec, Anjou, etc.

It is time to go to work, and I have just begun my day. Perhaps tonight, after work, I will sneak up to the editorial room and knock off a few lines while the front-page men play cards. You understand, there is a little feeling between us down in the basement and the fellows upstairs who write the news. We don't belong. Tant pis!

* * * *

Although the job is very unimportant it seems that everything centers about it. It forms the very core of my life, shapes it, directs it, permeates all my activities, my thoughts, etc. I would be unhappy, I think, if I were deprived of it, or if (and this is wholly impossible) I were transferred to the editorial department, promoted as it were. Honestly, I would not like to write news. I prefer this slavery. The very atmosphere of the place has gotten into my blood. I miss it on my night off. In the first place, it is a perfect maze of machinery. The air is fetid. And then there is the noise—a deafening noise, and the blinding lights. The compositors—all Frenchmen—are an interesting lot, far more interesting than the front-page men. Each one is a character. The old ones especially are quite adorable. They are like characters out of a French novel—and in them one can perceive the variety of blood that has gone into the making of the French people. There is one chap, for example, from the Midi, who has been a bullfighter, and now is studying for a career on the operatic stage. He has invited us all to go down to Nîmes next month to see the bullfight in the arena—the one where I saw my first bullfight. His favorite opera is *The Barber of Seville*. He has the body of a consumptive and lungs of brass. He is feeble-minded, too, I forgot to mention.

But this is neither here nor there. He is only one. There are dozens of types—Mephistopheles at the stones, for instance, who acts as godfather to Wambly Bald, who never smiles except when he is setting up "La Vie de Bohème" as it's lived on the Left Bank. And when Bald begins to blow about his potency he listens with both ears cocked and there comes over his face a sort of wistful, regretful smile, a smile full of condonement and admiration at the same time. Very often there takes place a discussion, precipitated by Bald, of course, as to the number of times one should cohabit weekly. And then there comes up too the question of the size of one's organs, and the opera singer will go behind a counter and unbutton his pants, show all and sundry what a virile cock he is.

Then there is old Captain Rush with the wooden leg who chews our ear off every night about Byron, Milton, Dryden, Dr. Johnson, Pope, Addison, Sheridan, Kipling, et alia. Like most Englishmen the captain has bad teeth, and not only bad but unclean teeth. In the lulls he regales us with poetry and his breath spreads a sweet stench over the place so that by comparison the smell of burning lead is aromatic. He and Fred are not on speaking terms. It happened this way: one night the captain brought his wife, a French woman, to the office. She was extremely homely. Nevertheless, the captain seemed proud of her. And the next night, when Fred met the captain, he said in his impudent way: "Well, captain, did you give her a good lay last night?" And the captain squirmed round in his seat and stammered, "What's that? Eh? I beg your pardon, etc. etc." But Fred continues blandly: "I say, did you fuck her last night? Was it good?" The captain muttered something about "disgusting language" and turned away. The captain doesn't understand modern verse either. He saw a poem once in the *New Review* about sandwiches which he found altogether mystifying. However, if there is to be a new issue of the *New Review* we are going to get the captain to contribute something on Lord Byron or else Rudyard Kipling.

Wambly Bald, of course, is the chief nut hereabouts. Wambly Bald is a misanthropist, if this isn't too dignified a term to use in connection with such a sad figure. Everything is futile to him. Everything but cunt. On our way home we indulge in guessing games. "Three guesses—what am I thinking about now?" Answer invariably and invariably correct: Cunt . . . cunt . . . cunt. Last night it was Ida's cunt. Night before, the Virgin Mary's. Very edifying pastime, as you can see. And every night there is a wail from Bald: "Jesus, I got a broad and she promised to give me a lay, but the concierge won't change the sheets. How can I give her a lay on those dirty sheets? Jesus, it's a god-damned crime that a guy can't make enough money to pay for his laundry. What do you do in a case like that?" And then another night: "Have you met my virgin yet?" The virgin has been screwed now day in and day out for the past two months, but she is still his "virgin." Or, after meeting a famous painter: "He gave me a lot of crap about art. I don't know what the hell he's talking about. What would you say about a guy like that? You can't talk about art in a column, can you? Besides, it's all been said before. There's nothing new in Montparnasse." Which is true, of course, but then it sounds so terribly pathetic and distressing when he says it. "Can't you give me a few names, at least?" he begs the night before the column is to appear. "Give me any names . . . your friends in America . . . anything. I just have to fill up space." And then, when you have accommodated him, given him names, dates, places, etc. the column appears next day with the usual rigmarole: The Countess was around again last night flirting with the Night Patrol girls. . . . Or, Kokoschka is going to New Caledonia to study the habits of the primitives. He sleeps on the floor. (Big question preceding night: why does he sleep on the floor? Is he just eccentric, or is there a good reason for it? Do you see what I mean? You can't say—he sleeps on the floor every night . . . you've got to document it. Otherwise people won't know what you're talking about.) And, after the paper is out, and the column is read, a little gathering at Gillottes's to discuss the whys and wherefores. Bald very sad because nobody sees his little jokes. "All right, you guys are so smart, let me see you write a column. You write it for me next week. Just try to say something funny. Just see how hard it is." So Fred and I, on a bet, write a funny one—a very funny one—about the Old Port in Marseilles. Show it to him. He grunts. "Is that funny? What does that word mean? You know god-damned well I can't use any big words in my column. Can't you write simply?"

There are feuds, intrigues, jealousies going on constantly. There is Stern, editor on the day staff, who is the bane of Bald's life. A pawnbroker, he calls him. "You're not a newspaper man," says Stern, after giving Bald a three-hour tryout upstairs. "Can you imagine that little son of a bitch saying that to me?" says Bald. "I don't know why I didn't crash him. Imagine, he gives me a bunch of names—French people, all of them, and the bastard knows I can't speak French—and he says, "Call them up and get a story—quick." "Jesus, I can't even call a number in French. So that's why I'm not a newspaperman. The dirty little bastard. Wait till I review his essay. I'll tear his guts out." It's all very childish and yet very amusing at the same time. There is a guy named Louis whom Bald and Fred refuse to walk home with. Not because Louis is a Jew. Oh no. But Louis talks too much. He's too enthusiastic. Toward two o'clock, when we're all down at the stones, screeching at the top of our lungs, Louis appears with his usual enthusiastic grin: "Are you fellows walking home tonight?" And Fred and Bald invent excuses. No, they're eating at Gillotte's. They know Louis hates Gillotte's. But Louis is lonesome this night and so he says: "All right, I'll meet you at Gillotte's. I want to tell you about a triptych I picked up the other day . . . wonderful bargain . . . really, you must see it." And before he has finished, of course, Fred is saying: "I'm sorry, but I'm too busy." So it's left for me to walk home with Louis. Funny thing is, Louis never suspects that they're shunning him. He always asks me: "What did they do? Where did they go to?"

I (should I say *of course*?) find Louis O.K. I like his way of living here in Paris. A crazy little hotel on the Rue Monsieur le Prince, with trick doors for the toilet, and the paint worn off on the stairs. Sometimes I go to Louis' room and stay all night. A bit of a collector, Louis. Bought the *History of the Jews* by Graetz the other day for a thousand francs. Has bound volumes of *Rire* and *Sourire* and books with engravings by Cruikshank, etc. Louis knows the Latin Quarter well. He has had a clap for a year. He gets credit at the restaurant around the corner. He reads Marcel Proust in the original with a fine East Side accent. He plays Brahms for me when I get up in the morning and shows me his clips—all the funny stories he's written since he came to the *Tribune*. "Some of these things ought to be preserved," he says. "Don't you think it's a shame for these things to be buried in newspaper files?" Josephine Baker and Peggy Joyce are good friends of his. They think he's a fine boy, and Josephine especially likes his funny little articles. Kokoschka likes him too. So there you are. Voilà, Louis Atlas!

But if I enjoy my walks home how much more do I enjoy my walks to the office. Take a day, for example, when I have been unable to rustle up a breakfast, when I have circulated about the terraces in search "of a friendly face" for several hours, and at last reconciled to the inevitable, begin to wend my way toward Gillotte's for the evening meal. Let's take an unusual day, when it is not raining. The twilight coming on, the sky lazy, tranquil, the fever of the streets dying down. After cutting through the Luxembourg, the quick descent into the Place St. Sulpice, through the Rue des Canettes, cross the Boulevard St. Germain through the narrow little street lined with whorehouses, the red lights already glowing, the windows slightly ajar, and then into the Rue de Seine with its art galleries and its sharp turn at the entrance to Cardinal Mazarin's palace. Along the Rue de Seine sombre hotels, people hanging out of the windows, a sort of dead glow to the street as in a Utrillo. For a brief spell the open panorama of the Seine, the quais, the quadrangle of the Louvre, the sentimental bridge that Napoleon had built expressly for his convenience—Pont des Arts, and then the court of the Louvre, the flagging alive with pigeons, the gendarmes pacing to and fro and the colored sentry box near the archway, and that glimpse through the arch of the angle of the Rue de Rivoli and—I don't know—is it the Rue St. Honoré? At any rate, a building there, in a sort of tutti-frutti color, which draws me on fascinatedly, but which before I have reached I forget in the welter of impressions created by the portals and facades of the Palace. An intervening space past the Banque of France and the Bourse, uninteresting except for a marvellous archway leading to Les Halles and the carrefour of the Place des Victoires where Louis rides horseback without stirrups or saddle, a grand, homosexual Louis with a chaplet about his crown. Then a few sharp hairpin turns through crooked streets—all before the Bourse . . . along the Rue Notre Dame des Victoires now, at night, staggeringly somnolent, grotesque, silent. Finally, that street of streets, the Rue Montmartre where life burgeons again, where every other shop is a bistro or restaurant or brasserie, where there is a Newsreel theatre and always a Parade de Nus, where there is the glittering Chope Nègre swarming with poules from early afternoon till dawn. The Fantasio, gaudy, gingerbread, an ex-pug at the door like Pat Maloney of the old Novelty Theatre, Driggs Avenue, Williamsburg. Scenes reminiscent of Bedford Avenue near the Fountain—the old Amphion (now playing Yiddish drama). And the big electric light arrow pointing to the Folies-Bergère. The street usually in a state of repair, the sidewalks crowded with tables, hawkers in the street selling cutlery and cheap watches. The Rue Cadet, whorehouses for homos, and cheap tenements where the Hindu pearl merchants live. Then the Rue Lafayette, one of the most congested streets in Paris, and particularly so in front of *Le Petit Journal* where are our offices. Continuing up and beyond the office, a steep ascent to Montmartre, to the boulevards, to the cheap Broadway of Paris, but to a Broadway however cheap which Broadway can never rival. (Strange thing is that as I write the name Broadway I ask myself is this right—is it Broadway I have in mind? Honestly, Broadway sounds queer to me suddenly, as though it were the wrong word.)

Let us imagine ourselves out for a drink during the break. Standing at the bar of the Trois Portes outside the Metro Cadet. A few beers and a contemptuous nod to the upstairs guys and then we're off for a brisk walk. A little way up the Rue Lafayette, toward the Gare de l'Est . . . a certain street to the right where there are hotels with blue glass shades over the doors. A lame girl standing outside, waiting for us every night to pass a few words. A very lame girl with passionate eyes, her face well rouged, her clothes somewhat frippery, and always the same pleading voice—just for a few minutes. Sometimes she bums a cigarette of us. And sometimes we actually debate whether we'll take her on. Bald is fascinated by her. "After all, she must have something to offer," he says. "She must get customers."

On payday she is standing outside the office, laying in wait for us. She has a friend along and her friend is a little jealous because we don't give her much attention. Bald arguing with the lame girl, trying to jew her down to ten francs. But it's not here that the fucking goes on. No, on payday, assuming that Bald hasn't had a lay for a few nights, we keep straight on down the Rue Montmartre until we hit Les Halles. Bald cursing now because the god-damned vegetables are in the way. Hotfooting it toward the Boulevard Sébastopol. Girls walking around with shawls, heavy girls, peasant girls, smoking and humming softly to themselves. Maquereaux standing by, taking it all in. One with a red dress, transparent, frail little legs, but teats and ass well proportioned. French to the core. Diseased. Brass. Ten francs—and Fred and I wait downstairs while Bald gives her a quick lay—on the edge of the bed, clothes on, no windows in the room, one towel for the two of them. She smoking while he jazzes her, calm, deliberate, uninterested. Go to it . . . take your ten francs worth. Customer at the door, waiting to get in the room while he's washing up. Door opens and customer watches. Timing him downstairs. Four and a half minutes. Satisfied? O.K. A drink in some little sawdust place. Cheap, ten francs. Maybe he'll take another one—just a quick, little one—standing up in an alley somewhere, if necessary, maybe for five francs. Whining about the futility of it all. Nothing to it. Just a lay. The flowers everywhere now. Châtelet. The bridge strewn with flowers. Notre Dame and the Tour St. Jacques. Old uns lying on the stones. More flowers.

Next instalment to follow in day or two.

Henry.

* * * *

I have a new ambition. I want to start an album of my Paris life. Buy some beautiful blank book, stoutly bound, with paper that will take a wash. Call it the "Book of 1 Bis"—on y boit, on y danse, on y pense. A sort of "Ah, que la vie est quotidienne." Reflections of Salavin, fragments of our night thoughts and the stir of the market, pen points by the compositeurs, snatches of French songs, Wambly Bald singing off key, objurgations by the rat (alias Fox our boss), wisecracks by the front-page men, errata, gouaches and caricatures, marginal notations, Instinctivist stories, interviews with distinguished cunts, remarks à travers la vie by Cresswell, Louis' enthusiasms, the sayings of the wise Jews of Paris, tintypes from the kiosks, idle hours in the Luxembourg, throwaways from the cinema, dreams, letters, clippings, menus, advertisements, memorabilia and incunabula. . . . You see, how the book shapes itself up. Simple. All I need now is: first the book, then paste, ensuite—red ink, green ink, violet ink, Conté crayon, a smudge stick, an eraser. After that I'll have my pants pressed and visit the dentist. Positively no contributions by Bob McAlmon. Positively no reference to Hemingway. A book of my life, my vagaries, my ambitions and my despair. With adequate decorations. And, of course, a preface dedicated to Barbey D'Aurevilly. Perhaps a word or two from Luis—Luis Buñuel. For, after all, besides Salavin, there have been only a few whom I cherished here in Paris—first Luis, then Nichols, and last Kokoschka. Yes, Kokoschka will have something to say, I am sure. And perhaps Vlaminck. As for the rest—fuck them! Whatever is missing Fred will supply. I think, therefore, you should send me something immediately—some testament of your undying affection, some little hollow squib without hip notes which I can insert toward the beginning of the diary. Some vaginary digitations would be swell, as a starter. And maybe Ned will have something to contribute about the donkeys in Van Cortlandt Park. That was delicious of Ned to choose such an occupation. I applaud it. Maybe I shall have something to say about the donkeys on the Champs Elysées, and the wooden rocking horses in the Luxembourg. Without the donkeys everything would fall to pieces.

(A suivre)

Henry

[October 1931]   The Dôme
                                                  Monday 6:00 P.M.

Dear Old Emil:
    I have just read your letter and everybody around me has been enjoy-
ing the reading of it. I am afraid to look at it again for fear of another
attack of hysterics. If that was meant to be a sad letter it was immense.
My guts are still shaking.
    Listen, Emil, everything's O.K. *O.K.* Tu sais? Don't think me cruel,
harsh, indifferent. Jesus, I love you—every hair on your head, your boozy
breath, your twisted smile, your delicious sadness which not even you
believe.

            *   *   *   *

    I'm glad you liked Fred's letter. If you don't get anyone to translate it
properly, why hold on, I'll be back soon and I'll translate it for you myself.
Meanwhile I'll tell Fred what you say. He'll piss in his pants. The poor
bastard, he's practically starving to death. His typewriter is in hock. He
can't shit. He has no friends, except me, and I've deserted him since June
arrived. Not intentionally, but worse—unintentionally.
    Just prior to June's coming I had been seeing him constantly. He
sneaked me into his room occasionally so that I could share his bed.
He fed me—tea and bread—swiped cigarettes for me, loaned me his
machine, etc. It was a frightful life for a time and Fred felt even worse
than I. Because he was powerless to do more. Yes, I think he's a fine
writer, particularly in French. (Did you ever get a copy of our manifesto—"The New Instinctivism?") In it there was a letter to Buñuel by
Ned which I think a masterpiece. The Manifesto itself is crappy maybe.
Nobody seems to appreciate the vulgar whimsical humor of it. It was
meant as a joke, the literature here and there being no more than a
little applesauce. Yet everyone accuses us of being dirty little boys. It
baffles me. I think we're quite grown up. Too much so. I think we were
really very funny in a crude, coarse way. But people don't want to be
amused with obscenity. Well, fuck them! You read it. Let me know if
you think it was too childish.
    I said I'd be coming back. I think it's pretty certain. It may be a month,
it may be two months. But I'll be returning quand même. June will
probably precede me. But I refuse to remain here stranded for long. I
would love living here forever—but not as a beggar. Two years of vaga-
bondage has taken a lot out of me. Given me a lot, too, but I need a little
peace now, a little security in which to work. In fact, I ought to stop living
for a long while, and just work. I'm sick of gathering experiences.
    There'll be a lot to tell when I get back to New York. Enough for many
a wintry night. But immediately I think of N.Y. I get frightened. I hate the

thought of seeing that grim skyline, the crowds, the sad Jewish faces, the automats, the dollars so hard to get, the swell cars, the beautiful clothes, the efficient businessmen, the doll faces, the cheap movies, the hullaba-loo, the grind, the noise, the dirt, the vacuity and sterility, the death of everything sensitive. June's got a cockeyed idea of France and the French. And I can't alter her ideas. One has to *live* here for a while to get it. As I once said to you, or didn't I, for my part it would be more interesting to go on living here even as a garçon in a bistro than live the routine life of N.Y. in a swell apartment. But maybe that's pure romanticism. Anyway, the swell routine-apartment life is quite remote. It would be better to say—where do you prefer to starve—in Paris or New York?

I'm waiting for June now. We have about forty francs between us to last until Saturday. In reality, it won't last till tomorrow. You can see, there-fore, why Paris loses some of its charm for June. I don't blame her. But it's not Paris we should blame. Well, it's an old story. *Full Stop.*

Votre Henri

P.S. Enclosed are two clippings on myself—send the one to George for me!

November, 1931
Chez Alfred Perlès
Hôtel Central
1 bis, Rue du Maine
Paris (XIV)

Dear Emil:

I was going to write you a letter asking if you could find your way clear to sending me five dollars a month—anyway I'm not writing it, so breathe easy and prepare to smile. What use in asking people in America for five bucks a month? The world is going to smash. Five bucks more or less won't help.

What precipitated this impulse is the fact that I am once again without a roof over my head, and now that winter is coming on, cold fogs, rain, catarrh, rheumatism—one hates to be left like that—alone and friendless. Oh ho! The sad music again, I know. This is just a sour wheeze and you know how to orchestrate my music.

I am writing this from Fred's room. He is still sleeping. I have come up here to keep warm. Looking at myself in the mirror I see an interesting face. Changing for the better. More character. More suffering. Fine lines, healthy tan, a little haggard around the eyes. Still under forty!

For a while I was living with a Michael Fraenkel in the beautiful Villa Seurat where lived Derain and still lives Foujita. We had a maid, Greta, and once a week Fraenkel invited me to have dinner with him. Suddenly he got a telegram and we all had to blow—that very day. Michael is going cuckoo. He is the author of *Werther's Younger Brother* which I will send you if ever I raise the postage.

Anyway, I have no room. I can only sneak into Fred's place once in a while—the patron is against it. Same with Wambly Bald. Osborn is tied up with a French cunt, and that's that. Kann, the sculptor, has only one narrow bed. I slept on his floor last night. Lowenfels, the poet, has a little cot in the kitchen, but there are mice and the baby's wet clothes. Zadkine I long ago ruled off my list. Voilà, c'est tout. Tonight I have dinner with Chadla, the Hindu girl who is showing Italy and Germany how to dance the *beguine*.

Meanwhile never a letter from America. June has faded out completely. Elkus is silent. You don't answer the beautiful letters we send you. Madeleine Boyd is recovering from an automobile accident. Christine doesn't love me any more—or else she is afraid. Anyway, she'll soon be going back to the Bronx. Mlle. Claude is still sitting at the Coupole but I still owe her a few francs. The *New Review* is either dead or dying. Tihanyi was attacked by bandits. Wilke is in the Rocky Mountains shooting wild geese.

What, oh what, is it all coming to? You know, I never even got an acknowledgment from June of the mss I sent. Instead a fairy comes to visit me—with some of June's dirty blouses in his valise. When I left the Villa Seurat I destroyed all the copies of my mss. Too much weight.

I have another book under way and Michael said he would publish it in Belgium. He wants at least a thousand pages. O.K. Whenever I get a meal under my belt I add a few pages. No machine any more. Sit in the luxurious offices of the Carnegie Institute for the Perpetuation of Peace and smash the world. Hey diddle!

Waiting now for Fred to get up so as we can have a cup of tea and some bread. Something's got to happen soon—or it will be the end. I'll be cutting one of my ears off, or a nose, and sending it on as a Christmas gift.

You see, the food problem I've solved fairly well. I get a warm meal every night by rotating among my friends. Fred gives me breakfast about three in the afternoon. Cigarettes come as a matter of course. But a room! Shit, there's the rub!

Christine has plenty of room to spare but her husband has dandruff and he can't see me coming in. Ned Calmer has a baby and besides the maid wants a place to sleep.

I thought for a time of asking you and George and Doc Conason to send me five dollars a month, but then you either wouldn't or couldn't. That would pay for a hotel room. Service en plus.

Anyway, I'm writing you and that's something. You can always address me care of Fred. If I get a break I'll let you know pronto. How is Muriel? And Ned? Still the donkeys? Jesus, this is a cockeyed world. Let's have more of it.

Henry.

IV

QUIET DAYS IN CLICHY

1932–33

After two years of the hand-to-mouth existence depicted in *Tropic of Cancer*, Miller settled down to a more domestic life when he rented an apartment with his good friend Alfred Perlès. With his food and lodging problems largely solved, he could now concentrate his energies on work and play, indulging in both with great gusto, leading the life he later celebrated in *Quiet Days in Clichy*. "When I think about this period," he reminisced in that book, "it seems like a stretch in Paradise. . . . even though the world was busy digging its grave, there was still time to enjoy life, to be merry, carefree, to work or not to work."

This was an enormously creative period for him, "the busiest, richest months of my whole life," as he wrote in one of his letters, reporting that he was working on four books at the same time. Indeed this was not only his most fertile period but the one in which he produced his best work, writing now in the liberated style found in many of his letters to Emil. As usual he sent installments from his works-in-progress, long sections of his three central books: *Tropic of Cancer* (which he refers to as "The Last Book"), *Black Spring* ("Self-Portrait"), and *Tropic of Capricorn*. At the suggestion of the publisher Jack Kahane, who was nervous about bringing out these books, Miller also worked on *The World of Lawrence* (the "Brochure" mentioned in some of the letters). It was Kahane's idea that literary criticism would establish Miller as a respectable writer before the *Tropics* appeared.

The move to Clichy was made possible by a new development in Miller's personal life, his involvement with Anaïs Nin. Married to a banker, she could afford to be his fairy godmother as well as his literary confidante and lover. She lived in a big house in Louveciennes, a village outside Paris, where Miller sometimes stayed; she also came to the apartment in Clichy. Miller, usually so explicit about his love life in writing to Emil, was reticent about this liaison, revealing it cautiously, little by little. Even years later—in 1969—he would have cut all references to Anaïs Nin from these letters. But now that her unexpurgated diary has told all (up to a certain date), his letters seem remarkably discreet.

In October 1932 June came for her third visit to Paris during these years, creating as usual a good deal of turbulence in her wake, which Miller sought to escape by going off on an abortive trip to England. To his great relief, June asked for a divorce as she left, yet he did nothing. Months later, when he heard that she had been seen in Greenwich Village in the company of a young man, his reaction showed that June still had her grip on him. Anaïs may have been his ideal woman, the one he hoped would be his next wife, but June remained the great love of his life. The conflicting emotions that appear in his letters to Emil explain why he had so much trouble telling that story and why it took him six years to finish *Tropic of Capricorn.*

———————

[April 1932]   Address: 4 Avenue Anatole France
                                     Clichy (Seine)
                                     (Don't put *Paris* as it's outside
                                       the city)

Old Emil, I got both your letters—the second apprised me that the first was there at the American Express, where I no longer go for mail—so never send any there. The above address is pseudo-permanent. I have taken an apartment with Fred Perlès which, except for the tax at the end of the year, comes to 5,100 francs a year, bringing the rent for each of us down to less than 300 francs a month, which is far below ordinary hotel rates. It's a new building in a row of modern apartment houses, the street, despite its fine-sounding name, resembling rather a New York street, some new Jewish section. Fred thinks it's rather swell, as he's never in his life lived in decent quarters. The bath and the kitchen fascinate him. For me it's an old story and leaves me cold. I would rather have a swell old-fashioned hotel or studio room, if I had the choice.

But we took it with the understanding that if either of us lost his job the other would do the supporting. And so I am happy to report that I am losing mine promptly. Yes, they gave me notice to quit on the 15th—economy! I may go downstairs again as a proofreader for the vacation period, but I don't know definitely at this writing. You can't imagine what a time I've had since I sent that frantic wire about Dijon. The night before I left I sat up all night in the Select, trying to raise the last fifty francs toward the fare. I thought everything was going to be hunky dory when I got there—a haven for six months. The first thing I learned was that I got no salary—none, none. Just grub and room. Well, now that I am reading Rainer Maria Rilke (his *Cahiers de Malte Laurids Brigge*) I sort of appreciate that old room with the dinky stove and the funny pipe that threatened to topple over on my bed. I don't remember how much I wrote about Dijon, if anything, so forgive the duplication. I enjoyed the young French guys, the maîtres d'internat (les pions, as they are called) with whom I was obliged to associate. We had some marvellous conversations and a few good sessions over the wine. The last night we made hot wine with sugar, just vin ordinaire, but it was magnificent. You must bring home a bottle some night and do that, Emil. It gives you a wonderful glow. Well, I have put some of the Dijon experience into my book, and if ever I get round to mailing you copies that I am sure I won't be calling for (as I usually do) you will have a good gulp. You see, Emil, this book (which I call tentatively "The Last Book") is like that beautiful big valise of yours, of stout leather, that expands or collapses, that you throw things into pell-mell regardless of whether they are starched or pressed or stained or not stained. (What do you call them again?—I forget a devil of a lot of words now, especially names of objects. When Fred asks me frequently, "How do you call that in English?" I am puzzled and some words are gone forever, or at least until I get back again. Nevertheless, the few I have will carry me through!)

About getting back. Oh yes, it would be splendid to see you—I think of you constantly—it has become a sort of joke with Fred and me— * * * * everything I see, circulars, theatre tickets, posters, jokes, funny objects, fancy whores, I say, "I'm sending that to Emil Schnellock." Albeit I send very little. But soon things will roll in. I am getting sound financial help of late—it's a long, long story, and I am almost afraid to go into it yet. Keep quiet about it, please. Some day I'll spill the beans—it deserves a letter all by itself. At any rate, come wind or hail or snow (Penn. Post Office) I'm better off here than in New York.

There is a big unemployment here (chômage) but it doesn't touch me. The *Tribune* is going out of business in a few months, so I am told. But that won't worry me either. After what I have lived through, since I said good-bye and took that ten-dollar bill, nothing will matter much—nothing in the way of hardships. In fact, during that sojourn at the beautiful Villa Seurat with Michael Fraenkel, when I had never a cent in my pocket, but simply a list of people with whom I dined each night, during that period, I say, I was never happier in my life. I was living! And everybody envied me my smile (rose et frais, comme dit M. Halasz); I had to support with my good humor, my courage, my recklessness all those miserable ones who were eating regularly but had lost their spiritual appetites. No, Emil, I don't want to return to America. Nothing but a catastrophe can make me go back. This is my world, and I knew it long, long ago, and I only regret it took so long to make the decision. What a different being

I would have been if, at twenty-one, I had gone to the Sorbonne or to Alt Heidelberg, or to Seville, or Madrid. Anywhere but City College. However, it hasn't been too late. I will never become a European, but thank God, I am no longer an American. I am one of those things you call an "expatriate," a voluntary exile. I have no country, no frontiers, no taxes to pay, no army to fight for. And I adore France. My one regret is that what I am now writing may cause me to be expelled from France. I am not exaggerating. I don't think there has been anything for several hundred years (seriously) quite as savage, as brutal, as frank, as sincere, as what I am writing. And I am going to preface the book with a paean to Luis Buñuel, the man who really made me discover myself, though he is unaware of it. As a matter of fact, I would have made the discovery anyhow, but those two films—Christ, there was a truth, an experience that simply split the clouds and I saw myself naked sitting on the right hand side of God and taking a good long look at his scabby buttocks. I've gotten all over the idea of writing literature, if you can understand what I mean by that. That too requires some explaining, and when I finish the letter that I am writing to Samuel Putnam (anent his *European Caravan*) perhaps you will get the drift. This is important, Emil. This means, in a word, that coincident with my leaving America I chucked overboard all my preconceived notions about literature. Almost from the day I arrived I sensed something different in the air, in my air. Looking at the shop windows, at the books, the manifestoes, the titles, the ideas germinating there like droning flies, I understood what it was that was driving me on—that my flight after all was symbolic—just as Van Gogh's flight to Arles was symbolic and Gauguin's to Tahiti. Oh, you smile—I am classifying myself with the big boys. Yes, Emil, I am. I'm there. I know what I'm worth. I say it quite humbly. I did a lot of farting around, I wrote junk. I listened too much, I was spellbound. But I am forty now and though I see the long declivity ahead I feel all my strength, my wisdom; I can accomplish things now—the way is marked out . . . I have a direction.

This must sound as if I had taken a dose of hashish, but no, I am sitting in the office, 1:30 in the morning, and all washed up on the stock exchange figures, Abitibi, Electric Power and Light, Wabash Common and U.S. Rubber Preferred. Fuck all these chiffres. Soon I am free again— April 15th. Fred will look after me. I will stay home like a well-kept mistress and polish my nails. Between times I'll do a little typing, read *Le Grand Meaulnes* or *Le Temps Retrouvé.* I scarcely ever read an English book any more. There are none that interest me. Faulkner I found a flat failure, and this is to inform all and sundry. Especially Buzby.

When you have been away from Paris it is a real experience to return. I was only in Dijon about three weeks—during which time I spoke scarcely a word of English—and then on a soft winter evening I sailed into the Gare de Lyons and was whisked through the streets. Jesus, what feelings it stirred in me. New York always gave me a sinking feeling when I came back. I used to hate that damned grim skyline, those crowds, those Jewish faces, that fetid odor in the streets. Paris is smiling—she welcomes you without distinction of race, creed or color. Her vegetables look brighter, her women gayer, her workers more industrious, her cops more intelligent. She is aged but not careworn. The roofs are so wonderful—all those fucking chimney pots, the black of them, the slanting studio windows, the walls with their traces of rooms which no longer exist, the bridges, each one like a poem, and the statues, hideous though they be, you get to like them, to admire them, they are part of the ensemble which your eye anticipates. And then that quick, bright exchange of tongues, the wit, the clearheadedness, the Gallic humor—Oh, I can't express it well enough, but you get me, I suppose. Well, it's like my home now, though I am still a foreigner and always will be. But whenever I make a journey it will always. be Paris that I want to think of coming back to—not New York. New York belongs in a finished past, a past like some evil dream. I go occasionally to the cinema and I see the American films, but how boring they are! (*Street Scene,* for example, now playing at the Vieux Colombier to élite audiences)—what a cheap, sentimental, false picture that was. How glad I was when I walked out and ran to a bistro, that it was Paris I was walking in and not some street on Brooklyn Heights. The other night I saw *L'Amour à l'Américaine* with Spinnelli. A beautiful parody on American woman, on American love. Altogether extravagant and far-fetched, but true, true. Much more deadly true than *Street Scene.*

*   *   *   *

Yes, woman dominates us in America, it is undeniable. I look around at these happy French people, and I admire the women, the wives. No better wives in the world. The proof is the Frenchman treats her well, like an equal, talks to her intelligently, loves her, fondles her, and she responds, she is jealous of him, but she is obedient too, and very affectionate, animal-like. It is beautiful. It is so because it is a union and not just some fake situation which busts with a little pressure. I must knock off here— Fred is waiting to walk home with me. Our way lies through Montmartre now—Place Pigalle, Place Clichy, all the night clubs open and crowded, the bars roisterous at three in the morning—oh, shit, if you were only here—if, if. . . . I miss you terribly.

Henry

P. S. Will continue this in a few days. Don't forget the MSS when you can. More to follow—*Frou-Frou,* etc.

[April 18, 1932]   4, Ave. Anatole France
                                             Clichy (Seine), France

Dear Emil:

Imagine, to begin with, that she has the wonderful name Mona Païva—
over the i two dots! That her husband is in North Africa and wears the
beautiful uniform of the Army of the Crescent. We waved good-bye to
him a few days ago at the Gare St. Lazare which I think of all the railway
stations I have passed through is the best in the world. You remember
how once in a violent storm I waited for Anatole at the Gare St. Lazare—
out beyond the glass sheds the rain beating through the smoke and
steam, the engines moving in slowly, their monstrous eyes cleaving the
murk, the violet haze clinging to their hot flanks. And tonight, in Clichy,
the rain is falling softly. The soft rain, Emil, and vino on my lips. All day
the rain and vino, vino, vino.

I should tell you first of all that she is Turkish. She comes from Stamboul and only a few years ago she still wore the veil. When I tell you that
I want to convey to you the sacredness that she brings with her sex. She
has discarded the yashmak but all the invisible veils of her race envelop
her still. She surrenders to you without giving herself. When I penetrate
her in the dark her flesh cries out in a mysterious tongue and wherever
I have left bruises there is the odor of rose petals.

I have been to the Boulevard de Clichy and back. The rain is still in my
eyes and the vino on my lips. On the kitchen table everything is standing,
as when she left. I can't bring myself to disturb the luxurious disorder
which she created. The fruit lies there, heavy and rich, as if waiting for
her hand to caress it once again; in the salad bowl a few leaves of lettuce
are swimming and through the spicy juice I can read the price of the bowl
which we forgot to wash off. I see her hands again, the pale olive against
the tender green of the lettuce, the ivory ring cool, *inoxydable*—hands that
were not made to wash lettuce. We are busy, the three of us, preparing
the humble feast. The walls are very white and there are two rubber tubes
of a dull hue hanging dejectedly from the faucets. Somehow I have an
insane desire to see her grasp the hose, the perverse jaded desire of an
aristocrat leading his mistress to a cow and bidding her to milk it.

We face the crisis of the orphic language. This is what I repeat to myself as
I lie down to sleep. Crisis of the orphic language. . . . Words treated
instinctively as a fluid medium of a vision. . . . The poet is not interested
in changing the world. He only wants to change himself. His form is in
movement. He struggles against nothingness. He composes the vision he
suffers.

This is the chaff I chew in my sleep, tattered phrases from "The Language of Night" which Mr. Jolas spewed out in hypnagogic hallucina-
tion. * * * *

* * * *

I lay me down in a wet dawn and the bells tolled peacefully. The strength which I had scattered recklessly in my two years of Paris awoke again in my veins. All along the fibers of my nerves the bells played and my eyes would not close, nor my heart cease pounding. How strange it was, I thought, that I should come to Clichy in order to meet this woman from Stamboul. But stranger still is the body bursting, this woman turned to night, maggot words gnawing through the mattress, all the fragmentary utterances, her groans, the madness of my writing desk, letters on the floor drowning in Muscatel, Nairobi and Timbuctoo, the Prix Goncourt for Fred and again the glass sheds of St. Lazare, his glass sheds in a French that turns to tears. . . . To walk to the Place de Clichy takes about thirty-five minutes. Arabs staggering home drunk, derailed at La Fourche. *Amour et Discipline* at the Legendre Cinéma. The Tragedy of Mayerling with Lil Dagover. Bertha, give me back my letters. Rose Cannac and Naples dying in the sunlight. All these women—Rose, Bertha, Tania, Mlle. Raymonde, Simone, Germaine, Odette, Brigitte Helm, Olga Tchekova, Lil Dagover, Marlene, Damia, Meg Lemonnier, Spinelli, all these women I take to my arms and I make a bouquet of them and I present them to Mona. . . . *The projection of a metamorphosis of reality.* . . . I open the window, and at Mr. Jolas' bidding, I throw out my *Biedermeier orderliness.* On the night of April the 18th, 1932, I apologize to the world for my orthodox use of language. I ask God to put his little finger into my wounds and derange the fibers of my nerves. *"Why should the poet be afraid to face the telluric aspect of the world?"*

Did you ever see the fleet manoeuvre in Pacific waters? When the bow of a dreadnought dips the weight of her sinking floods your ears; nothing is more majestic than a fleet of dreadnoughts washed by a heavy sea. Find the word for weight and give it a coat of gray paint. All the spices of Araby in the spectrum, the gunwales slow to sink, breasts punctured, weight and tons of weight, slimewash and emeralds and sapphires slipping, sluiced in gray, gray-neutral, neuter, neurology. The gun carriages turn, soft as lion-pad, vomit, drool a little; the firmament sags and all the stars turn black, black ocean bleeding, brooding, breeding, chunks of flesh swollen, bright uniforms, brass buttons, green pools of milk on the deck and birds wheeling hallucinated until the sky balances itself again. Nobody has sung the Equator, her red-feathered legs, islands dropping out of sight. A gun fired across the Pacific falls into space because the earth is round and pigeons are flying upside down. The water rushes into your ears and the bow widens like a face in fright.

Sitting at the table Mona's eyes turned green. Sorrow spreading inward had flattened its nose against her spine; marrow filled with self-pity had turned liquid. Her fingers bleed with anguish because she is so happy. Her corpse is very light; it would float in the Dead Sea. We are so happy,

Mona, to have even your corpse. But why do your fingers bleed when all
the life has departed your body?

Mona, before you came I walked by the cemetery wall. A boy kicked a
ball over the wall and it bounced on a grave. It was the street of Chance-
Milly, not far from the cemetery, where I stopped and said: "This is the
first cemetery I have ever enjoyed." And then I think of Minnie Imhof
lying naked under a crucifix. It was the first time I had looked at a woman
naked. A Catholic woman naked. Supposing battleships were naked and
wore crucifixes?

When three o'clock came and the rooster began to crow I felt that you
had given me back my strength. At five o'clock I was in Nairobi, Wells
Fargo. Green-jawed hyenas, jackals with silken tails, dick-dicks, jewelled
leopards, all left behind in the *boma*. When you come to Nairobi you have
left the Garden of Eden. Nothing in all the veldt is more hideous than the
laughter of a hyena.

Before going to bed I award Fred the Prix Goncourt. When you have
all your strength justice is an easy thing. . . .

This language of Fred's, how it affects me! He makes me hunger for
a sort of beauty that is absolutely out of my reach. A few nights ago he
said to me: "If you really knew what love was—it is the only thing you
lack—you would be a genius, another Goethe perhaps." Standing by
the window, reading his manuscript, I had an intimation of what Fred
meant. I don't believe that he ever loved Marcienne, or anybody for
that matter (it is *he* who is incapable of love), but I believe that he
loved what Marcienne did for him, how she made him expand, warm
to the world. When I read those opening lines about love and spring—
all that forest murmur and rustle, slightly blurred to me because the
meaning of his words often escapes me—I began to melt. I wanted
Marcienne to come here immediately and live with us, live with Fred,
of course. I would almost like to teach him how to love her, put their
two hands together and make Fred, who is so childishly selfish and
withdrawn, sacrifice his whole life for Marcienne and her kid. And if he
should refuse, why then I would do it! It is wonderful to know a Marcienne, to bask in her ignorance, to protect her and to say in your
dreams things totally beyond her comprehension. I do not need Marcienne, but there is room in me for all the Marciennes of this world
and all their brats, particularly if their brats are bastards. I love little
bastards. I should love to create a litter of bastards and be able to
roam the world saying hello everywhere to my sons and daughters.

But forgetting Marcienne—she isn't really important—let me come
back again to Fred's language. A magic language, so gossamer, so
ethereal and tenuous, so full of pale light and wistful sighs, so cerebrally,
slyly humorous. He bemoans the fact that he can write so easily about

anything at all, about nothing. He should be proud of it, proud to know that we will be enthralled whether it be of matchsticks, hairpins, or whatever it is he chooses for subject. It isn't to say that the emphasis is exclusively on form, on what is called style, etc. Not at all. It's that in his unseizable, imponderable, ever-fluid style he continually disperses himself, smears it out like toothpaste, an inexhaustible supply, always of the right consistency, always fragrant, always moist, always soothing to the gums. More—without knowing it, he has that sly, derisory, self-derogatory, deliciously tender way of dealing with himself that Hamsun at his best accords us. (Wait, mother will wash the spit off the walls!) He blows gently on the object and it floats, it breathes, assumes infinitudes of form. I think of soap bubbles when they are still glued to the pipe bowl, when they are refracted, bent, when they quiver and succeed almost in breaking away, when they become elongated and the colors inside change violently and all that is mirrored dances in a freakish deformity so outrageously pleasing to the senses. Oh, it is poor what I say about Fred's writing. The Prix Goncourt is not enough, but at least that, at least that for a start! I hand you these pages of his with the most delicate, chaste, reverent feelings. I think them exquisitely beautiful, matchless in a pre-hypnagogic way, and I want to say here and now that whatever it is I lack—love, gratitude, tenderness—Fred has revealed it to me through his language. My eyes melt before the magic of his words, and I know that there is a beauty in the world which is utterly out of my reach and I bow down before it. It is a world on which I have slammed the door and I will never try to open that door, but I must confess that sometimes, in the night, I go back and I stand wistfully before the door, knowing that I have left behind me one of the most cherished, precious gifts.

*   *   *   *

July 12th, 1932
4, Ave. Anatole France
Clichy (Seine), France

Emil:

I've got lots to tell you. Don't know if I can squeeze it all in this letter. In the first place I'm not leaving for Spain just yet. I am in touch with Paul Morand and expect to do some translation work for him these next two months—speeches, no less, for his next trip to America. I don't give a fuck about the work, but I am in hopes of establishing a real contact and enlisting his support—for what—?—for the future. I'll give you more solid dope on this in a few weeks.

I am also enclosing herewith a copy of the "New Instinctivism." What you said about the *Rona* letter made me think that you or George might find a way of selling it—as *smut*. Putnam had promised to publish it in his *New Review* and then he got cold feet—afraid of legal entanglements. We stopped abruptly when this happened—I say this because, if it seemed too slender we could go on and amplify it amply. It's meant to be humorous, you know. At any rate, please see that I get it back, as it's the only copy extant and we prize it for sentimental reasons.

I am sending you tomorrow a copy of Anaïs' book on Lawrence—it is for Buzby, as you will see, but I wanted you to have a chance to read it first. You'll send it to him for me, won't you? If you like it very much, I'll see that you get another copy. There are only a few left—and I wanted George to get it for diplomatic reasons. Did you get any MSS of mine from Dijon, thru my friend Jacques Renaud? I asked him to forward you some drafts on a Montparnasse article and something else, too, I believe. If you should receive other MSS from a Grace Flandrau, let me know, and I'll tell you what disposition to make of them. I'm using you as a clearing house because I know you'll enjoy poking your nose into these things. Everything I can afford to release I am giving you. Yes, I got the Buñuel thing and was delighted. You'll have it back in the next mail.

About my book—no, it isn't settled. It *was* a few weeks ago. Fraenkel was bringing it out in Belgium—then his cohort, Walter Lowenfels, came back from America with nettles in his ass (because of *Of Thee I Sing*) and the two fell out and my book fell between. But Anaïs is positive she will put it over. We are going to London together in the early part of August to see the big literary lights. Rebecca West thinks very highly of her book on Lawrence. And that failing, she will sell her fur coat and print it herself. Meanwhile I am dickering with Caresse Crosby and Peter Neagoe over it, and I'm going to give you a treat! I'm sending you, *as a gift,* the first hundred pages or so, the original draft. It has undergone some drastic changes in the rewrite, but loses none of its violence, obscenity, or defamation of character. But I ask you as a great favor not to show that around. Emil, this is a really swell book—and unique. I think it will cause a riot, and, at the same time, prove a seller—just because it is sensational in character. *But shit! I'll stop bragging.* More telegrams from Anaïs— private, Emil—*private.* I'm going thru some escapade. About the richest experience I've ever had. Anaïs left today for the Tyrol. I'm working hard and happy—and Spain can wait. Does the photo show it? * * * *
* * * *
About Buñuel—yes, what I wrote is substantially so. At any rate, the

impression is truthful. I am dedicating my book to him, you know. That's how much I think of him. More than anyone he made me realize what I wanted to say, and how to say it—that is, *with courage.* He is Surrealistic—and they will tell you over there that Surrealism is dead but don't you believe it. The orphic myth is being revived. Brother, that means something. I will send you shortly a copy of Fraenkel's article on "The Weather," which will give you a more profound idea of what I'm hinting at. I think that very few people will understand it. I had some difficulty myself, at first—but I have stuck to him and derived a lot from him. I regard it as vastly important—as a piece of work that follows inevitably upon Spengler. It is written like an abstract. He has sufficient notes to expand it to a very thick volume. (Check me up on all these promises. Keep after me until you get everything. I get indifferent sometimes, simply because the communication seems to have broken down. You are the only one I have any real correspondence with—on the American continent.)

Emil, I only wish you could come. I have gone thru the most important period of my life these last two and a half years. I feel so often what a pity it is to be alone here—because now is the time we ought to be sharing things. I see your position clearly, and I make neither reproaches nor suggestions. Each one has to make his own way, and in his own style. But write more often! I've got so much to tell you. It would buck you up, at least.

*   *   *   *

*   *   *   * That's Fred in the photo. The little prick who makes flower-pots all day. He's got a little cunt living here now—Paulette. She's between 12 and 14 years of age. We don't know what to do with her. We had to show her how to use a douche-bag.

Not a word to June about Anaïs. She knows Anaïs. I'll write you a whole letter on this subject shortly. It's about 90 degrees now and I'm sticking to the seat. I think, too, I'll be able to forward you a carbon copy of my novel. I'm waiting to hear from Buzby first. Did he ever show you the photos of *Brassaï?* I have some water colors to send you. *Write!!!*

                                                                    Henry.

Oct. 5th. 1932

Dear Emil:

* * * *

I expect you will receive from a Mr. Bradley (Paris) a copy of the first 60 pages or so of my latest book—*Tropic of Capricorn.* I have another batch which equals this in length and which I will forward you soon as I see Bradley again. This is a copy for you to hold—it is untouched—and I know it is safe with you. Should I ever lose my effects, as I have more than once, I could get in touch with you. There will be corrections and eliminations—that goes without saying. But in the main, I like it—I expect to carry on for about a thousand pages, at least. I would like to know, however, if it reaches you safely.

Another thing—did you get the "New Instinctivism"? Is or would there ever be any chance to print a brochure on that order in America (thru Buzby or Harold Mason or your L.I. friend, Tony Von Something or other)? We could carry on at this rate endlessly—*"against."* To me it seems good stuff from a purely "humorous" point of view—it would also have a *smutty* appeal to some, or many. Open up on this!

Then, too, did you ever receive the copies of the newspaper *Frou-Frou?* They are not supposed to go thru the mail. I have more for you in case they get thru all right. Among my notes enclosed you will find a passage or two on *Utrillo.* I think it was from Carco's *The Last of Bohemia.* I am going to make more excerpts soon—from Keyserling and from *L'Enfer* by Barbusse. Is Fraenkel translating things for you—do you still see him occasionally? Give him my warm regards. I am busy as hell—a great streak of creative energy.

Henry.

P.S. *This Quarter*—last issue is entirely devoted to the Surrealists—edited by them. You will find something by Buñuel in it. Look it up—it must be on sale in U.S. If you ever see Buzby would you ask him to try to get my MSS from Madeleine Boyd? And June—she's coming soon—I wish to Christ she would bring all my *papers.*

P.P.S. Just a bare possibility of my coming back "for a visit" in the Spring—with Anaïs. She and her husband have to go to N. Y. on business. If I come back I'll bring you back with me.

14th October 1932
4, Av. Anatole France
Clichy (Seine), France

Dear Emil:

Your letter just arrived and here I am, as usual, an hour later answering it—note the difference between us (you put off finishing the letter because it might interfere with your work, and I put off the work to answer the letter! No reproach—just a little difference—all for the little difference, popper! Of course you get paid for working and I don't—there's a difference too).

* * * * What strikes me immediately is the changed atmosphere of your "home." All these wild men coming in on you now—Harold, Fraenkel, Joe Gould, etc. You must have made a fundamental alteration in your attitude toward "society." It sounds good and I feel sorry for you because you must be *quite exhausted.* (I do wish I could foist on you two more guys—painters of the first water, in my opinion—John Nichols and Frank Mechau—both of whom are now in America. Fraenkel didn't know them—they belong to an earlier period of my Paris life. You ought to make inquiries about Nichols especially; he must be known about town. The Daniels Gallery man knows him well, if I am not mistaken. He had a shack in Woodstock for a long time; he has a big red beard and silver-rimmed glasses, wears fireman's underwear and is always well bundled up. One of the most fascinating guys to talk to that I have ever met in my life; and he has the goods. He would make up for all the dry areas, the lacunae in my writings on the subject of art, because, as you have noticed, I am paying very little attention of late to painting. Frank Mechau is another guy with a beard—he looks just like a Holbein, has a fine face, is a prince of a fellow, very simple, very wonderful disposition, and knows a great deal about art. I am afraid he is going to Colorado very soon; try to find out about him in the Village. Joe Gould probably knows him. As for Lionel Reiss, he's a water colorist—very pretty, adroit, etc., but no painter. He's confused and sterilized. He hates my guts now; I saw very little of him and the last time I hit him below the belt with a tirade against the Jews which he couldn't stomach. . . . He walked away from me cursing and swearing. No, June isn't here—he must have seen her in New York. Or is she in Paris and I don't know it? That would be like her—very funny indeed!

* * * *

I see the name Joe Gould! See that you showed him my writing. Very much surprised. Joe Gould seems an incongruous figure there. I never met him, but I am keen to get some of his stuff—ask him would he send me anything? Here in Paris I showed some of his stuff (which I gleaned from some crazy Village paper) and it amused people no end. I liked that postscript to one letter—"I am a megalomaniac. I have delusions of grandeur. I believe that I am Joe Gould." I roared when I read that. But when you tell me you read him from my manuscript I wonder. For the first time in my life I utter a cautious cry—remember that my books are not out yet and I have no copyrights! (It is just possible, you know, that they may be printed some day and there might be a few dollars for me. Now if one of those Village freaks should steal my thunder—that would be a damned pity. Of course I have a reservoir to tap—but I should hate to be *robbed* of something. So, popper, a little discretion. A little discretion about revealing the real names of the people too. I don't want to go to the Select some night and get a bullet up my ass, either.) Doubtless this is all unnecessary—you are probably looking after my interests thoroughly. Keep Anaïs' name out of things as much as possible. You might work her harm; I know you don't mean to.

Fraenkel knows that it was the last thing I wanted—to expose these poor bastards. True, I originally wanted to keep the real names; it would have been much better. But I haven't got the right to do that, as far as I can see. I don't mind what anybody writes about me—but then I'm rather unique in that way. Other people are still sensitive about themselves.

* * * *

I liked so much what you said—"It seems to me for the writer (substitute *artist*) the thing never collapses." Excellent. And Fraenkel's article on the "Weather" ought to bear that out for you superbly. He expressed it admirably. You don't mention that in your letters—haven't you read it yet—or doesn't it convey very much to you? Myself I regard it as extremely important—one of those very brief, very concise, very concentrated messages to the world which only becomes revealed in its true light as time goes on and the prophecies are fulfilled. His extremism is something that we need today. He pushes ideas to their limits—till they drop exhausted. He sounds crazy sometimes, and no doubt is, but it's magnificent, lucid insanity—the kind that builds up new worlds. He has always a fine, strong point of reference, a center, a core on which to fall back—he is not one of those peripheral, or centripetal crazy men who flare up like rockets and expire in dust. In a way he is the same man that Van Gogh was when he put his hand in the flame to prove that he loved the girl. Fraenkel does not hesitate to put his hand in the flame—there you have it. Cherish it.

Did Fraenkel use that phrase "my post-Spenglerian attitude?" Does he realize what's going on inside me now? I have a lot to tell him when I get to it. He fecundated me. I am anxious to know the impression made on him by *Tropic of Capricorn,* if you have shown him it. In this mail I believe

I will send you the succeeding pages—a batch about as large as the first—and this will give you a still better idea of the direction, the technique, the plan of the work. I ought to run on, I figure, for about a thousand pages—and sweat it all out of me. After that—only from the dream outward! After that maybe you'll shake your head solemnly and say—"He's going too far." Now the material, the content, the idea grips me. I might almost say I have a message. What I am doing, if I can explain it, is to free myself for expression on a different, a higher (?) level. I am working out my own salvation, as writer, thinker, human being. I am working it off on the world—even if that world is limited to the men who cross your threshold. It remains a world, nevertheless. In one sense I am deeply pleased, flattered almost, that you enjoy trotting out my pages and reading them to your intimate circle of drunks, models, bums, ranters, and what not. Couldn't have a better audience. I'd like to know the model's reactions particularly—would tell me more than Joe Gould or H.H. How does an ordinary little strumpet react to a man's attitude about cunt? This guy Menjou, whoever he is (can it be Adolph's brother?), he makes me feel good too, if it was he who added that little postscript when you were drunk. I feel good whenever an ordinary guy (rich or poor, educated or uneducated) gets a kick out of my pages. First I want to be read by the ordinary guys, and liked by them. Because I'm just the most ordinary guy in the world myself—a man living out of his solar plexus. All those big shots, with their theories and their white ink, are just pricks to me and whatever they have to say will only infuriate me, be it good or bad. I don't need them and I don't write for them. I'm writing for posterity, which is with us always in the shape of those who love us. (Fraenkel would say "cut this." But a little sentimentality here and there is like paprika, it flavors the meal. How I laugh when Fraenkel tries to protect me against myself. I don't give a fuck about being *right*, or *artistic*, or *clear*—I only care about what I'm saying for the moment. If I say that with passion and sincerity it's good for all time.)

I noticed that in listing my letters you make mention of two—"Oom Paul" and "Jamesian Droppings." I believe it is one of them that I was hunting for recently. (Don't worry, I don't ask you to send them to me!) But please tell me if in one of them I wrote about Henry James, and whether I said something good. * * * * I know this letter was written from Dr. Luttinger's ménage—Cockroach Hall—and had to do with Ned and St. Patrick's cathedral and Powys, among other things. My memory is getting poorer and poorer. . . . You will notice in *Tropic of Capricorn* that I touched on these scenes and on Riverside Drive—very cursorily because I had a better thing to exploit in that café scene and the dream stuff (which I hope you will like, it was white hot, and one of my best moments). But I am coming back to the Hickersons and to Bunchek

(Conason), of course; the latter will loom up large, as will yourself. This time I will do a *real* portrait of you—and I think you will like it; in the past I have contented myself with sketches and caricatures. But now my whole life is opening up, there is some kind of exfoliation going on, and I am happily able to recall the most minute details—where they affected me vitally. When I say my memory is poor, I mean it only in the sense that every creative individual has a poor memory. My "Proustian" memory is really excellent, if I must say so myself. And when you detect discrepancies in the narrative, lies, distortions, etc., don't think it is bad memory— no, it is quite deliberate, for where I go on to falsify I am in reality only extending the sphere of the real, carrying out the implicit truth in situations that life sometimes, and art most of the time, conceals. Do you follow me? And if I succeed with my aim and intention you will have a fine presentation of contrasting lies—June the pathological liar and myself the creative liar—points where we meet, explosions where we disagree, tangential approaches, logarithmic tabulations, parabolas, etc. I am the most sincere liar that ever lived. You will see that. But to myself I lie almost negligibly. I am writing out of my system, wiping it out, as it were, all that kind of lying. That is the real purpose of art—among all its real purposes, which nobody understands anyway.

"When Shakespeare painted a horse it was a horse for all time." I am in love with that phrase, wish I had said it myself. If you understand why that is true—and I know you do or you wouldn't have written it—then there is no use worrying about what Waldo Frank and all those spiritual muckrakers are trying to say. Keep your eye on the axle like that and everything will fall into whack. Anaïs enjoyed your letters (haven't shown her the last, naturally) because she saw in them a man who was an artist and who, despite the handicap of a strange medium, words, made himself understood. She is sending you the Lawrence book just as soon as she thinks of a fitting inscription to you in the flyleaf. And, apropos of her writing, which is not at its best in that book, let me say that only last night I was retyping one of her latest manuscripts and was overwhelmed with admiration. Undoubtedly she will be recognized as the most important woman writer of today. Fraenkel doesn't know yet—he hasn't seen all that I have—and there are volumes and volumes to be read. She has kept a journal since the age of ten, begun in French and later in English. I am typing some of it out for her. The last journals—since I know her—which contain a great deal about myself and about June—are the strongest kind of writing—almost unfeminine. I know no woman writer of any period who has had the courage to express herself as Anaïs does. Lawrence seems small by comparison—and how ironical it is that she should have immolated herself to explain him to the world. Lawrence would have been proud to explain her! I tell you (and I want Fraenkel to hear this) that the last twenty pages which she has written (about June) are heart-breakingly wonderful. I wish I had the permission to send them to you. Maybe I will some day. . . . And so when you inquire about "that most important phase of my life which I am now living through"—don't you see what it is? Can't you picture what it means to me to love a woman who is my equal in every way, who nourishes me and sustains me? If we ever tie up I think there will be a comet let loose in the world. Anaïs has great faith in me, but I have much more in her. She has all the energy I have, all the zest and inspiration, all the good will, the generosity, the frank-ness, the vision, etc. Circumstance has kept us rooted in our respective spheres temporarily, but I have no doubt that what there is between us will alter circumstances profoundly. More I can't say at present. But look forward to great things. Since I know Anaïs my life in Paris has become almost a dream. I work without effort. I live a healthy, normal life. I see things. I read all I want to. You talk about my correspondence filling one of your desk drawers; well, in the short time we know each other, we have amassed a truly formidable accumulation of letters. (I imagine there is already on hand a 900-page book of letters, such as they say has been recently published from the Lawrence guy.) Naturally, Emil, much of my writing is dispersed in letters. Much of what was good, is good. Very little of me will ever be squeezed between covers—in my lifetime. I know that. I'm reconciled to it. But the minute I'm found dead—it will be the old story of the art dealers. "Have you got one of Miller's letters around the house—any little scrap will do?" I know that before I kick off, and I'm enjoying it in advance. I may not have a fine funeral, but I'm one guy who's enjoying his own funeral. * * * *

* * * *
Soon I should like to begin another book (to run on in my off moments) about the cinema. I am trying to cajole Anaïs into collaborating with me. I see so many splendid films over here—and wonder often how does N.Y. fare for good films these days? There was recently an adorable, amusing thing called *Emil und die Detektive*—has that come to America? And *Pichler the Banker*—have you heard of that? Or have you seen a wonderful travel-ogue on India that is now running? This last is the nearest thing to a chapter out of Elie Faure that I can imagine: it explains better than words the reason, the necessity, for his grand flamboyant excrescences. No man could see a film like this and write pallidly. (That's why I am still silent about it.) And then *Maedchen in Uniform*—you must see that! There is Fräulein von Bernburg in that film who will knock you cold. The most wonderful Lesbian you have ever seen. The most beautiful handling of Lesbianism imaginable. Is it Lesbianism? It's bigger than that. It's some sort of unconscious, collective love which refuses categorizing and shat-ters all one's prejudices. If I were a girl I'd gladly be another Manuela—or

a Fräulein von Bernburg. Or both! But I'm a Henry Miller and my balls
get in the way of all that. Laugh that off.

    *   *   *   *   You know, Bertha, the damned bitch, destroyed my en-
tire correspondence with her. I wanted some of those letters badly when
I was writing *Tropic of Cancer.* How much I left out of that book! I wanted
to say so much about Paris and I feel I said only a tiny bit. But I suppose
there will come another Paris book some day. Now and then you get a
feeling of Paris, perhaps, in *Tropic of Capricorn.* I want to keep Paris
squarely before your eyes all the time—the books are incomprehensible
without a realization of its presence. What would I have been without
Paris? What did I know of all this that has happened to me on that cold
wintry day in February when I shook you down for a last ten-spot and said
good-bye. (In the meantime, since the last words, I have had a couple of
glasses of wine, some cheese and saucisson, talked to the gas man and
the electrician. I think the French are the greatest people in the world—
because they don't love you!—and that explains why I could never more
like H. H.) I am going to stop soon because I have wasted too much time
already, and I don't get paid for this. I am sending on my manuscript of
Crazy Cock to Covici-Friede, Inc., at Putnam's suggestion. He says it's a
Covici-Friede book and I think he's crazy, but that's all right. I had a good
letter from him which I answered with a better one. If I should give Pat
Covici permission to look at my manuscript *Tropic of Cancer,* would you
care to see him for me, or receive him at your joint? I don't know yet—it's
just a possibility. I feel I may have something in common with Pat. He
liked my Mlle. Claude story and the guy who liked that might be a good
egg. Claude was a real woman, the first cunt who put something above
cunt, made you forget it—first woman for a whore, I mean—or rather I
don't know what I mean because I'm a little cockeyed as usual and it's
only four o'clock in the afternoon. The day is just commencing. I see the
copy of my letter to Sam Putnam which I have kept for you—soit, here
it goes with the rest of the junk. Too bad you can't see his.

    Met Wambly on the train the other day coming in from Marly-le-Roi.
Fine talks of his new cunts. One is like an electric sign, he says—switches
it off and on. Glad I did him up brown in the book. He's a real character,
uninteresting as a human being—just a *character.* If that guy could ever
bring himself to write, what a book he would give! Cunt up to the ears.
Never heard such varieties on the theme as he expresses. He's really a
magician in this field. You were going to send a picture of *a cunt:* you
don't mean these little sketches on the margin of the letter, do you? Give
us something personal—"one cunt out of a million," like Rona! The
sketches were fine, as embroidery, but I want you to give me something
with hair on it, big gashes and all the convolutional melancholia that you
can pack into it. Not just pornographic, or obstetrical, but obscene—

something with red lust in it—sing the equator! Saw a book on that Jewish artist I like so well—can't recall his name—a sort of Surrealist from the old days. There's a biography of him now. He does cats on the roof and rabbis climbing out of chimneys. You must know who I mean. What made me laugh was that line—"Fraenkel through his rare mental endowments takes that away from me too." Oh yes, he'll take lots away from you. He'll take the bottom from under you. I would love to see the two of you chinning at a bar—where do you go for a drink now? Is Monte's still open? I haven't got to the heart of my letter and I won't now—I'll save it for the next. I'm going to talk philosophy to you. If you see June tell her I want *all my MSS* and a few of my choice books—the dictionary, Spengler, Proust, Elie Faure, etc. I'm going to get my bicycle out of the shop and go to Montparnasse tonight. What you see on a bicycle in the evenings is marvellous. Deserves separate treatment. So long.

HVM.

Oct 23rd.

Dear Emil:

June arrived just a few days ago, as the manuscript narrates, and I am hastening to write to you and advise you how to forward mail to me, because the war is on and I expect no mercy, no fair play. I am afraid your letter will surely mention something about Anaïs—and that would be disastrous, more for June than for me. So please in the future, until further notice, send my letters care of Alfred Perlès, Chicago *Tribune* (Editorial Department), 5 Rue Lamartine, Paris. You don't need to address me even—send them to him; soon as he opens it he will understand. Meanwhile if there is a letter on the way I will watch for it carefully. I hope to Christ you haven't broached anything about Anaïs to Harold or any of the other bums. Harold would love to get back at me, if he could. As for Fraenkel, I trust him—just tip him off to keep a closed mouth—at least until the storm blows over. As best I can explain it to you it's like this: I don't want to crush June. She thinks Anaïs is wonderful, they see each other frequently—it would therefore be a damned cruel blow, on top of her war with me, to learn that Anaïs too was betraying her.

* * * *

Not much use giving you a separate account of what's going on. I am going to endeavor to keep up with the book, despite the internecine strife, and through the pages of the book you ought to get enough to satisfy any curiosity you may have. I begged June to bring all my manuscripts when she left N. Y., but as you see I got nothing but old pages of my novel. And they are at the Hôtel Princesse, where June rented a room for ten days, instead of coming here directly.(???) Can't pay the rent for it yet. Manuscripts languishing. However, no discouragement!

I am eagerly awaiting a letter from you apropos these purple passages. Do you find *Tropic of Capricorn* better or worse than *Tropic of Cancer?* You can see what a herculean task I have ahead of me. But I like herculean tasks!

If I can maintain the poise, the courage, the serenity I have shown these last few days I will pull out all right. I am much bigger and stronger than a year ago. But I know it's going to be terrible. I dread it.

    *   *   *   *

Hastily, slyly, affectionately yours,

HVM.

Nov. 28th. 1932
4, Ave. Anatole France
Clichy (Seine), France

Dear Emil:

Just a note to say that in a few days I'm forwarding you a thick batch of manuscript—a new book I started about three weeks ago, dealing with Proust, Joyce and Lawrence *(et alia)*. Hope to have it appear at the same time as my *Tropic of Cancer*—which is slated to come out at the end of February. Am signed up, bound hand and foot, for three books by the publisher (Jack Kahane, of the Obelisk Press, 338 Rue St. Honoré, Paris.) Have a good suggestion for you—or if you can't see it, for Buzby—regarding the publishing of a pirate edition of my *T. of C.* in America. I will go into this in my next when I forward you the new pages of MS.

Would you be good enough, if you have any such, to return loose pages of notes—notebook size—so that I can include them in my notebooks on *Paris* which Anaïs is getting bound for me as a Xmas gift.

June has gone (tho' still in Paris, I believe). Big blowup—everything over at last, and a divorce in the offing. However, should you run into her in N.Y. don't reveal anything about Anaïs, please. I'll give you the harrowing details later. Am working furiously—all thru the *fracas* too. Feel I have *ten* books in me spilling out. Ever since I went to live with Fraenkel at the Villa Seurat my genie is expressing itself. (You will get an idea of the fury and scope when you see the critical work I am now on—it is in reality a statement of my own attitude.) Right now I can't afford the postage—that's all. How is Fraenkel? Give him my warm regards. The MS coming (which is in *rough* form) is for his eyes—I hope he can write me when he sees it. I would like his criticism.

Send me the looseleaf notes if there were any, will you? I would appreciate it. (Some day it will be put out like the Barbey D'Aurevilly perhaps.) *And write me*—I have been waiting impatiently to hear from you.

Henry.

P.S. In a few days Anaïs is sending you her book together with a swell brochure by Jolas called "The Language of Night." Merry Xmas!

New Year's Day, 1933
2 bis, Rue de Monbuisson,
Louveciennes (S. & O.), France

Dear Emil:

It's midnight and Anaïs has retired for the night in order to be fresh when Hugo returns from his trip to London. I am alone in the big room upstairs, under the roof, the former billiard room of this Du Barry house, which 200 years ago was bought for 16,000 francs and today is worth 250,000 francs. The purpose of this letter is principally to ask you if you would *immediately* be good enough to return me the "New Instinctivist" pamphlet. I have just finished collecting my notes for my first big Paris Notebook, and suddenly discover that I lack that. * * * * I know that you want to hold on to the souvenirs of Paris which I have sent you, and that is right. I am hoping that you might some day make books of them for yourself—I would be glad to look at them whenever I return to the native heath. If, therefore, once in a while I clamor for something that rightfully belongs to me, some little link in the drama which means a lot to me, I trust you will take it in good part. * * * *

Permit me to expatiate on this subject of my notes. It is in the forefront of my brain just now. The first time I have ever considered such a preservation of material. Looking over these tattered pages, very much like the "tattered schizoidal self" itself, I get a glow of pleasure. I know that on the day when I land in New York and press your doorbell that book will arouse in you keener emotions than any artistic endeavors of mine. It will be the raw, living imprint of my Paris life, that Hegira on which I em-

barked so fatefully and unknowingly one raw February day when I asked
you to eke out my "frais" with a ten-dollar note. So don't be hard on me
in my hour of need. What you have from me must constitute several
volumes. All I am looking for now is this pamphlet and, if possible, a few
scattered items, handbills, clippings, menus, anything that you want to
give away to me which glowingly calls up again the rollicking picture of
these times. For instance, in sorting out my pages on the Cinéma Vanves
I was amazed that I had not saved even one program from that place. Not
one menu from the Restaurant des Gourmets, where I ate on credit and
talked of Tibet with my friend Kann, the abstract sculptor. Not one
handbill from the Société des Savants or the Tribune Libre in the Salle
Adyar, nor anything like a program from my Studio 28 reminiscences,
Buñuel, Rocambolesque, etc. To Buzby I think I sent the program notes
of *Un Chien Andalou,* which is a pity as that bastard is a total washout.

All this comes home to me with grim earnestness when I realize that
now that June has left me for good (the last item in my notebook is a scrap
of toilet paper on which she wrote, "Please get a divorce immediately"),
there is no chance of my getting back all the papers, letters, books, notes,
manuscripts, etc. etc. which she has in her possession. A great mass of
data, invaluable to posterity, which she in one of her morphine moods
may throw in the fireplace. And Elkus too has a wealth of material from
me. And Harolde Ross and Bertha and Joe O'Regan. I am wise, you see,
in appointing you my literary executor. You are like the Bank of England.
England always pays her debts. Emil can always be counted on. Sometimes, when I get in a funk, I think quietly and contentedly of all the paper
stored away in your studio, and I say to myself, "Well, at least they can't
rob me of that."

Do you begin to get the drift? Much has happened since I last wrote
you. A big drama with June, which ended definitively, June having sailed
the other day, knowing all, and threatening to take it out of me if I dared
to publish that book about her, etc. Claiming that Fred and Anaïs tried
to poison her, that's why she vomited and had diarrhea all the time she
was in Clichy. Great big scenes, Emil, which naturally I can't do justice
to in a letter. All this will go into *Tropic of Capricorn,* which has been
shelved for a while until I finish with the Brochure. And, by the way, not
a word of acknowledgement to date from you. I sent you four or five large
envelopes by the same boat train, containing all I had written on the
subject, together with clippings and all sorts of data which would interest
you. Can it be that you didn't receive them? That would be a calamity of
the highest order. Please let me know, when you answer this letter.

One funny thing, in passing, was my experience in trying to visit England. Had a visa, a return ticket, all my manuscripts, a typewriter, etc.,
two valises of stuff, and when I came to the immigration authorities at

Newhaven, England, I was turned back. In fact, I was jailed overnight, in charge of a constable, because I had only 178 francs in my pocket and did not know what hotel I would stop at when I arrived in London. They grilled me for about three quarters of an hour and handed me back to the French authorities in Dieppe as if I were a political prisoner. Considered me irresponsible, likely to become a public charge. Couldn't convince them of a damned thing. When they asked me to name some of the books I had written I mentioned *Tropic of Cancer* coming out in February by the Obelisk Press, Paris, Rue St. Honoré, No. 338. Fiddlesticks! "You don't mean to say, Mr. Miller, that you are writing about diseases?" "No," I said, somewhat shamefacedly, "this happens to be about geography," and I explained what Tropic of Cancer meant. But my inquisitor didn't seem to recognize that either. At the end I think they took me for a nut. When I got back to the French side I was treated swell, like a real human being—not a word of interrogation, merely looked at my passport, asked me a few perfunctory questions, suggested that I put my French visa in order (it has expired) and that was all. The whole procedure was so exactly like Fred had described in his book, when he spoke of his own entry into France, I recognized the French spirit so clearly, and sympathized with it so much, that at the end, when I shook hands with the man, and he escorted me to the train and wished me well and called me by name—"Monsieur Miller"—Jesus, Emil, I had tears in my eyes. I was the happiest man alive to think that they permitted me to return to Paris. If I had been rejected by France, deported to America, I would have cried. Then I knew that America was the last place I wanted to go to. (I don't mean that I wouldn't like to go home some time, on a visit, but to be shunted off there permanently—no, that would have been the worst calamity of my life). France is where I belong. Or somewhere here in Europe. I am no longer an American. I can swear to that. What got me about the French authorities there at Dieppe was the doddering way they went about the examination of my papers. So human! The desk was old and battered, the ink wouldn't work, the man's derby was gray, his whiskers were stained, his glasses fell off his nose, his teeth were falling out, his pants were shiny and threadbare, his hands were black, his breath was foul, his eyes were watery, everything dropped on the floor and everything was not in its place, out of order, etc.; but that guy was a human being, he had under his ass the whole weight of French history, French civilization, French culture, going back to Rome and Greece and Carthage and Crete and Mesopotamia and still farther back, back to Paleolithic man, to the Cro-Magnon type. Jesus, there was something venerable, something to respect as a force, a value. He didn't give a fuck if I were an artist or a bricklayer, he didn't ask if I had a sou or anything: he looked at my passport and saw that the date had expired and he asked me like a civilized being if I would care to have him renew it, since he was endowed with extra-temporal symbols, etc., and for my own benefit in case I wished to travel out of France soon again. And when he said fifty francs I wanted to throw myself on his neck. I would have taken him for a drink, sure as my hat, but the train was leaving any moment, and I was still worried about those Blimeys on the other side, whether they would have me yanked off the train and shipped back to America. . . . Well, all this because I was trying to escape June until she would leave for America. The night before I am to leave for London she visits me by surprise and asks me for dough. Pulls a melodramatic scene of the most intense variety, and it ends by my giving her the contents of my wallet, which I had already changed into English money. When Fred arrives later he won't hear of my staying; he forks over his salary to me and packs me off. And he ships my bags direct to London, with all my valuable papers, manuscripts, personal records, etc. Jesus, what a sweat getting those things back again in Newhaven. Tipping the telegrapher, tipping the constable, tipping the waiter who brought me my breakfast in jail, tipping the Blimeys right and left, the buggers who said to me on the boat, "We'll never *twist* you." But they fucked me all right. Fucked me good and proper. I think the payment of the debts had a lot to do with it. I had to pay for America's political blunders.

But as I say, it's all over now and it only remains to go through the monkey business of a divorce. Says June to Fred when he sees her off (she thinking I'm in foreign parts), thinking Fred has raised the money for her ticket, etc. Says June: "I feel like Alice in Wonderland . . . tell Henry to send me a divorce as quick as possible"—as though it were a money order or a calendar. And now that we're through with June there's Jeanne, Osborn's old flame, and she tries to tell us she's going to have a baby soon, blows herself up with a bicycle pump to look like a pregnant woman. No address—just Poste Restante. Walking around, waddling like a duck with an imaginary stomach, threatening to all and sundry to drop a kid in the Gare St. Lazare or the Metro Barbès-Rochechouhart.

A relief then to spend the last ten days here at Louveciennes, just a stone's throw from Mme. Du Barry's old estate on the Seine at Bougival. The last 50 pages of my brochure, which I mail you herewith, were done here. I hope you find them exciting. * * * * My best pages are still to come, I imagine. Form and language, psychology, function of the artist, geological I, etc. And as soon as I get through with the rough outline which you are receiving I will insert some final pages in *Tropic of Cancer* before it goes to press. A truly Joycean picture of the cunt, equals sign, putting back into the equation all that Wambly Bald missed when he turned his flashlight on it and found it wanting. No philosophy of hair this time. The mother longing. Incest. Convolutional melancholia. Etc. Get me?

As I sat down to write I looked at one of Anaïs' old diaries (1926) and saw in the index: Florence, Fiesole, Tours, Carcassonne. . . . My life for the next twenty years is to franchir these frontiers. Next notebook will be Spain, Capri, Stamboul, Bali, if I have anything to say about shaping my own destiny. And a trip to New York for a month, at least, if possible. This depends solely on finances. If you want me badly, brother, help me to buy a return ticket. Otherwise I shall cross the Apennines, and make the historic trajectory as did Hannibal, Napoleon, Caesar and all the other men of destiny. I have lived out my Pension Orfila in Paris. It is Tahiti or the Mediterranean shores. The Romantic Age began with the Sermon on the Mount.

Do write immediately. I am enclosing a few items from *Frou-Frou.* I have finished the last of the Anjou. The fish are made of glass here and the water is dirty. I go down to lie in a bed of state with red velvet covers. I have my own toothbrush. My own toilet. And I have Jung, Freud, Spengler, Rank, et alia to keep me company should I fail to fall asleep. I do nothing but take off my pants. Life is like that. Nothing more than taking off your pants. The rest is an alibi. I am waiting to hear from you. Don't forget "The New Instinctivism." I have a news item on Monsieur Faux Pas Bidet who died the other day.

Henry

Postscript

Emil:

A little drunk after a discussion of cosmological problems with King, the racetrack man, but here are a few things I forgot in my letter. First, a copy of letter to Covici-Friede, saying that you will call for my rejected manuscript of the novel, *Crazy Cock.* If a man named William Aspenwall Bradley should call for same, call on you, give it to him; he is my literary agent and is O.K. Second, I enclose a copy of letter from Mme. Boyd; if I could get hold of my "Cinema Vanves" article at least, I would appreciate it; she says she will surrender thing if not sold. Well, why not? And if she won't surrender it maybe you have a copy, or Buzby, any way will do. Sending you herewith a few clippings from *Frou-Frou.* On second thought am not sending you the carbons of the Brochure, it costs too much money and I'm almost broke and I want to go dancing this evening. Feel pent up, haven't been in Paris for ages it seems. Will send you with carbons a story from the book called "Bezeque, Inc.," which maybe you can sell to someone. If not, have a good time with it. Am finishing notebook and it looks swell. Some documents. King, the racetrack man, was too sober, and I got drunk.

What I want you to write about at length is plans for a pirate edition of *Tropic of Cancer*. You might make something out of it. I am too drunk to go into this now. Some other night, but not tonight.

I may be in N.Y. this Spring. It depends on whether I can raise enough dough. Want to come badly, if only for a month. If you see June, she has arrived by now, say I am willing for the divorce. What I would like is to lay hand on my possessions. How?

Yours in dire perplexity and good will,

HVM.

April 11th, 1933

Dear Emil:

It was awfully good to get the postscript to your last letter. Because if I have convinced you of my genius (?) that is a great deal. After all, you are almost my sole audience. And a terribly critical one because you know me so well and are naturally blinded by my closeness to you. How much I should like to write you of all that is going on in my head these last nine months or so—the busiest, richest months of my whole life. A sudden turn to an interior way of living which marks a great turning point in my career as man and as artist. When I write you now about myself it is hardly as though it were about myself, but about someone I knew intimately, just as you knew me. For over six months now I have been immersed in "The World of Lawrence" (the precise title I have chosen for that portion of my brochure which is devoted to him). In that universe I have lost my-self—and *found* myself. I don't mean that Lawrence is entirely responsi-ble; the process of losing myself began at the Villa Seurat. The great importance of *Tropic of Cancer,* as I now see it, lies in the fact that it summed up (alas, all too incompletely for my satisfaction) a whole period of the past. I suppose, nay I am quite sure, I shall never write another book like that. It was like a surgical operation. And out of it I emerged whole again. Though when I embarked on it, it was with no intention to cure myself of anything—rather to rid, to divest myself of the horrible wounds that I had allowed to fester in me. (As it now stands, this book, it is much much better than you know—I have added to it considerably, revised, excised, etc. I am very impatient to see it come out and have you possess a few copies for yourself and your friends).

As I was saying a moment ago, I am now immersed in Lawrence's world, and as soon as I finish with him I move on to Joyce and then to

Proust. I have accumulated so much material, have made such gigantic plans, that God only knows when I shall come to the end. The study of the three men only forms half of my projected brochure, its illustrative side; each study is really a small book, and perhaps eventually that is how the work will appear, in a series of books. I go into this only because there must be some confusion in your mind, seeing the rough manuscripts—a very tangled morass. My job now is to make some order of these chaotic fragmentary exurgitations (to use one of Osborn's favorite words).

So often, in studying Lawrence (and how I have racked my brain over him!) I have a desire to write you and recall old discussions. Recently I have thought principally of one night in Prospect Park, when we had first renewed our friendship—you were trying to explain your impressions of *Aaron's Rod*—the symbols he had used, etc. How happy I am to be able now to present to you some of my most mature reflections on these very obscure details. And how amazed I am also that we grasped so little then, we who were already mature, as men, and yet infants with respect to these things that Lawrence held so dearly. Some of this you will perceive when you get the completed manuscript. I have a feeling that I am plumbing him deeper than anyone has—and why should I not, since there is so much in common between us, even to the obscurity. But I have been terribly slow in maturing—that I see. And yet, I do not regret it altogether. The vast experiences in which I wallowed ought to mean a tremendous lot when this process of unloading, which has now commenced in earnest, finally begins to be understood.

I have enough work in preparation, in hand, that is, to last me three full years at least. I am working simultaneously on four books—because a vein has opened in me and I must exhaust it. For the moment I have been lending the carbons which I usually send to you to Lowenfels, but I will get them back soon and you will be able to get a perspective on my projects.

* * * *

The enclosed pages on the "Cinema," the germ of another book, may interest you. A great relief to let myself wander imaginatively and critically through all those silent sessions of the past. It won't be a *tight* book, nor even perhaps a profound one, but it will be highly interesting to you. Through everything I can relive my whole evolution, and to understand what it is that actuates me to write about so many things at once, please understand that I stand at some peak now from which I survey past and future, gather up both worlds with two hands, preparatory to making another descent. Hence everything is even more wonderful, more mysterious to me. For once I feel a united being and that ecstasy which you speak of burns steadily. The only fear I have is that I may be cut off before I say all that I wish to say. I feel that what I have to say now is important—

more for the future than for this present. I am living outside the age. I expect nothing of any tomorrow. I have it all here inside me and it suffices. No more losses for me—it is only the world which stands to lose by my death.

Death! That major theme running through everything I am engaged on. I owe it to Fraenkel. But here is the strange irony of things: in accepting it I have found a new life! I am truly resurrected. To me death is the greatest thing of all—it inspires me constantly. It is my one great joy.

More soon.

HVM.

Thursday, April, 1933
4 Avenue Anatole France
Clichy (Seine), France

Emil:

More notes. . . . Remind me, if you don't get them soon, that I am sending you these: *Paris de Nuit* by Brassaï, *Dali ou l'Obscurantisme* by René Crevel (containing photos of Dali's wildest paintings!), *This Quarter* (Surréalisme), a Grosz Album. Not all at once, but peu à peu. In exchange I want: a photo of the house, #662 Driggs Avenue, Brooklyn, where I was raised (the Old Neighborhood). Maybe some day you will wander down that way, amidst the Ufa settings, and be enticed into doing this for me—it is a souvenir that I would greatly appreciate. If you go there, wander left or right along Metropolitan Avenue (the old North Second Street), wander through North 3rd and 4th Sts, Berry Street, Wythe Avenue, Kent Avenue, etc. I guarantee you will get some startling reminiscences. (All near the old Broadway Ferry.) Stand at corner of Grand Street and Bedford Avenue—look at the fish market (Daly's), at Vossler's Drug Store, at the Beer Saloon on corner opposite, look at Cinema on Grand Street, near Driggs Avenue (the old Unique, or the Bum). If you make any sketches of shanties or saloons or ferry-slips send me one or two. And if you feel extremely generous, send me a good water color some day—one of your finest! I would love to have something around me of yours. I can't get up the courage to do a water color; I know if I pick up those brushes I will be lost again. And I can't afford to wander off the path.

*   *   *   *

Should you ever bunk into June again—dubious!—try to tactfully broach the subject of my manuscripts, letters, files, etc., all contained in my big file-case. I would give the world to recover these things—half my life hangs there in those papers. They mean nothing to her, nothing whatsoever. I don't ask for *her* letters, or the ones I wrote her (God knows they would be interesting!)—but just my petty, personal things. Shit, I suppose it is futile. But it gripes me. When you say "genius"—there it is! Always hankering after impossible things, always creating messes, always sundering bonds, etc. Fred is reading Verlaine's letters—he asks his friends now and then for sixty centimes, a few sous, a penny even—and makes the most eloquent promises to repay them. Sometimes he just asks for a clean shirt to leave the hospital in, or a pipeful of cheap tobacco, or even a postage stamp. Heart-rending. But so familiar. Verlaine, Rimbaud, Van Gogh, Gauguin, Villon—what lives! Strindberg! (Did I include that fine passage I rewrote for *T. of C.* on the streets of Paris and what they mean to the madmen? The Pension Orfila business enlarged? I doubt it. Wait till you see it all. It's swell—it *explains* Paris for all time. I'm proud of it).

    * * * *   I am also sending you in a few days some forty or fifty pages of my rewrite on Lawrence—it has to be rewritten once again, alas, because I am constantly expanding the frame. But some things will remain—it is quite solid, only it is too fragmentary. And with it I shall doubtless send another fifty pages or so of a new book I write on the side, called *Self-Portrait.* That contains more hallucinating stuff—streets again—and cracked ideas—the slats of things, the warped, twisted aspect, the universe which has fallen a little to one side, collapsed, gone kerflop. I like it very much and mean to carry it along.

When you say *Last Book* I don't know any more what that means. Perhaps *Tropic of Cancer.* Perhaps. You know that I have a companion book underway—*Tropic of Capricorn.* That is last in point of time, relatively at least. Since then there are a few *last* books. I am going on six cylinders and a little harassed by the task I have set myself. I dream a lot—and I am recording these dreams, with my own interpretations and origins for posterity. What dreams! In other words, believe me to be a little mad. Yours truly, etc. Write on anything you find to hand—preferably paper napkins, tablecloths; get your friends to add a word—I like crazy names on the letters, like that brother of the movie star, what's his name. Put mustard on it and vinegar. How is the new beer and the diluted wine? How is Joe O'Regan and Ned? How is the advertising world? Did you read *Challenge to Defeat* by a young American optimist?

                                                                                  HVM.

4/28/33
4, Ave. Anatole France
Clichy (Seine), France

Dear Emil:

* * * *

Alors—in the pages of the *Self-Portrait* I hope to let off that effluvia which ordinarily went into my letters. Regard it as such. I keep you in the back of my head while writing. Remember that my idea is to make it in 4 Parts—the *four* Seasons! This first batch is still Spring. I want to get in a lot of *street* stuff—the physical, sensuous Paris—*plus* my warped moods, introspection, ghosts, etc. Follow me? Above all, the captivating, motivating idea is *"marginal"* thoughts. If Picasso is the pioneer, the experimenter—he who moves on from one problem to the next without getting *mired*—then that is one of my chief goals also. The art is a by-product, the incidental. Any and every means to preserve the inner flame—the gusto— the vision.

That's all for the present.

HVM.

* * * *

5/19/33
4, Ave. Anatole France
Clichy (Seine), France

Dear Emil:

This may sound mad, but it is absolutely sincere, sincere as a man can be who is weeping and at the same time examining the carbons to see if they are inked enough! Sincere anyhow as a lying buffoon of an artist can be. The great exultation of this morning has been succeeded by the blackest misery, deep, deep anguish. This evening, at dinner table, I received a 42-page letter from Osborn; on the first page I read that he has seen June in the Village, in a restaurant, with a "man considerably my junior," etc. And June is very bitter and will hear nothing about me—except to know if the book has been published.

That bitterness of hers rankles in me. I can't go on living with that woman hating me. I can't. You're the only real friend I have, and I don't think I have asked too much of you in the past. Perhaps more than I should, but I have tried to give what I could in return. And now I need a friend—more than ever in my life. You know my life with June—all it meant to me. You know how I came crying to you one afternoon, begging you to do something for me. Now it's all over. I know it's finished. But she hates me. And I can't bear that. I can't understand why she should. After all, it was she who committed the crimes against me, not I against her. I was kind to her, generous, forgiving. I loved her as I believe few men have ever loved a woman. I loved too much. I can never get over it, not if I live to be a thousand years old. Only to mention the name to me and everything turns over inside me. She was everything I wanted in life—and she failed me—or I failed her—what difference does it make who is to blame? I don't blame her. I don't even blame myself. Nor life. It was just the human fatality of things, a cancer worse than blame or hate or love.

I thought I had rid my mind of her. I have found another woman, a far better woman that June, a woman with whom I have never had the slightest quarrel, a woman who has sacrificed a great deal for me and who demands nothing of me. And yet there is this June, this damned Jewish vulture gnawing into my vitals whether I want it or not—first with her possessivity, her jealousy, her overwhelming sex and clawing beak, and now with hatred and malice and vindictiveness. God knows, I am through with masochism, with self-torture. I have had more than my share, first with B and then with June. I have been miserable in all my love affairs— with Pauline, B, June, Muriel, Fedrant, all of them. Up till now. Now I feel free. Free to love a woman in a normal, healthy way. And just to prove it to you I will mention that this evening I was smitten by the loveliest whore I have ever seen in Paris—*until* suddenly I realized that she was a prototype of June. And then the bottom fell out of me. I wrote her a long letter in the café, in my poor French, an ardent, wistful, tender letter, as only a mad Ludwig knows how to write. I would go without food to love her a little while, to receive her tenderness.

No, I don't want to recommence with June. But I want her to stop hating me. I don't want this bitterness. And I ask you, as the only friend I have left in this world, to intercede for me. Forget my papers, my letters, my manuscripts. I don't really need them. If I live long enough I can produce all that over again, tenfold. But between you and me, Emil, and this is no blarney, I am not going to live very long. I know it. I feel it in my bones. I don't know what I have, but I have something—it's deep inside and it's eating me out, and you may call it imaginary or what you will, but that won't wash it away. I have a few years, and I am trying to make the best of them. For whom? I don't know. I am driven from behind, a blind force impels me, and I obey it. It is no longer fame, vanity, reward, success. None of these. Maybe I want to immortalize myself. I don't care what it is. I am pushing myself on, driving with all the steam that's in me,

to say what I have to say, before the curtain falls. And when I have said
it all, I will fall over. I know it as sure as Fate. I am built along those lines.
It is a classical fate for such as myself. (Vide—Gauguin, Van Gogh, Strindberg, Nietzsche, Lawrence, Proust, Dostoievski.) Just enough strength to
convey what they wanted—and then finis! Well, that's me. Life hasn't
been too kind to me, as an artist. Maybe I am not an artist, as the world
judges art and artists. But in my soul I know that I am—though there is
very little to prove or justify myself. Anyway, the few who knew me can
testify as to whether I was one or not.

I lapse unwittingly into the past tense. I am writing at top speed. *I was!*
Read what you like into that. At this moment, or rather a few moments
ago, when I was sitting alone in the kitchen, after coming from the café
and the beautiful whore whose eyes kindled me with such a flame, such
a thirst, I was thinking of my whole life, all my abortive actions, all my
failures, all my sad attempts to assert my real being, all the foul blows
below the belt that life seems to have dealt me—I am sorry to confess it!
And I have loved life so and still do. I know how to laugh, to forgive, to
be generous. But I am hurt, so dreadfully hurt that the one being on earth
whom I loved—and I love her still, God help me, though I do not want
her any more, and only because I can't stand that cruelty any longer, that
foul injustice of flesh against spirit—I am hurt to the very quick, I say, that
she of all beings should hate me, should not know who I am, what I am.
Sometimes I think of myself as being almost a God. Certainly a saint.
There is that fine side of me, which you know, and which I need not blush
in mentioning so forthrightly, since it is a fact which even I can see. And
June ought to know that, as indeed I am sure she does. But she will not
see that side of me. Her damned petty, little ego, her feminine vanity, gets
the better of her. Emil, so help me God, one of the greatest moments in
my life was here in Clichy, just before the crash. It was an afternoon and
June and I were rushing to the post office to call Anaïs. They were great
friends, you know, until the very end. Indeed, the end of that affair is
something almost impossible to believe. Who would believe me if I told
the whole truth? Not even June herself. She would deny it, as she has
denied all the great moments in her life, most of which I brought her. I
tell you, Emil, I am not crazy, and I am not vain or boastful. I am weeping
as I write this. I can hardly see the words for the tears that are running
down my cheeks. And I don't mind if you shed a few yourself—for the
little boys we were who once thought we could take life by the horns
perhaps and make a fair name, etc., etc., etc. All the et ceteras! But that
afternoon! We were going to the post office. And in the street June
clutches me in that frenzied way of hers and says—"You are a great, great
man, a saint, a genius, I love you, I worship you, I'll do anything in the

world for you"! Christ! Christ! what mockery, these words. For only a few hours later we were separated—forever. Only a few hours later I listened to the worst vituperation a man can ever listen to from the woman he loves. Everything turned to stone, to ashes. All the sacredness gone out of life. Dirt. Dirt. Vulgar Jewish display. Vulgar histrionics. I look at the woman uttering her blasphemies and ask myself is it the same woman? And what miracle has wrought the change? Is it I? *Could* I alone have wrought this change? I do not believe it. If I had committed the most heinous crime, still I would not be deserving of all those foul accusations which she heaped upon me.

* * * *

Do you know what I really want of June? I want her to get down on her knees and *beg me to forgive her.* I want her to weep until her heart breaks, her dirty little mean petty Jewish heart that failed to recognize a great soul when it had one. Who is June, *in reality?* Don't you think I know? Don't you think all your little sarcasms and ironies, your petty innuendoes lodged in my brain? Don't you know that I have a brain? That I am a sensitive organism? Sure I knew who June Smith-Smerth-Mansfield-Miller-Cunt-Balls-Whore was. I know her down to the roots of her insatiable cunt. I know her soul inside out, because it was so thin that you could turn it inside out like a sleeve. I knew June, better than any of you did. But I loved her. That was a misfortune. That is something one has no choice about. I loved her because when I met her I was already a desperate, hungry soul. I had nothing to lose. I hated my wife. I wanted tenderness, love, joy, expansion, life, ecstasy, illusion. I loathed that foul son-of-a-bitch who bore my child. I loathe her still. I loathe the whole American tribe of women with their false virginity, their false love, their dirty Lesbian masturbating tricks. I loved June because she was a Jewess—and I knew that before ever I admitted it to you. I loved her because she represented another race, something wholly alien to me, something I did not know. And June loved me, there is no doubt about that. Had I not been a fool artist I might have held her. I might today have been happy. But I could love her and at the same time I could ridicule her. I had to tell her the truth about herself, and she could not stand that. I knew all along that I was being fucked, I was not so naive as you may have imagined. But I loved her! If she had come to me rotting with syphilis I would still have loved her, loved her all the more perhaps. Who can say about love? Why we love? There is no logic in it. One is a slave. One is mercilessly bound. Helpless. A victim. I was a victim of love. And still I saw clearly. The day I left America was the most horrible day in my life, and perhaps that is why I never want to see America again. Oh yes, I would love to go back—in imagination—but when the moment comes I feel I always shall renege. I can't go back. I hate America. I hate American women. I hate what America did to me, through June, through B, through Muriel. . . .

Emil, I am no homo—you know that. And you are the only fellow I really care about, really count on, really have confidence in. Osborn says you laugh at me behind my back—you joke about my philosophy of death and other things. Well, I forgive that. Good God! There is much to laugh about in any human being. We are all ridiculous in the ultimate. But I have great confidence in you. I know you tried to save me when I was in the toils of June. But you couldn't save me. And now I say, help me! But how? I don't know how to save myself. I don't know really what I want. Only I know I don't want her to hate me. Upon my word of honor, if she wanted it badly, I would kill myself. She doesn't deserve it, but I would do it. Who am I? Am I so important that I should destroy another's happiness? Ask her that. What does she want me to do? Does she want me to stop writing about her? I can't do that. That is my life. Unfortunately. All too unfortunately. But if killing myself will soothe her conscience, if putting this miserable Henry Miller who loved her so much out of the way, will help any, I will do it. I can't bear to have her hate me. I wish you would show her just this. I wish you would believe that this is not just the inspiration of a drunken moment. Tell her that I loved her and that *I love her still but do not want her.* That I am happier without her, though God knows what kind of happiness this is—without her. It is ghastly. She can never know what it meant to me, our life together, all that I planned, all that I dreamt. My June! And she is just a little Jewish cunt, whore, a trollop running around with some good-looking collegian very much my junior. Ghastly. When I think of how I pushed her in the streets, cold bitter nights when we were selling the leaflets, or selling the candy, pushed her with love and vengeance and God knows what. I was mad, crazy. I loved her, and I was hungry. I was desperate. Nobody understood what I was, who I was. I wanted to be somebody. I thought I was an artist, a poet. I was a dreamer. I believed so in human beings that I pushed them about. I beg her to forgive me for that. I never really wanted to push her. I pushed her into everything. I see it all too clearly. I pushed her away from me. I was a coward. I don't deny that. I was a coward because I loved her, and didn't love her enough. I loved myself too. I wanted to be somebody. I was glad that she sacrificed herself for me. I hoped to sacrifice myself for her some day. It was all twisted, tortured, all crazy, wrong, from start to finish. I've lived through a whole world since then and I know better, but poor June, she only remembers that I pushed her, when it was cold and when she had only too little courage of her own. Christ, Emil, there is nothing too much to say for a woman when she has done all that June has done. And there is nothing too bitter to say against her when she has done all that June has done against me.

Perhaps I'll never again write a letter like this in all my life. But Osborn's words cut me deep. June was in a restaurant. June was alive. June was with a young man, "considerably my junior." Etc. The et ceteras! I wish the young man luck. I hope to Christ he will be happy with June as I hoped to be. I wish I was that young man. I wish I was young and naive and stupid so that I could sit opposite June in a restaurant in Greenwich Village and hang on her words and believe in her as once I believed in her. I wish it were possible to make June understand what all this means. June *won't* understand. That is the trouble. I wish instead of writing this long letter I could be transplanted to America and just see June for a few minutes. How can that woman hate me? That woman ought to get down on her knees before me.

Emil, I am very sad, and very drunk, and very ill. Ill at heart, and it is this illness which carries me off. Once I wrote a long letter to June saying that I would commit suicide if I could not have her. I wrote it in the kitchen at 224 6th Avenue where you and I laughed so boisterously one night when we read the crazy letters from the Western Union messengers. Well, tonight, I say again, I am ready to commit suicide, if that will relieve June. She may not believe me, but I am serious. She has only to say the word. And nothing I have written need see the light of day. I will take everything with me to the grave, like the honest Dutchman that I am. I am a fool and I know it. But I put love high. I would have liked to think that she loved me for my own sake, for all the defects I had, as well as the virtues. I would have liked to think that it was eternal, this love of ours. But since it isn't, or wasn't, what can I do? I can blow my brains out or jump in the Seine. For a Jewish cunt. Oh irony! Oh fate! Yes, I can do that for a little Jewish cunt whose pride was hurt. I can do that for June Smith-Smerth-Mansfield-Miller. Tell her that. Tell her that I will do anything to make her little Jewish cunt twitter again. She can lie in bed with a young athlete and tell him how a romantic Hans Castorp, a delicate child of life committed susensryup for her.

Drunk . . . Drunk . . . Drunk . . . I loved her. That's the whole story. All the rest is twaddle. Love. Love. I'm bursting with it, and before I commit susensryup tell her that I am going to fuck some of the grandest cunt in France. Tell her that I found a little black-eyed whore in the Café Wepler that is up my street, and that I love her and that means LOvve. Love. Tell her that I find French cunt so much more intriguing, tho I'm a goddamned liar when I say it. I can't see the keys any more, so goodnight and good luck and here's hoping the next world is bright and merry and no catarrh or rheumatism or adenoids or cancer. . . . Just love. I loved her. Tell her that. The cheap little five and ten cent store son of a bitch.

But I'll do it for you if it'll make her happy—she and her five and cten
tencet store athlete with his "considerably my junior" etc. Et cetera.
                    Do you know what is meant to be hurt? I'm hurt.
            That's all¾

                            Three quartes¾ Hurt. Hurt.
                                I loved her.
                                    Tell her.
                                        Sunsensryrpup
                                        HVM.

                                        May 19th, 12 hours later

Dear Emil:
    You can disregard the enclosed letter. Read it for your own amuse-
ment. Enclose a rough outline for the "Palace of Entrails" which should
lose none of its flavor because it is slightly discordant. Copied it off for
you this morning just to prove that I am in fine fettle after last night's
Sorrows of Werther. Everything is O.K. Just a temporary spasm—because, as Wambly Bald would say, Osborn's damned letter left images in
my mind.
    This morning I read it over and laughed my head off. Never trust the
author, trust the tale. If I say my heart is breaking, never believe me. It
is just literature. Should you ever see the said Mansfield-Smith-Smerth-
Miller woman tell her to go fuck herself—tell her I said so! Don't show
her anything—because none of it is true. All that stuff lives only in my
imagination. Organically, functionally, metaphysically, I am intact. I will
not live a hundred years, but I am not dying yet. Nor do I intend to
commit susensyrup. Not until I've done a few water colors as well. (I'm
now about to do a column for Wambly Bald: he gives me a picture of a
nut with a phallic tree beside him and an aureole around his head that
looks like a rolled-up condom. *Inspiration.*)
    * * * *
    I haven't much to say this noon except that I am slightly bilious. That
letter gave me a good shock—I enjoyed it. So write me once in a while
and tell me about June because I don't give a fuck about her. Tell me what
color dress she wore and if her eyes were painted green or blue.
    The young man considerably my junior—what a phrase! I think that

started all the trouble. That must be none other than Stratford Corbett of the N.Y. Life Insurance Company. Now I know why June used to say, whenever she came to Paris and went to bed with me: "God, Val, how *thin* you are!" He must be a fine, athletic, healthy-looking specimen. The artists are always a bit seedy, run down at the heel, wormy, neurasthenic, flyblown, yellow-bellied, etc. Et cetera. I never knew there was so much meaning to et cetera. I am making discoveries. I love you, June . . . et cetera. No thank you, I have had sufficient . . . et cetera. Will you have a little snifter? . . . et cetera. Werther's Younger Brother . . . et cetera. Always God . . . et cetera . . . *et Cie.*

You see what a fine, cheerful, healthy mood I am in. * * * * If I get any dough today I'm going on a rampage. My black-eyed whore will be at the Café Wepler between cinq et sept—with a gray dress this afternoon, so the garçon says. However, my note is addressed to the dame in blue. I wrote her that I loved her with violent passion. Do you think that sounds all right? Can one really love like that any more? Regards to Fraenkel. Under the sweatband you will find the universe of death.

HVM.

<table>
<tr><td>(For Self-Portrait)</td><td align="right">May 20th, 1933
(24 hours later)
Clichy—Seine. Death</td></tr>
</table>

Dear Emil:
* * * *
Fraenkel! If he were here I would put my arms around him and hug him! Where is that little man with the bright glancing eye, the flame in his guts, the fire in his brain, the fierce, inquiring mind, the shameless arrogance and humility that makes one weep, so deep is it and so genuine. Fraenkel? Why little Fraenkel, so despised, so misunderstood, so tortured and bound up with his inner conflicts—Fraenkel is a man very much alive, a man with the Holy Ghost in his bowels, where it belongs, and if he is the philosopher of death he breathes more life than all that crew combined—that vile, healthy, rosy-cheeked piratical crew you picture to me—Boyd, Hale, Smith, Van Vechten, etc. Smoking, steaming shits, these are! I borrow the vituperative language from Lawrence. It was a favorite expression of his. Smoking, steaming shits! When it comes to life

and death, you are all over there a lot of smoking, steaming shits! I must say it, Emil. There is no use hedging about it.

　＊　　＊　　＊　　＊

To my friend Emil Schnellock　　　　　*Anno Domini 1933*
who taught me all I will ever　　　　　4, Avenue Anatole France
know about painting!　　　　　　　　　Clichy (Seine), France

The Genesis of a Masterpiece

As near as I can possibly remember I want to give you the history of this remarkable water color which is now drying in the wastepaper basket. I may never do another one like it in my life. Not unless I can recall the technique I just employed.

To begin. . . . It goes back a ways, the origins of this masterpiece. In the morning I looked over my folder called "Materials" which is composed of odds and ends that will be cemented into my *Black Spring.* I look over my last will and testament, over my enthusiastic letters and—finally I come to my notebooks on "The Novel"—the novel that has never been written, which I excuse myself for not writing because it will take the rest of my life and I don't know if I will live that long. By noon my head is bursting—with ideas. All my life comes up in one gush, like a geyser that has just broken through the earth. I don't want all these ideas—I want to sit down and write. But I am powerless. While I am eating lunch I cover the whole tablecloth with notes. My past life. My future. La Fourche, where I sit on top of all the roads and go schizophrenic. Chez Richard. But never mind. I come home and take a short nap to let the blood ooze back into my feet and legs and stomach—any place but not my head. All right, you son-of-a-bitch—if it's ideas today then I'll devote the day to being my own amanuensis. After dinner I copy out a little of Goethe to relieve the pressure. Goethe was possessed. He believed in his demon. He obeyed it absolutely.

I clean my bicycle thoroughly, screw all the nuts tight, oil it, polish the spokes. Then I clean off my desk, arrange my books. I sit down to write—but it's impossible. I have too many ideas at once. Among the books I arranged on my desk is a brochure, about three inches square, called *L'Art et la Folie.* Fine. I open it. I see a boy and a girl kneeling close together and they are holding a big lock between them. Instead of a penis and vagina they are equipped with big keys which penetrate each other. They look very happy. This is a drawing by a "fou." Not bad. Page 85 is a *paysage.* It looks exactly like one of Hilaire Hiler's—in fact, it is better than Hiler's. The only peculiar thing about it is that in the foreground there are three miniature men very deformed. They look as if they were too heavy for their legs. But that is not at all disturbing. (I have just made copious notes about the "monsters" I saw while sitting on the Rue de Rivoli yesterday.) Maybe these three birds are fairly normal, as monsters go. Anyway, it is an architectural picture, a study in Neo-Naturism. It is midway between Giotto and Santos-Dumont.

Quietly it is beginning to dawn on me that I ought to do one of these crazy drawings myself. At first I wish to copy one of these for you, Emil—to show you how good they are. But I am a little ashamed to be copying the works of men in the lunatic asylum. This is the worst form of plagiarism. These devils have no redress. Just the same, I'm at a loss for ideas.

Finally I decide to draw a horse—just to begin with. I am thinking vaguely of the horses I saw yesterday in the Etruscan Wing of the Louvre—a special trip to follow out a note I made three years ago. Well, I begin with the easiest part of the horse—the horse's ass. I leave a little opening for the tail—to be stuck in afterwards. But the moment I start the body the trunk becomes immediately too elongated. I am not drawing a liverwurst—I am trying to draw a horse. I recall that some of the horses on the vases (Rhodesian period) were very elongated and that the legs began inside the body, with a fine stenciled line—the beginnings of Cubism and Surrealism—about 4,000 years ago. O. K. then—I'll make it a Rhodesian horse. But now comes the hard part—the legs. The shape baffles me entirely. I only know about as much as from the fetlock down, which is to say, the hoof. To put the meat on up above is a delicate operation—and to make the upper leg join the body naturally, not as if it were stuck on with glue. I've already given the animal five legs—one of them I turn into a cock—when I suddenly realize that you don't see all four legs at once. I try turning the front legs up—sort of prancing like. It won't work. Then I try to fix up the stomach which has become dilapidated during the leg work. Finally the stomach looks like a hammock— that's the best I can do. I leave it at that. If it doesn't look like a horse I can always change it later—call it a hammock and put a man in it, asleep. And now the head. I have the ears, but the skull looks like a feed-bag. When I put the eyes in I notice the horse is laughing. This is the first human feature about my animal. And then I'm disgusted. I want to do it all over again. So I sit down calmly and close my eyes and try to picture a horse in my mind's eye. I rub my hands over his mane, over his shoulders, over his flanks. Seems to me I can remember how a horse feels, how he curves here and there. (In Chula Vista I used to curry-comb the jackasses every morning before going to the fields. Even if it were only a jackass—looked like a jackass, I would feel better.) So I begin with a mane. It looks a little silly—like Zadkine's drawings when he wants to be smart and pretend he can't draw. The mane is already beginning to look like a pig-tail. Well, maybe a little color will fix it up when I come back to this part. I go on. I change the lines of the stomach completely. That is, I make it concave where it was convex and vice versa. Now the horse is galloping, for some reason. He's fiery and his nostrils are snorting. But he looks funny with two eyes. I rub one out. He looks a little more horsy. Suddenly he's gotten kind of cute-looking—like Charley Chase! I decide to put stripes on him in case I want to make it a zebra later. But I forget that the stomach is round and that the curve should break in the center. He looks now as if he were made of cardboard. (I recall the Cinzano horse—he has stripes too—a beautiful animal. And he's only an advertisement for an apéritif.) If I could find a picture of a horse done by a fou I would do a little plagiarizing. But there are no horses. Only Greek goddesses, rivers, bridges, epileptics. Well, a bridge then. I look at page 85 attentively. It's a fine composition. Has a Japanese quality about it. Very mechanical, very geometrical. But you can see it's a bridge and you can tell what are houses and what are trees and what are mountains.

Also. . . .

Right under the horse's ass, where his croup begins and ends, I draw a straw hat, a melon. Under it I put a head—roughly. I take the big horse-cock and twist it into an arm—so! The man is tickling the horse's stomach. Fine—I can always say I was imitating the work of a *fou.* (And right here I ask myself for the first time if there can possibly be something wrong with me for wasting my time this way.) Not being able to draw the feet well I cut off the feet by a parapet which I can copy from page 85. The man is leaning over the parapet and tickling the horse's belly at the same time. Compositional effects. (I recall that in the fresco designs recovered from Portugese Africa some 17th century slave drawings of the Crucifixion were terrifically fine composition though very bad crucifixion.) And now, as I'm getting a little tired from my exertions I decide to shorten my labors by putting in diagonal stripes of flooring for the bridgework. This kills at least a third of the picture, so far as detail goes. Now the terraces, the escarpment, the three trees, the snow-covered mountains. It's like a jigsaw puzzle. Wherever I don't finish a cliff properly I make it the side of a house, or the roof of a hidden house. I'm gradually working up toward the top of the picture where the frame cuts short my labors. Only the trees and mountains remain. The trees look like bouquets. I put lightning inside the leaves to give it structure, but that's no go. I put clouds in to cut off some of the foliage—that's always a good dodge. But the clouds look like pieces of tissue paper that had been torn off the bouquets. . . . Well, the mountain at least. A mountain is easy. Too easy.

I decide to make mine a volcano. Shit, I can take a few liberties—especially with the work of a *fou*. So I put the crater in first and work down toward the foot of the mountain to join up with the bridgework and the roofs of the houses below. I put cracks in the mountainside to represent the damage done by the volcano—this is an active volcano and its sides are bursting. When I get all through with it it looks like a shirt. I can recognize the collar-band and the sleeves. All it needs is a Rogers Peet label and size 16 or what have you. One thing in the picture stands out unmistakably however—and that is the bridge. It has three arches and no shadows under them. I suppose the sun was directly overhead. The bottom of the picture is unfinished. It's scraggly. I put in big portals, as though it were the entrance to a cemetery. Later I can make grillwork if necessary. And oh yes—I almost forgot. In the upper left hand corner, to ease my conscience of all the plagiarism I had committed, I decided to put an angel. It didn't turn out well either. The stomach was too big and the wings looked like umbrella ribs. But you could see it was *symbolic*. At least that much was original.

And now my theory is—get the drawing out of the way as quickly as possible and slap in the color. After all, you're a water colorist, not a draughtsman. (Not a workhorse, pobba!) So out with the tubes. I commence with raw umber, for the side of the house. It looks weak. I put some Crimson Alizarin into the wall next to it. Looks too pretty. Fuck it! I'm starting off bad with my colors. I get out my penknife and decide to experiment. (First—knowing what's up my sleeve—I put a gondola alongside the bridge, which makes it automatically in the water.) Now for the palette. I take the tubes and squeeze them liberally. I dip the knife into the Laque Carmine and apply it to the windows. Holy Jesus! The house is afire at once. (Now if I were really mad, instead of silly and wasting time copying the works of a *fou*, I'd start putting firemen into the picture, turn it around and make the flooring look like a ladder. I could even turn the cliffs into burning houses.) But instead I start to build a big fire. I make all the houses on fire—first with the carmine, then with vermillion, and then with some bloody concoction by mixing four or five paints together. This part of the picture, which is almost the center, stands out fine and bloody. It's a fire or a murder, according to whether I let the houses stand or turn them into human beings. And just to calm down a bit I go toward the water and decide to paint that. As I'm still pretty fiery I make the water a clear gamboge—one swift streak without a retouch. Fine. It looks clear. It's mineral water.

Emil—at this point I left off, realizing that it was a part of my book. In a few days I'll send you 135 or so pages of the *penultimate* draft (there never being a *final* draft)—and you will see for yourself what I did with this theme. This is just a souvenir for you. 50 years from now you can sell it as an "authentic" document. Sell *all* my possessions—but first wait until they put a price on me.

Yours,
Henry.

*   *   *   *

On the terrasse of Café Wepler   June 16th. '33
Place Clichy—hot night   4, Ave. Anatole France
                                                   Clichy (Seine)
                                                   France

Dear Emil:

I'm sitting here, midnight, waiting for my new cunt, the fancy-priced whore, to show up. Apparently she isn't. I must have paid her so well the last few times that she can afford to lay off for a few days, get sunburned or what not—for which God be praised. Believe me, I've gone with all manner of whores here in Paris, but this one, the moment I get within striking distance, my guts tremble. And that's an infallible sign—*that's love,* or infatuation. That hurts.

I'm waiting impatiently for an answer to a long letter I wrote her—Fred really wrote it!—I just gave him a few ideas. If whores were sensitive, intellectual, if they had souls (?)—such a letter as this one would finish them. But they're not—and that's why imbeciles like myself go chasing after them.

I come in from Louveciennes after fucking my head off (and working hard too) to fall into her clutches, hand over the money that Anaïs gave me with which to buy a Summer suit. I lay with her and tell her in bad French all about my life. *She listens marvellously.*

I don't really need to fuck her. I like the way she sprawls out on the bed, one leg poised in midair, her foot resting on a flower painted on the wallpaper. I like her body. Talk of Renoirs! She's one, if ever I saw one. A magnificent *torso*—she posed for some American sculptor in Montparnasse. I can imagine what it was he sought in her. The other whores around here tell me she's too fat. They ask me to feel their thighs, etc. But I don't want their young, firm buttocks, *etc.* I want this one—her huge rolling torso that's like a cradle for me, the massive limbs that inspire me just to touch. I like bending down beneath her when she's undressing, her foot resting on a chair. I look up at her crotch, dark, mysterious, *big,* and I'm in heaven. I wouldn't take an ounce off her. Just as she is.

But it's her language and her looks that get me. Fine eyebrows, natural ones, delicate, like brushstrokes. Her face heavy, Spanish, Russian, if you like, but losing its weight with the slightest gesture, slightest emotion. When I came up close to her for the first time—I had been eyeing her from a distance always—I got a shock. How the human face can change when you get up within six inches of it! It's almost like looking at a familiar object thru a microscope. A new world opens up. And hers was so lovely up close, so soft, so gentle, so really dark and enticing. I was happy just to stare at her. I devoured her with my eyes. And then to think that it's so easy to go with someone you really desire so strongly. Just a little dough. Hell, what do I care about suits or meals or this or that? If she wants me as a customer, O. K. If she wants me as a lover, O. K. If she wants me as her *pimp*, O. K.!!

* * * *

You said you were touched by the letter about June. Christ, yes! I was *real* for a half-hour. Falling apart. I hope some time to describe those sensations in full. It was very "Albertine." *Very.* Anyway, it's a horrible deep wound, and I know it will *never* heal. *Never.* There are things one doesn't recover from. Despite all my lechery, my waywardness, my self-ishness, my childishness—I loved June terribly. I do still (but I would never admit it to her again). I dream sometimes of having you meet her and talk to her. Of your giving her one of those frank, bitter talks which you know better than I how to hand out. Of seeing her wince. I wish her heart would break somehow. Not because I wish her ill, but because I am afraid she has no heart. I would like to imagine her *real* for five minutes. Anaïs has done a marvelous portrait of her in a book that no one wants. A book that antagonizes immediately. But she penetrated June as I never could. (And not thru hatred or jealousy—she *adores* June, believe it or not.)

I guess what got me was the image of June beside someone else—some young collegian, some empty bladder with an athletic body. She didn't even give herself time to grieve a little bit. She dropped me like an old coat. *Mentally.* Well, maybe she did, and maybe she didn't. Maybe she has a little private grief and anguish. Maybe once in a while she remembers what I was to her. What I can never be again to any woman! The way I am now is like stone. I can go off with anyone almost. This fancy-priced whore, for example. Why, I would follow her into hell if she said the word.

June crippled me. There's no getting away from it. I don't know what to tell you to tell her (Tell her to go fuck a duck!), should you ever see her. I notice she keeps clear of you. Tho' I know also she has a very high opinion of you. It was a long battle. There were times when I damned near sold you out. Anything to pacify her. Treachery, arson, theft, mur-der. Anything—just to hold her.

What I wouldn't give to run into her in the Village some night—
unexpectedly. I'd give her a hellful. But here I am and here I'll stay,
sucking off whores. (Greetings to Dr. Perry—"Dear 85, dear 85, we'll
honor thy fair name!" Ho ho!)

Well, I look forward to hearing about Renoir and Cézanne and Piero
della Francesca and Titian and even Rubens! These are the only things
that matter. *Cunt!* What's cunt? It's what we *feel* about cunt, what we work
off on the margin, as it were, that has value. *And only that!* I won't give
up the ghost for any cunt ever again. If they want to give me syphilis—
O. K. I shall write even with false teeth, even with a hole in my neck to
pour soup into. Even with my balls missing. There's something that
belongs to me—and no cunt will get that! (1:30 A.M. and my fine buxom
Renoir is surely sleeping in a dirty bedroom.) But do you know what she
said to me after the last session—"I was thinking of you all night!" And
I, the jackass, I believe it literally. So help me God, I believe it! That's
my weakness. And that should tell you how much of a thinker, how much
of a philosopher I am. "The master of pink toilet paper." O.K. Wipe your
ass!

HVM.

*   *   *   *

July 21st. 1933
Clichy

Emil:

I expect Fraenkel to be leaving for America tomorrow and this letter
will probably go with him on the boat and be mailed from New York or
delivered personally. There are other letters for you, in his care, and two
books (in manuscript, carbon copy) which you may read and then pass
back to him. He is going to try selling the novel for me in New York; the
other book, which is the last one I wrote, and which I like best, I want
to show to Buzby. *   *   *   *

Listen, about my book—the worst coming to the worst. Anaïs will sell
her fur coat and publish it privately. But I would prefer some kind and
noble gentleman with a little faith in humanity to step forward and as-
sume the risk. I would like that! But, if we publish it privately, don't forget
that we will clean up some dough. It is certainly sensational enough—and
it is only the first volume. The decks are all clear now and I am ready to

start the second volume. Treat Fraenkel well. He is an excellent fellow, and you will learn a lot from him. He likes hard liquor.

Henry

P.S. The Buñel MSS I will mail separately in case the boat sinks with Fraenkel.

Sept. 7th, 1933

Dear Emil:

Tonight America has charmed me and I want to tell you why—you the only American I ever knew who had what we call charm. All day I had been using high explosives. And I suppose there are still a few grenades left in my pockets which I forgot to fling at my tattered pages. Know to begin with that I am ploughing through the final draft of that *Self-Portrait* which, with amazing emendations and additions, now becomes *A Black Spring*, the heart of which I sent you from Louveciennes some months back. I felt this evening when I knocked off that I was entitled to a little relaxation, and wanting only a few quiet hours of repose I chose the cinema. And wanting a bad picture rather than a good one, because a bad one relaxes me more, I chose an Ernst Lubitsch—*Haute Pègre*—something like *Fancy Crooks* (I enclose the program to enlighten you).

As the picture opened I thought—good, it is starting off as usual with American pictures. Venice . . . a gondolier collecting the garbage cans and singing "O Sole Mia"—so absurd, even if it be realistic. But so American! But instantly I must tell you that, with the exception of this bloody gondolier serenading the garbage cans (he appears twice), the picture seems to me faultless. And not only faultless, but of a degree of perfection which I had never wished to attribute to said Ernst Lubitsch whom now I recall very vividly your having praised one night in front of a cinema on Atlantic Avenue—a Pola Negri-Emil Jannings picture—title gone.

Yes, tonight America exerted the full force of her charm and I must eat certain words and very gladly. Grâce à Ernst Lubitsch, a Croat or Hungarian or Viennese, the hard, brittle surface of our American ways attained to an almost Mozartian grace and dignity. Grâce à Miriam Hopkins also—perhaps the only truly charming female I have seen on the American screen. What added perhaps to the high brilliance of the picture was a strong unexpressed tension—for the audacity of these Americans. To

make that clear. . . . For thugs, crooks, gangsters, imbeciles there are no
actors to beat the American. The French have accepted that, bon gré, mal
gré. But to present a spectacle of manners, to move amidst the bric-a-brac
of high society, to soften that athleticism, that brutality of the Americans—for that they were not prepared. I take it that the principals were
Miriam Hopkins and Herbert Marshall. I do not know them—never saw
them before. * * * *

    * * * *

You have wanted to know what Anaïs is like. Well, in the person of
Miriam Hopkins you have as near a reproduction of Anaïs I can give
you—photogenically. The same wave and part of the hair, the same
lustrous quality to it; the same regal sway of the body and the elegance
that befits it; the same breadth of shoulder as contrasted with the slender,
willowy flanks; the same oval lines of the face, but not the same expression. If you put the two together I am sure they would not resemble each
other, but fragmenting them and then recomposing them at distance one
from the other, there is a peculiar similitude. Anaïs has a more serious,
a more pensive, a more tragic quality of face; it can turn to stone when
she is moved. The Hopkins woman remains on the surface, but with all
the surface depths that might be expected of a full-blooded woman raised
in another climate, another soil.

I won't bore you with details of the film, as you probably know it. I give
you a few reminiscences only, which certain gestures, scenes, poses
stirred in me. I was almost going to say—this Hopkins woman reminds
me of The Dark Lady of the Sonnets. But I am not thinking of Shakespeare's enigmatic figure at all. I am thinking rather of a woman whose
name is completely faded from my memory, she whom I think of as the
dark lady of the screen, the most intelligent, the most charming, the most
noble woman we ever produced on the screen. This ought to summon
her for you at once. She belongs to a period of about ten years back, I
should say. She was better than Miriam Hopkins—perhaps not quite so
good-looking. You went to see _her_, not the film. Her name should have
been Maud, because she was dark and tragic, and everything she touched
was poetic. She was one of the few women of stage or screen who knew
how to sit down, how to open a door. She knew how to do things—savoir
faire. She had everything, except genius. There was something lacking,
something which removed her eternally from the ranks of Duse, Mod-
jeska, and the others. Perhaps just that she was an American. Perhaps just
that.

I come away from the movies and I am sitting at a café in this cool
September Paris and my mind still dwells on the charm of this picture.
I recall nothing definite any more, but I seem to recall this other woman
of the screen and how she could lean against a magnificent panel, and

with scarcely a flexion of the finger, scarcely a turn of the head, convey to us in that glorious mute fashion which the old films sought all the richesse of her moods, all the inexpressible stirrings which no amount of dialogue can now give us. I never heard her speak—fortunately! But her body spoke—and perhaps it wasn't even her body, but something that emanated from her body, some mysterious, tangible, odorous essence which bathed her gestures in unforgettable eloquence. And as I sat on the terrasse, thinking of her and of all the beautiful silent films I had seen, it seemed to me that the great change which has come over us—of America particularly—is the change of tempo. Even then we were not back in the days of the horse and buggy, of the narrow cinder path where the bicyclists wheeled along on Sunday mornings. We were in 1920, let us say, or perhaps a little earlier. But with every year that elapses since the war the pace grows sharper, the music more strident, the manners more gauche. We are being screwed up to a pitch where with every slightest turn we create a rasping noise. The machines are well oiled, but not ourselves.

I talk to you about these times because when I come to write that book of the cinema which I mean to do at the first opportunity it must be that this background forms the springboard. I beg you to take this seriously and to aid me with your rich memory of what we like to call the golden days—such days, for example, as when we came away from a Jannings picture (that early one of the Polish wars, I think it was???) and we were in tears. I want to dig up, revivify these memories of the pictures which once meant something to us—because I have a bad memory in some ways, it does not fix with precision on dates, places, titles, plots, etc. I remember only what I myself created of value in these emotional reactions. And so I am filled with impressions, with moods—but I lack the form and detail which belongs to them.

With this period—somehow Atlantic Avenue figures strongly in it (you must have just returned from Europe)—belong our walks in Prospect Park in the evening, when glad to free myself from the Western Union and from B, I used to call on you in the near neighborhood of the Park and we would start on one of those leisurely ambles which are engraved in my memory because, I imagine now, your talk was saturated with the aura of a world I had never glimpsed. And how strange it is now that, from this little outpost of Clichy, I should be filling you with the contents of that same vessel which created in me such a fever, such a restlessness—such a despair, I should say—for never once then did I dream that it would be possible for me to visit these shores. * * * * What commenced in Prospect Park, with your blind stabs, is finished now—finished for me, at least, for the utmost of my capacities. There remains the soft Summer nights in which the whole question of Lawrence is enveloped—

the dark, lonely paths by the lake, the melancholy in which you wrapped everything, the beginnings of creation in myself, those god-awful empty streets of Brooklyn afterwards, those horrid brownstone stoops, those dreary lights on Flatbush Avenue and that scar of the Fifth Avenue-Sea Beach Elevated Line which makes the turn at Third Avenue and Flatbush. Many the night I turned under at Third Avenue to go to 284 Sixth Street where my friend Stanley would scrape together a meal together with insults and discouragements.

But about Lawrence . . . another thought occurs. If then I dreamed some day of writing, it was never to rival a man like Lawrence. When I would think of *Sons and Lovers* I would think of it as occupying some eternal place, classed with other perfect works of one time or another. To criticize him—far from my mind was that. Yet here was a man almost my age, older than me by only a few years. And I hadn't even begun to bud. And he was famous. He had already roamed all over Europe; he spoke Italian like a monkey, he introduced French locutions now and then; he wrote poetry, he painted. My God, he did everything. Courage, my lads, it is never too late! I remember a time a little later, when I had commenced in earnest—to be exact, I had been at it five years. And that night, in one of my exalted moods when I knew of what I was made and for what I was destined, I wrote a little note to June—don't worry, kiddo, we're coming through, etc. . . . We were then pretty well estranged. The Kronski woman had appeared—things were rolling on to doom, rolling merrily, as everyone could see except yours truly, the mad Ludwig, who believed in his friends, in June, in the world, etc. And so you know what I saw written on the back of that note when I filched it later from her bag—after a violent quarrel? *Five years!* Like a black mark against my good name, against all my serious efforts, against my good will, my high purpose, my desperate struggle to come alive. I never mentioned to her that I had seen this—but it took the wind out of my sail. It was eloquent, those FIVE YEARS. Nothing to show on the credit side, don't you know. No books published, no name, no money earned, no slightest recognition. And I was writing here in high fettle, signing off Ludwig or something, promising an eternity of bliss, etc. Always an *et cetera* with me!

＊　＊　＊　＊

When I was sitting on the terrasse I had other thoughts too. So happened that I was taking a fifty-franc bill from my wallet to pay for my drink. I'm sitting there kind of large and expansive, still imbued with the spirit of the 18th century as it filtered through the sinuous loins of Miriam Hopkins. (She wore a dress in a garden scene, with puffed sleeves, exactly like one Anaïs wore the other day—which is why, perhaps, when Paderewski saw her he said: "You have the beauty of another time.") I was thinking at the moment of how different it sounded in the French version when Miriam says in finest French: "Mais nous aurons beaucoup de temps devant nous, mon cher ami . . . des semaines, des mois, des années." Have you any idea how lovely that sounds in French? How that restores the original Lubitsch motif? Because, what is it that constitutes the charm of his direction? Is it not that his delicacy, his pursuit of fragile surface contours, lends to every movement, every object, a musical value which is expressed by the words "18th century"? He not only retards time, not only arrests it, but he imprisons it in a mirror whose lies have a perfection of their own. . . . Be that as it may, at this moment when I am courting the grace of Mozart, a whore espies me lifting the fifty-franc note from my wallet. She knows well that it is a fifty-franc note. She smiles in recognition of its full value. I smile. I smile because I think there is a charm too in this frank recognition of values. There is something 18th century about it. For we are living now in an age when all values are confounded. The incident passes off with this mutual smile, based on a profound misunderstanding. The next moment I am thinking of horses and buggies, of the tempo of before the turn of the century, of the period which marks us as men of another generation, and I am proud that I was born in the 19th century and not in the 18th or the 20th. I think of the spires of Martinville which Proust glimpsed from an open carriage, and I think to myself—that is how one must always see the spires of Martinville—from an open carriage. I remember then all the turns in the Delaware River as we rode one Sunday afternoon from Narrowsburg to God knows where. I remember the horses farting and the yellow shit full of bird-seed tumbling over the harness and staying there all afternoon. I remember this, that it never seemed bad taste, never seemed offensive, ill-bred, when the horse farted in your face. Even the odor he left behind, as he trotted briskly forward, was pleasurable. Such is the horse.

When I leave the café to pursue my usual way along the Avenue de Clichy towards the Porte, I suddenly come upon a drunkard dancing in front of another café—Chez Richard, at La Fourche—and now again a fine feeling of approbation comes over me. On the edge of the curb is a blind man strumming the strangest instrument I have ever seen; the terrasse is crowded with working men and women . . . we are approaching the low quarters of the city. And a few paces off, moving with imbecilic rhythm, is this drunkard, and the crowd on the terrasse watches in amusement, an amusement finely differentiated from derision or scorn or disgust. And then, Emil, by Jesus, the curious thing happens that on the other side of the street, a whore who had been standing against the shutters waiting for her prey, suddenly grows inspired, grows intoxicated by the music and by the crazy drunkard's antics too, no doubt, and she lifts her dresses with a grand whoop-la and commences to do a jig. And there, by God, you have the real spirit of Paris. The man of the streets, the woman of the streets, the open café, the tolerance, the amusement, the wasting of time, the indifference, the common humanity. . . . A soft, gentle moment which in America would produce a jagged note. The suffering that could create this is sponged off. One forgets that the whore is going to stop jigging and begin that unspeakable muttering, that desperate pleading of three in the morning on an empty street; one forgets that the bum who is dancing on the curb is going to lie down somewhere in a dirty alley, on an old newspaper and snore the night away and get up with dirt in his eyes and hold out his trembling hands for a few sous. One forgets all that, as one forgets in the Lubitsch presentation that this world of Venice and fancy crooks is an imaginary limbo invented by Hollywood.

I had intended to write more. Made a lot of notes, but the typewriter, like the paintbrush, and the daylight lamp, takes it out of you. Call it a letter—for the time being.

"What by that?" says Aaron.

"Why, just this—that I'm tired."

Is that a good enough excuse?

The Cabinet Minister.

V

THE OTHER HEMISPHERE OF BEING

1933–34

During Miller's fifth year in Paris the letters reflect a change of mood, a lowering of intensity after years of turmoil. June had finally disappeared from his life. His rage and hunger were gone, replaced by a sense of achievement. He was sure of himself as a writer now. Although he maintained his Spenglerian view that the world was on the brink of disaster, personally he was serene, taking a detached, philosophical, "Chinese" view of things.

In 1934 he was still preoccupied with the four books he had begun two years earlier. After many postponements *Tropic of Cancer* came out in September, and he sent copies to friends in New York; one letter shows him anxiously awaiting Schnellock's reaction. He continued to struggle with the book on D. H. Lawrence but set aside *Tropic of Capricorn* for the time being, though he was still going over his past life with that book in mind. Mainly, though, he was making progress with *Black Spring*, sending part of the "dream section" that eventually appeared as "Into the Night Life." He had already sent a piece entitled "The Genesis of a Masterpiece," which was an early version of another section of *Black Spring*, "The Angel Is My Watermark!" And his friend Walter Lowenfels, referred to as Jabberwocky Cronstadt in one of the letters, was the subject of still another section, "Jabberwhorl Cronstadt."

His personal life was still centered on Anaïs Nin, who continued to provide moral and financial support. Thanks to her he was able to move into a studio apartment in the Villa Seurat, a street of new buildings designed for artists and writers, where he had stayed once when Michael Fraenkel took him in. Anaïs still shared his passion for writing—his as well as her own—but she had become increasingly absorbed in psychoanalysis, first as a patient of Otto Rank, then as a collaborator. Rank, who had been one of Freud's earliest and closest disciples, had broken with Freud and moved to Paris in the 1920s. In 1934 he decided to move his practice to New York, and Anaïs followed him there. Everyone seemed to be going to America; all the Paris friends, and now Anaïs. Suddenly

Miller decided to go too. His last letter to Emil before leaving registers very mixed emotions as he contemplates his departure from Paris, perhaps forever, and his return to New York. As it turned out, he was only to stay a few months and to spend the rest of the decade happily ensconced in the Villa Seurat, but he had no way of knowing that at the time.

[December 16, 1933]   Saturday—16th
                                       4, Avenue Anatole France
                                       Clichy (Seine), France

Dear Emil:

   *   *   *   *

Just this morning Anaïs stopped in to bring me an electric heater (we are still in the grip of zero weather and these houses and the heating are inadequate). *   *   *   *   You know, of course, that she has been taking care of me all along—otherwise where would I be? Dead, no doubt, for there is no way of getting along otherwise. Seriously speaking—if you do take the bull by the horns, and decide to venture it over here—for a year or so—I can do a lot to curtail your expenses, if you think you could share a place with me successfully. I am just about to move out of here, and take a place near her. She is coming in to Paris for three months, a furnished place for the winter, as Louveciennes is almost unbearable in dead winter. That means that I will find a semi-studio place for the time being, perhaps indefinitely—in the Passy section, which is the ritzy section of Paris—just off the Trocadéro and Eiffel Tour district you know. All new, practically, chic, modern, expensive. When spring comes and she returns to Louveciennes, I shall either remain in Passy or go out in the country near her—around Garches, Marne-la-Coquette, etc. Delightful country! (On the general road to Versailles, St. Germain-en-Laye, etc. Wonderful old forests, 18th century houses, and so on.) You see, I can cook pretty well—damned well, I may say. Without slaving over it, of course. Always a fine wine with the meal (I have a bottle of Vouvray cooling now), good cheese, the best cuts of meat, and whatever you like for vegetables—with salad mâche and betteraves (beets) included. Fred is not coming with me—in fact, I am glad to be free of him—though we are good friends still.

   *   *   *   *

Anaïs has lots of friends, lots of connections—in the social world. She has just finished her analysis with Dr. Otto Rank, whose book, you said, gave you a pain in the head. But I think you would change your opinion if I could talk to you about him, or have you meet him. I expect to get quite close to him this winter—only my natural timidity prevented me from doing so sooner—as he has pressed me to visit him on a basis of friendship. Now he knows all about me. And he is a man, Emil, who, unlike the other psychoanalysts, is almost entirely interested in the "artist." He is considered an outlaw, practically, and is very much against Freud and Allendy and the other scientific spirits who are stratifying the theory. I found him marvellously flexible, subtle, sympathetic—a mind like Spengler's, very, very human, very modest, very curious. And, owing to his interest in the artist, he knows all the big painters and writers here (he has their canvases on his wall, he has treated many of them as patients, etc.). You see how things interlock. What I am driving at is this—that never in my life was I more favorably placed—to make the right contacts (*contacts!* I hate that word—it smells like America, like the advertising lingo—but take it in the best sense). I have kept rather aloof, free of entangling relations, free of bores and pests—which I never could do heretofore. A little lonely, at times, but inwardly content, richer, surer of myself. I can meet the biggest now and swap blow for blow. No false modesty, no false timidity. And a certain hard, tough deliberate gunning to make only those who are worthwhile to me—*who can nourish me.* And why not? Why should I waste myself on the lesser fry? The others are just as human, just as interesting, and as sympathetic—and just as eager for the proper companionship. (Understand, that out of my heterogeneous relations in the past I gained a great deal—it was gold for me. But I don't require it any more. My "anecdotal life," as Zadkine puts it, is finished. My future adventures will take place in the spirit. (Is *that bad, pobba?*)

* * * *

You asked about "horoscopes." I enclose a rough draft of mine, as I copied it from the original. The elaboration of this is in process—and when I get it you will have a copy, if it amuses you. Anaïs is a lot more interested than I am, and through her her husband has become quite expert on the subject. He has a whole library on it. And they have decorated the walls of the studio, in Louveciennes, with their respective horoscopes—and very interesting it is to see. I merely repeat, that as horoscopes go, mine is considered remarkable. But I don't attach much importance to it. I am still skeptical. Only, I do admit the most remarkable correspondences. And whether it was the influence of the stars, or the working out of a blind inner process, I do also see how my life-pattern has altered in the last few years, and the part that I myself played in influencing my own destiny—I mean where I *abetted* it, as it were. Rank, in his book, *Art and Artist,* has some marvellous things to say about the old astrology, its place and significance in human life. Chapter called "Macrocosm and Microcosm." A big subject, and a revelatory one.

*   *   *   *

Alas, we are witnessing the death-throes of the individual life. Spengler is unfortunately too right. But we, as individuals, as men, can at least register our protest. I do not want to belong to this Communistic future of nobodies, where it is all peace on earth and good will to man, at $7.50 a day and no overtime. The present is bad, the past is irretrievable—but the future is black, black, Emil. *Black Spring!* Alors, merry Christmas, just the same, and do tell me what you think about yourself, your plans, your future, and what I might do for you.   *   *   *   *

Henry

*   *   *   *

Feb. 15 (?) 1934
24, Rue des Marronniers
Paris (XVI), France
This is the Passy district—
all the swell shits live here!
Write here. O.K.

Dear Emil:

The above is my address for the time being—another month or so. I shall be writing again before leaving here. Should you by any chance pack up and come over, and not find me, just get in touch with Fred Perlès at the Chicago *Tribune*, Rue Lamartine, off the Rue Lafayette—the main plant—downstairs in the basement—the proofreaders' department. He will always know where I am.

I am now living in the ritzy section of Passy—just the other extreme from *Clichy.* Moved just before the Revolution! Suppose you have read all about it by this time. Paris was very strange, weird during the few days of suspense. The first night—when they nearly stormed the Chamber of Deputies—I didn't know that a demonstration was about to occur. I had not read a newspaper for a week or more, was engrossed in my Lawrence book, thoroly isolated—and the very evening when the crash came I walked right into the middle of it—instinctively. Walked in and out again—in a hurry. I thought at first, seeing the streets so empty, so sinisterly bare, that a parade was taking place. Gradually it dawned on me that something *real* was about to happen. I was at Richelieu-Druot, on the

Grands Boulevards, hemmed in by police and soldiers. Had the queer sensation (so true when you are in danger) that I was a target. Saw the mob pressing me flat against the walls and the bullets mowing us down. Realized that I was in a net. Looked frantically about for an exit. Got home just as the thing broke loose. And you know by this time that the fight at the Place de la Concorde and all along the Boulevards was very very real. Paris changed in those few hours tremendously. One could feel all over again the bloody drama of the Revolution. The crowd was ugly. Had the Cabinet not resigned I think the city would have been burned down. Terrific damage occurred in a few hours.

The queer and perhaps fortunate thing was that the crowd lacked a leader. Not a man on the horizon. ("The *untragic* age," as I say.) On Friday night, when the Communists staged their little war, the scene was even more terrible. One of those winter nights of thick, choking fog, every shop and bistro boarded up, the lights floating in a murky halo, the sound of police whistles, shots, windows crashing, etc. All in a thick fog. Quite a few killed—about a thousand wounded. Barricades up. But a complete fiasco. I suppose the newsreels are showing it over there. Here they have been censored and suppressed—hardly anything is given. The public is still uneasy. Queasy. It isn't over yet—Doumergue and his coalition cabinet won't last long, I fear. The thing will crack open again—and more organized this time. When you know how comparatively well off France is, in comparison with America, one wonders how America ever staved off a revolution. (Not that I think France will go Communist! Not yet! Fascist more likely!) Here and in the U. S. the middle class is still powerful. But gradually, it seems to me, we are moving towards the Roman stage of dissolution—the mob and the tyrants. The battle between *money* and *blood,* as Spengler says. A long drawn-out affair. In America I can see the makings of wonderful tyrants, wonderful sadists, degenerates, perverts, etc.—rising from the gangster world. And that army of wage-slaves gradually turned into robots who must be fed and amused—because they surrendered what inner life, what individuality they had, to the machine. The middle class will be ground to dust between the millstones, disappear entirely, and with them the notion of "democracy" and "freedom"—*illusions.*

* * * *

You were quite right about your view of psychoanalysis. Don't you perceive more and more that I am *exposing* the whole thing? (You will, when you see more MS.) But first I had to know, to *understand* clearly myself, what it was all about. I feel I have gone to the bottom of it. (When the middle class is abolished, the neurotics and the *"soul doctors"* will go with it!) For me, as for Lawrence, everything had to be personally and passionately experienced, tested. I can't dispose of things just intellectually. Anaïs was again impressed by your letter. She gets your personality remarkably well. She likes you—and understands why there is such a strong sympathy between us. She thinks you're always intuitively right, that you're a person of fine feelings, of sound judgment—she likes your attitude towards life. * * * *

* * * *

As I already told you, when you get ready to come over, we can arrange a way to live. You put it on any basis that satisfies you and leaves you easy in your heart and mind. I quite understand your feelings. *Even I* experienced those qualms, you know. (Where do you suppose all the violence and bitterness of my books comes from?) But the more I live the more I can get beyond that—I mean the feeling of humiliation with its constant reaction of bitterness. I have gotten a better slant on people—that is, I don't expect too much of them, don't overestimate them. The root of all idealism! With its consequent guilt-sin-neurosis circle of viciousness. I don't accept the world, and never will, I suppose—but I can live in it! Maybe that's something. And furthermore I won't have my books being an excuse for not living. I'm not going to live vicariously, in Art. How to live accordingly, and not be a hypocrite, not surrender, is in itself an art. I think already I show a great deal less ranting, in my work, than Lawrence—but keeping the *explosive,* the *dynamic,* the rebellious quality.

My work on Lawrence has been *enormous!!!* Can't begin to tell you all. The book will speak for itself. I practically smashed it to pieces in order to get a more secure foundation. Now I have it—but it cost me a year of intense effort. And to say one does this for art, or for the world, is foolish. *I am the gainer. I* fought something out—to a conclusion. Not just tackling a problem, as so many *finished* writers do, but living through a thing, body and soul, till one almost dies of it. That is what I mean by *creative effort.* That is a surrender which yields a certain eternal sort of triumph—not paid for in fame or money or success. In two years I have learned much. I have established myself, for myself at least, as a real artist, one with the best. I mean it! I know my own worth now—the world will catch on slowly, maybe never—but I think it will. What I've got is vital and durable—in this rotten age or any age. I don't fear. I've won my battle—the rest is tinsel, whether it be recognition or ignominy. And this, you will see, makes of me, or designates me, as a profound optimist. If I die tomorrow it won't matter. *I won't die.*

Alors, pobba—am I patting myself on the back again, and too much? I want to see you come over. I'll guarantee the *privacy* of your life. I won't talk you to death. I won't criticize. We're getting to be ripe old codgers. I think once I used to be rather "interfering." I'm cured of that. The philosophy is gradually getting converted to deed and gesture. More and more I talk and act as I write and think. The inner reality and the outer get more finely, adequately adjusted. Why, for all I know, you may find a Chinaman on your hands when you arrive. You may not recognize me any more.

(*China!* That's a very significant word with me now. I've *created* a whole new China!)

I don't understand all about your coloring scheme, and your enthusiasm and confidence in it—but I do hope it pans out some. I don't think I'd worry much about what you have to do for a living. Don't let any job or mode of living get you to a state where you look down on yourself. Serve God *and* Mammon—if possible. Inwardly you're all right. Don't make too big an issue of things. Take it more nonchalantly. If you stop fighting with yourself, stop worrying about your pride and all that, the water colors will come of themselves. It's the terribly false outer world that gets you rattled. Settle with the world—throw it its bone—and be clear of rancor. The sun, the spring, even the birds, pobba, it's all *in you*—or nowhere. Think of the marvellous things that came out of the Black Plague—always out of the blackest times. If you face death and accept it—whatever death means to you personally—you will live again. It's not Lawrence I'm giving you—it's what I really believe and know to be so myself. A man doesn't live *many lives*, as they say, unless and until he dies many individual deaths. Everything is won with pain and sacrifice, at the cost of bitter illusions.

Sign here _____!

* * * *

It's now Feb. 26th.—never had a chance to finish this, so will sign off here, and continue in next. Haven't even reread it—so it's all Greek to me.

Am sending you with this *part* of the "dream section"; there are over 90 pages. I'll put the balance in the next envelope. Have dropped work on *Black Spring* to finish the Lawrence book at demand of publisher. A marvellous book, Emil—I'm going nuts. It's the pivotal point of my career. "The soft bloom of being!"

Henry

P.S. Anaïs is here with me for a week and working her head off for me on my vast notes and materials for the Lawrence book. It looks like a prison camp here. * * * *

May 12th 1934
Grand Hôtel de la Havane
44, Rue de Trevise, Paris (9)

Dear old Sock!

You can't imagine what a tremendous relief it was to get your "note of evasion"! Except for the tortures June put me through I must say that never in my life have I waited so feverishly for news from home. * * * *

And so, even tho' I learn you are broke, ill, desperate etc. (a relative *schnellochian* desperation, I take it!), it is something. If you had a nice long illness I could look forward with pleasure to writing you regularly. * * * *
* * * *
* * * * Don't die on me first! I know how desperate everything is—but I was *so* desperate long before this world-disillusionment that now I can scarcely take interest in the universal calamity—hardly even in yours, if I tell the god's truth. And that is hateful to admit. It doesn't mean indifference—it means that with respect to certain emotions the rubber band has been stretched to breaking. I am less sentimental, less clownish, less *personal* maybe. I have no illusions and no hopes—therefore everything is jake and each thing is a gift. If I ever became self-supporting (or won a lottery ticket!) I would indulge my emotional self and do something drastic about your miserable condition. As it is, I only see in you a previous incarnation of myself—and at some time or other in the last four years *I definitely died*—and what lives on is a cruel jester who feeds on catastrophes. *But no indifference*—underneath! Do you follow me at all? One thing after another I saw smashed, done for, buried. How can one care greatly any more, in any *personal* way? Everything does become truly *symbolic.* (I liked that bit in the Lawrence MSS.) Means a great deal to me.

But take it this way always, Emil—the fact that I write you and practically only to you is significant of my rock-bottom sincere emotional being. I cling to you desperately—you are the last link between me and the world I departed from. (I never knew when I left how fateful and irrevocable was the step. In *Tropic of Capricorn*, which I hope to *start next year* (!), I shall make this point clear.

I couldn't sleep all night after receiving your letter. Went over my whole life, year by year, almost month by month. A fantasia of dates and incidents and people and dramas. But as tho' someone else—*not me*—had done these things. Wondered would I ever again see the scene of these 38 years. By a curious piece of irony I had my palm read the other night by "Bijoux," an ex-whore, who is crazy now, or "eccentric." Predicted a life till 80 or more, no accidents, great voyages, much **much luck, mar-**

riage to a beautiful young girl, etc. Everything superlatively swell! Of course I don't believe this crap—I did it to give her a few sous. But I did think to myself—strange, but this sounds almost like what I have already experienced. Down to the last detail.

And tonight, leaving Jabberwocky Cronstadt, I was speculating on whether I should take the studio-apartment he offers me—just to put you up for a while!

It is a marvellous place—with sun parlor, bath, steam heat, space, etc. and the price has been reduced to 700 francs a month for me, *tout compris*. Now in America that's a ridiculously low sum for such a place. Here it is still high (about twice what I now pay in my hotel). Funny, I like my cheap hotel—like its crazy wallpaper, the stains on the wall, the odor of mildew, the broken things, etc. Even the noise! For I have selected the very busiest district imaginable—one short block from the Rue Lafayette, from Chicago *Tribune*, from Folies-Bergère—etc. I like the bustle and smell and sweat and dirt—for a while anyhow. But to come back to the studio! Where do you think it is? Fraenkel's place— Villa Seurat! I am almost afraid to go back there—ghosts! And especially since everything connected with that place is broken off. Jabberwocky is the last of the Mohicans. Incidentally he showed me a letter from Fraenkel in which the sorrowful Werther recounts that to date he has done $35,000 worth of business—could retire if he could collect all outstanding debts.

*   *   *   *

Part II

Terrasse of the Trois Portes Café

Full sunshine—paper itself is hot! 11:00 A.M. Breakfast. Metro Cadet, Rue Lafayette. Sunday morning. *Catholic* Sunday! Wrote you in bed last night—and have hay fever this morning. There's only one ambition I have as age creeps on—to find a quiet spot in the *sun!* Believe me, I never noticed the weather or climate heretofore, but four years of interior living—within the damp walls of French houses—makes you weep when you get full sunshine. France has her Midi of course—south of the Loire it begins. In my way of looking at things it is there, on that French Mason and Dixon line that the earth has its true axis. The more you read about the great ones the more you find that the decisive turning point in their lives is that period when they discover the South in themselves and live out the other hemisphere of their being. All wisdom, as I see it, consists in reconciling these two faces (*our* European life). The fusion of the Romantic and the Classic spirits. In the northern world idealism, striving,

Idea. In the South life for its own sake, hedonism, action and contempla-
tion, ideas related to living. Goethe is a marvellous example of the blend-
ing of these two hostile spirits and his triumph over them.

Still thinking of your letter. What you said about the *Dreams.* Can you
say any more? I wanted your reaction to this Section as a piece of literature. It was an experiment. Does it come off? Does it convey the dream
quality? I am dubious of it. I expect to rewrite, condensing the episodes
but expanding the dream-state itself. The *Black Spring* has architectural
dimensions. I have it all clearly charted out—and the greater part done.
The *Dream* motif is like the nucleus. In each section there is a repetition
of the principal motifs, each time with a new emphasis—Streets, Violence, China, etc. There were parts of the dreams I thought superb
myself—the Brooklyn Bridge thing, the cock and scissors (Gertie Imhof),
the edelweiss in my heart, the return to Decatur Street, etc. Where I left
off I had expected to explode into life—to give, in a way, a sensation thru
words of the *"trauma of birth."* So tell me!!

*   *   *   *

Meanwhile I am rewriting *Tropic of Cancer* over again, as I told you. Hard
job. Hard to imagine that empty belly and the fever and the agony and
the suspense and the nightmares. Mostly it's the construction of it I'm
altering. And eliminating, as usual. Weeding out the useless shit. Putting
in new shit.

*   *   *   *

The menus are just a beginning. I will write my letters now and then
on the backs of menus gathered from all the joints I patronize. When you
come you bring the menus along and try out these places. In that way you
will quickly get to know the city.

*   *   *   *

So long.

Henry.

P.S. Try to fill the page next time. Always a mystery to me how a guy can
end a letter in the middle of a page. Make postscripts. I like the ragged
notes. Like everything that's calligraphic.

*   *   *   *

14th July, 1934
18 bis Ave. de Versailles
Paris (16)

Dear Emil:

* * * *

Voici un menu séduisant! As I told you I have been saving them up for my correspondence paper. It may serve to recall some old scenes. This one from a little street just around the corner from Les Folies-Bergère and my last hotel—Havane. A few doors from a good whorehouse.

* * * *

You ask about the *T. of C.* It is in the press now—I am reading proof—will be out in September now. I didn't get the least kick out of seeing the proofs. No emotion whatever—unless disgust. If I do a lousy water color it gives me pleasure to look at it—even for the thousandth time. But a book! Bah! It's so dead, once you've got it out of your system. Perhaps a good painter feels that way too about his paintings. I don't know. I never met any.

* * * *

I really have a curiosity to see N.Y. since Prohibition is finished. Must have changed a bit, eh? You will see from the backs of the menus (I forget, I am not sending you those which have wine lists on the back—because there is no room to write), but anyway, from the wines you see listed, I wonder how many you can buy over there at a reasonable price? Is the vin ordinaire any good? Can you get a half bottle of Beaujolais, for example, for 25 cents? That is a good average red wine, as I suppose you know. A Macon is still better. And a Châteauneuf-du-Pape encore mieux. Tell me about them, Emil. If I thought I could stroll up Broadway and find a little restaurant where there was good wine and good food, and where one could sit indefinitely and watch all those swell females (which Céline writes about—*where are they?*) I would perhaps feel fairly content. Sit there discussing old times with you. That's one thing I've learned to do here—sit and do nothing. Just eat and drink and watch the crowd go by. And I must have my Gauloises Bleus—can't smoke an American cigarette for the life of me—haven't done so in over three years now. * * * *

Yes, lately I've thought more than ever that I might like to go back for a visit. Just to see the big change. To hear English on all sides. To see nothing but million dollar legs. To visit the Roseland and the Irving Burlesk. To sit under the Brooklyn Bridge. Ah that, especially. One of the first things I would do is to grab hold of you and put on the walking shoes. Go to Wallabout Market towards dusk, along by 23rd Street Ferry, down on Second Avenue. . . . Und so weiter. . . .

* * * *

I notice, in rewriting the *T. of C.* that it abounds with food and drink. Uterine hunger! Anaïs and I are just struggling over a preface—the editor insists on one, because he says it's too hair-raising and must be explained. So we begin: "Here is a book that should restore one's appetite for the fundamental realities." Appetite. That's the key word. And a good digestion. The rest is literature. "My idea up till now in collaborating with myself has been to present a resurrection of the emotions." Soit. Evil to him who evil thinks. * * * *

Or I could say: My aim has been to present an erection. Without a preface. The bat, penis libre. Jesus, I had to sweat some in rewriting that book. Rewrote the whole god-damned thing from beginning to end. Only left about thirty pages intact. * * * *

Faithfully yours.
Paint me a line or two soon.
Henry.

Friday, 1934. Paris

Dear Emil:

* * * *

Osborn just sent me some clippings from the *Telegram*, I imagine—a series of articles by a certain M. Liebling dealing with the expatriates who have returned to N.Y. and meet back of the Gotham Book Mart. And behold Wambly Bald figures therein, as "a brilliant wit"—and his last column is quoted—or a good part of it—the part I knocked out for him, because he was empty and at his wit's end. (Don't mention this to anyone—just between ourselves.) But it's so funny to see my own words quoted under another man's name. And I'm about the only expatriate left over here. Lowenfels and Hiler are returning shortly. I'll be the Last of the Mohicans. I'm rather proud of it too—because when I left I had no exile complex and have none now. I feel free of all cults, isms, movements, countries, latitudes, and philosophies. I am alone, a man, an artist, by Jesus, and I want nothing to do with these sap-heads—Putnam, Gillespie, Bald, etc. *Cripes!* Nor with Pound or Eliot or Joyce. They talk like weather experts who always manage to predict sunshine when it rains.

* * * *

You know, occasionally you walk about like a ghost, searching for familiar faces. It's almost five years now. Everybody's leaving. It's like being left in a desert isle. I can't make any worthwhile friendships. Either something wrong with me, or with the world. I'm getting fucking critical of people. At present I have a semi-friendship with a German Jew, Heinz Liepman, who just wrote a big success—*Murder in Germany*—perhaps you've heard of it. He has only a year to live—they busted his kidneys with their blackjacks and their thick boots.

Henry

* * * *

This guy, Michonze, whom I took a lesson from—I don't give a damn about his lessons, but I would like to help him. So I pretended I needed lessons in order to buy him a meal or hand him a suit of clothes. Etc. Poor bastard. He's been here 12 years and never had one exhibition. He never has a cent. Lives in a wretched garret, sleeping on the springs of the bed. No water. No heat. Frightful. And yet he's optimistic about the future. Believes in his own genius. (The other day he and I called on Hiler while the latter was in the midst of a job. Hiler asks Michonze if he would like to help. Michonze says yes, grabs a brush and goes to it. Afterwards Hiler gave him *ten* francs. That's worth about a half-dollar here.) Michonze blushed. Hiler blushed. Hiler says—"Do you want more?" Michonze says "No!" But I could see he was mortified. And Hiler too was mortified. It's terrible. What value has an artist's time when he is unrecognized? Less than nothing. But the saddest part of all is that Michonze is not a genius. Or if he is, he gives no proof of it. You would think that 12 years of struggle and suffering would reveal itself in some way in an artist's work. Often nothing is revealed. Michonze paints Jewish literary scenes of a fantastic medieval quality—neither Surrealistic nor crazy nor anything else. They are all Michonze, but Michonze is nothing. If the wrong man suffers it doesn't count. Even a dog can suffer.

* * * *

One night I heard some old tune that sounded so American that suddenly, before I knew what had happened to me, I began to weep. The other day too, sitting outdoors at a restaurant, I broke down hysterically over the mention of some familiar episode of the past. One never knows when it will bob up. This last was occasioned more particularly by a talk about N.Y. Anaïs was offering me the chance to go back for a month. It was so vivid in my mind that I was already walking the streets and holding conversation with everybody. Then suddenly I realized that I would never go back unless it was with some prestige. A vain thought, but there you are. If I ever come back for a while it must be in a different way than I left. Otherwise I'll stay here and die here and the hell with the past. I couldn't think of flopping at Decatur Street, for example. When I think of that neighborhood, that life, I go crazy. That *would* drive me completely nuts. No, I'm going to stick it out a while longer. If things don't

turn for the better soon I'll be amazed. It's ten years now since I started
to write. And though there's damned little to show for it I don't feel like
a Michonze. Not yet! I'm sick of being a Romantic figure. That's just
literature.

*   *   *   *

Henry

8/28/34
18 bis, Ave. de Versailles
Paris (xvi) France

Dear Emil:

*   *   *   *

It is just possible I may make some dough out of *Tropic of Cancer.* (It
comes out in September and I may send you a few copies thru Hiler who
is returning for good early in September.) I have just written a preface,
by the way, for some expensive albums of his, dealing with his Indian
paintings and designs. He expects to open a café in N.Y. for artists—with
library, bar, and other things.

To get back to my book. As you know, it can't be distributed either in
England or America. If it proves as sensational as I imagine, some clever
guy over there will be getting out a pirated edition. I have always thought
Joe O'Regan just the guy to do that sort of thing. But of course he is
always broke. Maybe my friend Doc Conason would finance it. ? ? ? Once
I thought of Buzby, but I doubt now if he is sufficiently interested, or even
in a position, financially, to handle such a venture.

Even if I only sell out the first edition I feel quite confident Kahane (the
publisher) will put out the 2nd one—*Black Spring.* He's just cagey and
waiting to see what will happen. Once he had me contracted for three
books, but then he got cold feet and let the contract run out.

Fred is now dickering with a printer to get his first novel—*Title to
Follow*—published. It can be done for only 3,000 francs (about $175.00).
That's not much, is it? It would be excellent if both our books came out
together, as they are really companion books, written at the same time
and almost in the same place. He has used my real name throughout—it
seems very strange to see it that way. And some of the episodes dovetail.
If Anaïs got hers out too that would be ripping. Shit, I'd be a celebrity!
But there seem to be a lot of *ifs* here.

There is another book, by a friend of mine named Edgar Calmer (a

Virginia fellow) who calls me *Irving Brace* in his book *Always Summer,* which is being published by Harcourt Brace & Co. He has me killed at the end of the book—run down by a taxi while in an ecstatic mood. (Not to mention that he plagiarized a few paragraphs from *T. of C.*—which I thought a good joke, particularly because he didn't think I noticed them.)

If I mention all this crap it's only to show you that eventually there may be a way of publishing my own stuff at my own expense—a thing I have no hesitancy in doing, as I don't propose to wait all my life to be recognized by the idiots who rule the book mart. That's why I am willing even to practice psychoanalysis if necessary. I want my say, and I won't compromise in how I say it. I think myself that eventually I'll get an audience. It only needs courage and persistence.

*   *   *   *

                                                                Henry

                                                Oct. 25, 1934
                                                18 Villa Seurat (xiv)
                                                Paris, France

Dear Emil:
    Your letter came the other day and I held up answering you thinking that you might have received the book meanwhile and be writing me again. Had a letter from Osborn and one from Buzby, the latter enclosing a check (!—swell), so theirs got through all right. I do hope you got yours, because I made a special little water color on the title page for you, as a proof of my affection.

*   *   *   *

In case I don't get to New York in December, as I hope to, Anaïs will surely look you up. She must go—it's an official visit. Myself I want to go terribly. I want to go terribly; I feel it would do me good. Especially the *Tropic of Capricorn!* It would renew all those old nerve centers which are withering slowly. Just a peek at Wilson's joint, at the Palace, at the Roseland, at Minsky's.   *   *   *   *   I spent all last Sunday afternoon at Walter Lowenfels' joint singing at the top of my lungs—the first time since I'm here—singing all the old records, from "Old Bill Bailey" and "Monkey Land," and "Aren't You the Feller," etc. down to "Mandalay" and "Poor Butterfly." Haven't had such a joyous release in ages. With a worn out old piano, full of sour notes. The windows open on the big court and all the French bourgeoisie craning their necks with fright and merriment. I'd like to sing that way again—even if off key—when I hit your place. Have you still got all the old songs? Do you remember "Lorraine" and "Put on Your Old Grey Bonnet"!

Interruption.

Continuing at Lipp's Brasserie on the Blvd. St. Germain. . . . Want to reply to some of the points raised in your letter. Do you know, that line of yours—"All you have to do etc. is to convey your quality to the reader"—why that is practically what Walter Pater said, in writing of Botticelli. The letters are probably much better than my finished work for that very reason—there are no barriers then. Certainly there are several good books in that stack of correspondence. Bet your ass! The hell of it is I have to die first. Maybe not! Maybe I'll get so fucking famous one day that we'll publish them in a deluxe edition—*Letters Before Death,* or some such title. *And you'll illustrate them!*

* * * *

You said another strange thing in your letter. The line was—"The first question is—Am I an artist?" Now, if you have the *T. of C.* you will see how I had to answer, or dispose of, that question too. Several people have told me they were much impressed by the way in which I stated it. I wonder if it struck you the same way.

No, you're an artist all right. You were from the very beginning. I mean from the days of *"dear old 85."* Never forget my first impression of you. Don't seem to recall previous meetings—only that day shortly before Christmas when you stood up and quietly and efficiently proceeded to cover the blackboard with Christmas trees and Santa Clauses. You should have gone straight from 85 to Paris or Italy, to an academy—even tho' they say it's bad for one. The atmosphere of Europe would have permanently cleared up all this fog and miasma of doubt and futility which seems to hang over you. I blame America and her ideas of "progress"— especially this fucking advertising racket, which undermines a good young man because it provides him too early in life with a quick and material success. If you were only an illustrator (as you sometimes call yourself), if you were only a good advertising man you wouldn't be worrying about painting *other* things. You'd do your work and get drunk regularly. *America will create doubts in any man.* Because fundamentally the whole psychology of the people is *against* art—real art. America is profoundly conservative in these things, as she is primitive in religious matters. No doubt about it. A man is nourished by the atmosphere he breathes, not by money, success, etc.

As for myself, I'm going on with head down, like a bull. I *will* do what I want. I'll write what I want, how I want. Fuck them! I have one life and it belongs to me. They can rob me of everything but this—*I will!*

I'm not reading Thomas Mann any more, any more. No Sir! Thru with him! Reject him! He's a polished, finished craftsman—and that's why I drop him. He's 30 years behind the day. * * * * Every bastard like Mann who remains alive and turns out more and more books is a nail in our coffin. They smother us. Dead leaves. Fine autumnal russets, etc.—but of what use? Whither and what? Ho! He's made his grave and now he must lie in it. *To the worms!*

The studio here is swell—perfect! except that it gives you neuralgia. Always a fly in the ointment. If you have light and air and space you have *draughts* too. And I have no covering any more on top. No shag-pate, what! I work with a hat and shawl on. Just got out of bed today—after a severe cold. Must get acclimated. Have steam heat, but the French are slow. Had to wait too long. Like that they'll be the death of me some day. That's what caused poor old Barthou's death. He had to go get a taxi and find a doctor all by himself. Imagine it! Such things can only happen in France. Freedom! Liberty! to *croak!* * * * *

* * * *

I enclose a few things to amuse you, comme d'habitude. * * * * More soon. Maybe I'll see you soon in ole New York. I do hope so.

Henry

Dec. 29th. 1934
18 Villa Seurat
Paris (xiv), France

* * * *

Maybe the last time I'll write on this stationery!
Dear Emil:

Little did I know when I got your last letter that I would be bringing the letters you requested myself. I have scarcely the time to take a last look at Paris, as I would have wished. Am still trying to clean up things— add pages here and there. Hard to believe that I may never see these people again—the French. I catch the last somnolent notes of Paris wistfully. Five years here! A long time. It does something to you. And though I'm going to be happy to see you I don't think that way about New York, its people, its activity. Not love of country, not homesickness brings me back—but love, just love, as old Fraenkel used to sing. I'm going to feel like a queer guy there, I think. I don't want to meet the returned exiles or even see their haunts. I was never one of them and am not now. * * * *

Emil, I don't know how much I can bring with me—nothing of much account, I assure you. I'm traveling fairly light. Anyway, I'll bring some trifles and big bag of reminiscences. I don't know America any more. I feel timid a bit, shy as a horse. * * * *

* * * *

Maybe I'm somewhat changed. The five years count—the life, the meetings, the hardships. (Never too terrible, the hardships, but wearing, eat you away, you know.) I'm quite intact as regards the fundamentals. And I don't go back on all I wrote you—about the artist. I may have to stop being an artist, for a while. That's all.

* * * *

I'll have a wild impulse to weep when I see you. Maybe better not meet me at the dock. I'd like to be strong. I'd like to burst in on you with a hearty cheery voice. You're the one person back home I always kept in mind. I thought of you more than you will ever realize. * * * *

These are the last hours. The last ten days have been refined torture. I almost caved in. The voyage will do me good, I hope. A rest. Fresh air. Wind. Sunshine perhaps. You don't know what five years of steady drizzling rain does to one. It drizzles inside you finally. Today it was beautiful. Just would be! Like spring. The old bitch puts on her loveliest countenance.

Anyway, à très bientôt.

Love,
Henry.

* * * *

ACKNOWLEDGMENTS

Publication of these letters was undertaken with the blessing of Henry Miller and of his friend Lawrence Clark Powell, then University Librarian at the University of California at Los Angeles and guiding spirit behind the Library's Miller Collection.

Brooke Whiting, then Curator of Literary Manuscripts at UCLA, was unfailingly helpful and cooperative. More recently his successor, David Zeidberg, has also provided timely assistance.

I am greatly indebted to Linda Wickes for preparing the text for publication and grateful also to Michael Stamm for his assistance and persistence, often with nagging details.

Rupert Pole, Executor of the Anaïs Nin Trust, and Philip Nurenberg have provided photographs, most of them previously unpublished.

Françoise Calin, Richard Heinzkill, Ian MacNiven, Jay Martin, Roger Nicholls, and Robert Potter have answered all manner of questions and done their best to preserve me from error.

Peter Glassgold has once again been a thoughtful editor, thoughtful in every sense of the word.

My thanks to all these collaborators and friends.

INDEX

Dewey, John, 5
Dietrich, Marlene, 72, 97
Dog of Andalou (i.e., *Un Chien Andalou*)
Dos Passos, John, 29
Dostoievski, Feodor, 4, 6, 71, 122
Doumergue, Gaston (French premier in 1934), 145
Dr. Caligari (*The Cabinet of Dr. Caligari*), 34
Dreiser, Theodore, 7, 29
Dryden, John, 81
Du Barry, Madame, 111, 114
Dufresne, Charles Georges, 43, 48
Dufy, Raoul, 28
Duhamel, Marcel (French writer, subsequently translated HM), 38
Dulac, Germaine (French film director; HM interviewed her and hoped she would star June in her first talkie), 32, 38, 52, 63
Dun, Jacobus (Western Union messenger hired by HM), 11
Durrell, Lawrence (English writer, co-author of *The Durrell-Miller Letters, 1935–1980*), viii
Duse, Eleonora, 136

Eliot, T. S., 42, 152
Elkus, Abe (Brooklyn merchant, friend and benefactor of HM), 40, 53, 60, 66, 89, 112
Ellis, Havelock, 5
Emil und die Detektive, 107
Eugene (Pachoutinsky, Russian emigré who worked at the Cinéma Vanves and let HM sleep there; appears in *Tropic of Cancer*), 61
Ezra (*see* Pound)

Fantin-Latour, Ignace, 23
Faulkner, William, 94
Faure, Elie (author of a monumental *History of Art* much admired by HM), 32, 75, 107, 109
"Fauves, Les" (Matisse, Rouault, Dufy, & Co.), 27
Fedrant, Camille (HM's secretary at Western Union), 121
Flandrau, Grace (American writer living in France), 100
Flaubert, Gustave, 11

Folies-Bergère, 84, 149, 151
Forel, Auguste, 5
Foujita, Tsuguhara (Japanese-French painter), 68, 89
Fox, Robert (proofreaders' boss at Chicago *Tribune*), 86
Fraenkel, Michael (friend and benefactor of HM in Paris; prophet of doom; portrayed as Boris in *Tropic of Cancer*), vii, viii, 89, 93, 100, 101, 102, 103–105, 106, 109, 110–11, 127, 134–35, 141, 149, 157
France, Anatole, 5, 11, 36, 69
Francie (*see* Wood)
Frank (*see* Mechau)
Frank, Waldo, 106
Fred (*see* Perlès)
Freud, Sigmund, 5, 115, 141, 143
Frou-Frou, 49, 95, 102, 115

Gauguin, Paul, 94, 119, 122
Gautama, 30
General William Booth Enters Heaven (Vachel Lindsay), 4
George (Buzby)
Germaine (prostitute who served as a model for HM's first published story, "Mademoiselle Claude"), 50–51, 97
Giddes, Archie, 78
Gide, André, 49
Gillespie, Abraham Lincoln, Jr., 152
Giotto, 129
Girtin, Thomas, 73
Goethe, Johann Wolfgang von, 98, 128, 150
Golden Whales of California, The (Vachel Lindsay), 4
Gorki, Maxim, 5
Gould, Joe (Greenwich Village character, raconteur and wag), 103–105
Goya, Francisco de, 23
Graetz, Heinrich, 83
Grand Meaulnes, Le (Alain-Fournier), 94
Granich, Irwin, 4
Grosz, George, 71, 118
Guitry, Sacha, 32

H. H. (*see* Harold Hickerson)
Haase, 13
Haeckel, Ernst, 4